OUR WORK, OUR L
OUR TOWN

Burnley People, Pakistani Roots

Edited and compiled by Sobia Malik © 2013

OUR WORK, OUR LIVES, OUR TOWN: Burnley People, Pakistani Roots
is a project led by Jinnah Development Trust Ltd,
and funded by The Heritage Lottery Fund

Published by
Jinnah Development Trust Ltd
2 Brougham St
Burnley
BB12 OAS

Edited and compiled by Sobia Malik © 2013

Portrait Images by Andy Ford photography 8Imaging

Supplied images by contributors

Design & production by Graphics, Burnley Council, Creative-Council.net

ISBN 978-0-9926591-0-3

Front cover montage - Top left clockwise: A. Majeed, G.N. Chowdhary , Maulana Qadri, A. Anwar,
M.R. Malik and N. Malik, F. Sharif, A. Sharif, R. Ahmed and team, S. Malik, Dr A. Haq, N. Khan.
Background image: I. Chowdhary at Blackpool.

Back cover - Top left clockwise: A. Khan, W. Khan, M.R. Malik and family, M. Yaqub and nephews,
Maulana Iqbal and A. Haq Mian and M. Waheed and son, M. Najib and family, Mr and Mrs K.
McGeorge, Dr M. Hassan and family, M. Younas and family.

Printed in East Lancashire, UK 2013

Edition 2

Contents

I gratefully dedicate this book to mum and dad, with love.

Acknowledgements

A book that I estimated would take one year to complete ultimately took more than two. A fascinating challenge for which I am grateful.

It would not have been possible without the Heritage Lottery Fund (HLF), especially the patience and support of Rebecca Mason. Edward Lee at the Burnley Community and Voluntary Services (BCVS), his guidance in the early stages of applying for funding was invaluable. Local historian and Councillor, Roger Frost, for sharing his knowledge in this field to support the first ever book on the historical contribution of Pakistanis to the town. The University of Central Lancashire (UCLAN) volunteers support and the North West Sound Archive (NWSA) for their training services. Burnley Council Local Authority Officer, Mike Waite, made a generous contribution through all stages of the project. Gary Smales, MJ Hindman and the Graphics Team at Burnley Council, for their design creativity and steadfastness despite tight deadlines in the book production process. Mike Townend, Senior Curator at Towneley Hall where the exhibition based on the project will be held, his expertise informed Jinnah's Communication Group from the outset. The gem otherwise known as Philippa Gillatt for giving her time selflessly to proof read the book in the final stages of production. We would also like to thank the Burnley Express and Lancashire Evening Telegraph for the use of articles from their archives.

On behalf of Jinnah Development Trust I want to thank all the contributors to this book and their families for their kind co-operation.

Finally, I cannot thank the Jinnah volunteers, Ibrar Syed, Shahzad Hasan and Alamzeb Khan enough for their administrative support, often required at very short notice. I could not have composed all the precious stories in this book without time sacrificed by them and all the people mentioned above.

Sobia Malik
Burnley, June 2013

Preface

'With faith, discipline and selfless devotion to duty, there is nothing worthwhile that you cannot achieve.'

The above quotation by the founder of Pakistan, Mohammad Ali Jinnah, encapsulates the vision behind the creation of 'Jinnah Development Trust Ltd in Burnley' (Jinnah), Lancashire nearly forty years ago. The first generation of Pakistanis to settle in significant numbers arrived in the 1960s attracted by the economic opportunities presented by the cotton mills central to the working lives of many Northern towns of the period. As a registered local charity based in the Daneshouse ward of Burnley, the organisation acted as a bridge between both English and South Asian cultures, through a range of services it offered new arrivals to integrate as they made the town their home.

Over the intervening decades, one of the founders of the organisation, Mohammad Rafique Malik, wanted to document this period in the history of Pakistanis in Burnley. This book is also a chance for younger generations to capture a glimpse of those early days as elders now share their stories of leaving their homeland to become pioneers. They built a sense of belonging guided by key tenets of Islam and established a British way of life encouraging them to contribute to the town through their working lives, making them role models for subsequent generations. Britain is a successful pluralistic society that has welcomed their traditions, enabled them to work hard, flourish and to give something back to the town they call home, Burnley.

Above: Mohammad Ali Jinnah, Qaid-e-Azam

Below left: Jinnah Advisory Service volunteers 2010

Below right: Pakistan Women's Association celebrate Pakistan Independence Day 2011

'Jinnah' successfully bid for a heritage project from the Heritage Lottery Fund. The aim of the project was to showcase successful contributions by these pioneers in the local community and beyond, specifically through their chosen professions or voluntary work, focusing where possible on individuals who were the first Pakistanis to serve in a wide array of fields from politics to the postal service. In the 1960s, the majority of Pakistani people in the workforce were men and this is also reflected in the larger number of contributions from men than women in the book. Despite limitations in funding, 'Jinnah' thought it desirable to allocate some time to record continuity in the attitude and work ethic among the second generation of Pakistanis. The organisation wishes to celebrate those histories and achievements and tell the stories to a wider audience through a DVD film and touring exhibition, as well as this book. The emphasis

Above: Sobia Malik
interviews Shahid Malik 2012

Below: Sobia Malik discusses
project with UCLAN
volunteers 2011

is on social history and civic engagement by looking at different professional and social areas of the town. It is hoped this community cohesion endeavour provides a timely highlight of what makes British society richer.

The context for this is the way Burnley people with Pakistani roots have established themselves in the borough. The number of residents born in Pakistan grew from a few dozen in the early sixties, with most pioneer immigrants arriving for work through the late sixties and early seventies. By the time of the 1981 census, there were 1,235 Burnley residents who had been born in Pakistan; by 1991, there were 1 447: and by 2001, the number was 1,948, slightly over 2 per cent of the total population of Burnley then.

By this time, of course, the community which is the focus of this book had grown through families forming and children coming along: most of the 'Pakistani' people in Burnley were British citizens born and bred in the town, and could not be identified as Pakistani through their place of birth. In the 2011 census, which no longer recorded country of birth, the total number of 'Asian' or 'Asian/British' residents in Burnley was 5,924: around 6.8% of the whole population. This would of course include those people with roots in Bangladesh, India and other 'Asian' countries - though most Burnley people with connections

back to 'the sub-continent' are of Pakistani heritage.

This fact itself needs unpacking: Pakistan itself is a large and diverse country, with different regions and cultures, which simplistic media stereotypes do not capture. The ancestors and families of some Burnley residents are from the big cities of Islamabad and Lahore; others from the North West frontier area which borders Afghanistan; and many are from the Mirpur region. People featured in this book include those born or who lived in the cities of Faisalabad and Rawalpindi, as well as those from villages in the Jhelum district or the Punjab province. 'Burnley' is the place of birth mentioned most often – with one Burnley person of 'Pakistani' heritage citing Copenhagen, Denmark as their birthplace, and another admitting that they were born in Yorkshire!

The stories and traditions of this diverse group of the Burnley community are documented not only to establish enduring evidence of their contribution but also to act as a catalyst to create a network to conserve and share this local history.

The project is a vehicle to bring the community together, dispel a few myths, create local pride, enhance civic virtue and actively preserve a community in partnership.

As the co-ordinator of the project, and having been born and brought up in Burnley, my personal journey with 'Our Work, Our Lives, Our Town' started a number of years ago when the idea was first raised by Mr Malik in conversation - I was immediately interested. Over time, I realised his vision was to remind us all of the value caring for your community can add; not only to the quality of life for others but to the individual making the contribution, irrespective of age, colour or creed. This philosophy seemed in keeping with my experience of 'Jinnah' over the years, as many of the people I interviewed for the book and film were part of my childhood too. Observing these adults as a child they taught me social values that I'm not sure we can take for granted anymore; being kind, offering help to those who are vulnerable, and sacrificing personal time for no personal gain. They demonstrated the meaning of community through their actions. Personally, I cherish these memories and still feel inspired by their quiet humility and spirit of generosity which shaped the society of the Burnley I grew up in. Those of us who have benefitted from the challenges these pioneers undertook owe them a debt of gratitude and of humble remembrance, which should lead us to ask ourselves what more we can do to honour the example they have set and indeed rise to the challenge of the standard they have set. Every individual's story is unique and so we look forward to learning from those who have been willing to share their story with us.

Sharing personal and family photographs can be a sensitive matter for any individual, despite this people were still willing to share some with us. We were very grateful for their kind permission allowing us to publish their photographs and share them with a wider

audience. Each person was asked a series of questions in one-to-one interviews I undertook at Jinnah Development Trust's office in Stoneyholme. The book is conversational in tone because it is based on the edited transcripts of those interviews. If the editing process had prioritised formal English more associated with the written word it would have lost the authenticity of the voices best captured through the spoken word. I wanted to convey the character of the personalities interviewed which meant retaining some grammatical anomalies and instances of non-standard English used by the interviewees; this can sometimes also be a feature of speech when English is used as an additional language. The hours of research, interviews and filming has taught me a great deal. Most starkly, I learned about a generation of Pakistani men and women who came to this country, made it their home and in doing so created a richer community that has had a real impact in shaping the town itself and its history on many levels. The way they did that; the sense of brotherhood, sisterhood, solidarity showed to one another and engaging the wider part of the town with Islamic good will was something I feel almost nostalgic about. The subsequent generation of South Asians are arguably more educated about their faith because

Above: Burnley Council of Mosques raise money for Palestinian Aid 2010

Below left: Sobia Malik promoting the project on Pendle Community Radio 2011

Below right: Sobia Malik interviews Basri Chowdhary in 2012

Above: Sobia Malik delivering a Confidence Building workshop for Asian women

they have more access to Islamic knowledge via British born Imams and the internet; and yet in some ways this second generation of Pakistanis seem more separate, or are intent on doing 'their own thing.' With the passage of time this was perhaps inevitable and natural as the community integrated culturally and the need to be interdependent gradually diminished along with the language barrier. Still, I find myself reflecting back on a time when this generation of pioneers first came to Burnley because there are lessons to be learned about the spirit of a community from the example they set.

The spectre of death was perhaps one of the first catalysts for an organised community when new arrivals realised they had to facilitate burial rites in adherence with Islamic doctrine now they were truly in another country. The first burial committee was created which then became subsumed in to the responsibilities of the first established mosque. That historical process was a familiar pattern across the towns in England for migrants who came from South Asia at that time. In Burnley the first mosque/masjid was built on Rectory Road in Stoneyholme and then moved to Brougham Street when the old Majestic Bingo Hall was purchased for the purpose of establishing a communal worship site. It was finally named Abu Bakr Masjid with Shia as well as Sunnis on its committee; that spirit of love and care was in abundance amongst the men who were trying to cultivate an Islamic community in Burnley society, quite evidently looking beyond doctrinal differences. That holistic outlook is something that doesn't need to be entirely lost. However, how we hold on to that spirit in a tangible way is something more challenging, the timely reminders to reflect on this are at the heart of the stories the elders share in 'Our Work, Our Lives, Our Town' listening to the pioneers of that generation and appreciating the doors that they literally opened for us - foremost by their advocacy for representation in different sections of society and professions. The impact of their work is such that we are empowered, have a legal

awareness of our right to equality and citizenship in a way that had they not done the ground work we could not enjoy today.

A recurring theme by people interviewed was the desire to help others through their work whether they were Imam, community workers or footballers; many referenced the Islamic teaching to 'love thy neighbour' having a huge impact on their working lives. Second generation Imam Abuzar of Abu Bakr masjid said,

'I feel that it's a duty of every person to help and value others, and obviously ourselves as Imams and community leaders, we are being examples to the people, and the people then follow in the footsteps of the leaders, so we try and live and do everything according to what Islam has said. To understand Islam truly... you need to look at the life of the Prophet, peace be upon him, and then the life of his followers, how they lived, and even in this day and age we have people who are truly Muslims and those true Muslims are those who are generous, kind, helpful. We need to actually look at Islam not through the eyes of the media but we need to look at Islam through the eyes of Islam itself.'

The English heritage elders interviewed were clearly open-minded and forward-thinking for the 1960s, anarchist and priest Father Jim Petty said,

'But with the influx of Asians I couldn't understand people... we'd just had a war where India had produced anywhere between 2 million and 3 million soldiers, everywhere the British army fought there were Indians there, Egypt, Asia, Malaya, and so on, they were as worthy to be reckoned as Englishmen as we were after all, with all these Scots, and Irish and Welsh, and what have you rather than to sort of single these people out for no good reason at all which people did...

I believe, obviously being a priest, if you believe in an Arab saviour, I would find it very hard to be discriminatory against an Asian or an Arab.'

Others spoke of witnessing the positive impact Pakistani neighbourliness made to change the attitudes of people around them. Iris Verity was asked to join the newly formed CRE (Commission for Racial Equality) in 1976 and said,

'Working with the community was the best time of my life really. I worked about 20 years with the Association. Of course in the beginning it was very difficult, for me it was very difficult, I mean my parents didn't agree; my parents were quite against it. As I got better known then it became respectable towards the end. Even my mother saw it as respectable at the end but in the beginning they just didn't... But it was the children that motivated me.'

A few of the first generation Pakistanis in Burnley who were interviewed were invited on to the Commision for Racial Equality (CRE) and recounted the impact of the Race Relations Act in 1976 in improving the ability of ethnic minorities to access jobs and gain representation in all aspects of public life. Prior to these changes in the law, some convey the barriers surmounted by their determination and work ethic. First generation Ghulam Nabi Chowdhary said,

'I started as the first Asian bus conductor, first Asian driver and first Asian staff instructor in Burnley, Colne and Nelson Joint Transport.

In 1967 I saw advertisements at the bus station, jobs for conductors. I thought I should give it a try as I had worked for a long time in the mills. I went for a test and my application was not successful but they didn't give any reason. I went to the Citizens Advice Bureau... Actually there were union bans. It was the General Transport Union. They had decided not to employ any coloured people... There was no Race Relations Act then. They promised everyone that they will look into it. This issue also came into the media with headlines saying race discrimination on transport. That was difficult for the transport union... The union said they will have to start letting some coloured people apply, only 6%... They were also threatening those people who were willing to train us and they were sending un-named letters to the press that anyone who co-operates with the Asian people, we will send them to Coventry. We carried on through this, got the training. When I started my own job I had to go with the driver. The first day the driver refused to work with me. So they had to change the driver. This was at the beginning but many years later, they found out that Asians, we were very hard working, good time keepers and they added some more. The union couldn't stop it.'

Many commented on the soul-searching experience after the disturbances in 2001 and the impact faith had in building bridges and a community actively working in partnership. Mr Malik had been on the CRE nationally in its early days and was also the first Asian Mayor of Burnley, he describes setting up the 'Building Bridges' organisation,

'We set up Lancashire Council of Mosques; I was elected as secretary in 1990, for ten years I was the secretary and I retired when I became Mayor of Burnley... We are still trying to overcome the difficulties but the good thing is that when I was Mayor the Bishop of Burnley, the new bishop who is still Bishop of Burnley, Bishop John came and I invited him to the Mayor's parlour and we talked about setting up a sort of partnership of mosques and churches so that we could understand and celebrate what is common and work on it to give a positive note, a positive aspect of the religion to the community as a whole. I'm very pleased that it has grown from strength to strength and it is doing its best to bring all the faith and non-faith communities together in different activities, celebrations of festivals, of Christmas or Easter or Harvest Festival or Eid and people from different faith groups visit each other's places of worship. So it's quite fascinating that what we want to see happening in the whole world, it is happening in Burnley and in several other towns in England, but especially in Burnley because that's what we are concerned about primarily.'

Safdar Baig Mirza, teacher and present Chair of Jinnah Development Trust said,

'We did some community partnership work after the 2001 riots, there were several organisations which were formed and one of them was Building Bridges... And we enjoyed being together, with Christians, other religions as well with Islam, people getting together, these imams and these priests hugging each other... And there were

so many people from Christian communities who used to come and visit mosques and their misconceptions about Muslims and about Asian Pakistanis or Bangladeshis, those misconceptions literally vanished. Some of them made comments that we now know that you're genuine people; you are genuinely nice people… Faith can play an integral role in bringing communities, people, together, keeping them calm… Islam does persuade you to go out and see people, meet them, greet them and invite them towards you. But I think as a society it's our responsibility to do what you can do for the community.'

This is echoed by Abdul Hamid Qureshi, former chair of Lancashire Council of Mosques, commenting on his contribution with Building Bridges.

'I thank God that I was able to contribute in its development and some of the work which we did was acknowledged nationally and internationally. People were becoming comfortable with one another and they started to get the confidence that it is not all talking about differences; it is that you can live and understand the differences and differences are not always negative. You don't have to be same, you can be different and yet cohesive.'

It isn't possible to go back in time as community volunteer Alamzeb Khan, reminiscing on his late father observed wryly,

'I realised that growing up in my family the front room of our house used to always be occupied and my mum used to be cooking for ever…

Then when we had the shop my dad used to sit upstairs… and every single day people used to come in from all over, relatives, friends… since the 60s and 70s. They've been friends, they've lent each other money, money's a valuable thing nobody gives it you, I realised that these people, our house, my mum was telling me that where we live on Clive St, we didn't have much money so your dad's friends paid for the house and I was thinking I wouldn't pay for a friend's house now - I wouldn't get it back!'

And it isn't about looking through rose-tinted spectacles because the negatives about South Asians and Muslims in the past and present are well-documented. This is a rare moment to reflect on historical community activism and civic engagement so we can be inspired to build on that heritage, something the younger generation are clearly trying to do. As Nazia Khan a trained pilot describes,

'Pathans, those from the North West Frontier of Pakistan, are very strict and they focus more on the men, well they used to and for a girl having achieved something like I have - I didn't expect them to be this happy for me, but I think it's woken them up a bit as well having a woman, Pathan woman, achieve something like this. I was saying to my mother the other day, because the focus is always on the men, most often whether we like it or not. I think most of them are helping their own daughters now, into whatever they want to do, not piloting of course but I think they're more open minded.

The only thing I would like to say is if anyone wants to pursue their dream, it is possible. They should go and do it because whether it's piloting, law, anything I think it's all down to you. And nothing is impossible, I actually believe that.'

Uppermost should be a duty of care to one another alongside the wider community, ensuring in ethical dilemmas our sincerity is touched by consideration for the greater good and our actions an example to others. No mean feat. In Muslim, Non-Muslim, South Asian and white British heritage people interviewed, the overwhelming humanitarian instinct demonstrated what power an individual can make to create positive change for themselves, those around them and for future generations. Many highlighted the importance Islam plays to integration in society and the need to be a useful citizen to your town and country. To describe

this Islamic passion in words is challenging and yet Mrs Anwara Shahid, a first generation Bengali lady and the humble symbol of the volunteer expresses the oceanic spiritual heart of Muslims when she said,

'I was a bridge, someone has to be a bridge of love, understanding. It was only language that was a barrier. It's the secret for people; we have to give to everybody. Everybody should give, it's who we are. We as Muslims, we love each other. And people should respect and love, not from our outside but our inside. Love is the true colour of Muslims and we are the messengers of our Allah and this is the way we can share with others.'

The privilege of growing up in a town where the elders worked with spiritual altruism focusing on education and community activism is not lost on me. They provide wealth beyond the material to the people of Burnley who inherit their legacy.

Sobia Malik
Education Consultant,
Community Cohesion expert and Writer
Burnley, June 2013

Introduction

A brief history of Jinnah Development Trust Ltd

Jinnah Development Trust made a policy decision towards the end of 2000 to recruit more individual members, particularly second generation Pakistanis. As a result of that policy I was approached and I readily joined it as a member because I wanted to do voluntary work. I was elected its Board Member 10 years ago. Six years ago, I was elected its Vice Chair and last year I was elected its Chair. Therefore, the earlier part of the introduction is based on my research and the latter one on my personal observation.

Jinnah Development Trust set off on its journey towards the end of 1965. There were a couple of hundred Pakistani heritage people resident in

Burnley, mainly single men and teenage boys. Most of them were not literate particularly in English and didn't understand the British social security, income tax and employment systems and were constantly in need of information, guidance and advice to understand, to cope with and to adapt to a new way of life.

The newly arrived Pakistanis established The Pakistan Association in 1966 and the late Mr Mohammad Yaqub was elected its first President. Because a few schools needed a bilingual teacher to help non-English speaking pupils, he was appointed as the first Pakistani school teacher in Burnley. The Association had no offices in

Above: Mohammad Ali Jinnah, the founder of Pakistan, also known as Quaid-e-Azam

those days. They operated from the front rooms of Pakistani residents and ran the temporary offices mainly on Saturdays and Sundays to deal with personal, family, tax, employment, passport and immigration matters of the members. They first called this initiative Burnley Pakistan Advisory Service and later extended its scope to the whole of East Lancashire because no town had such a service and named it as East Lancashire Pakistani Advisory Service.

The Association organised a reception and invited Alderman Newlove and Mrs Newlove, the then Mayor and Mayoress of Burnley as guests of honour in the church which is now North street Mosque and in return Alderman Newlove invited Mr Yaqub to the Mayor's Ball. This was the first official contact between the Pakistani community and the Town Hall.

The people who mainly ran this advisory service in the 60s' and 70s' were the late Mr Mohammad Yaqub, Mr Ahmed Khan, Mr Ziarat Gul and Mian Abdul Waheed led by Mr Mohammad Rafique Malik who had acquired a lot of knowledge about the Government systems. He had also been elected as the Chair of National Federation of Pakistani Associations in Great Britain (NFPA) in 1968. The then Home Secretary Mr Reginald Maudling MP appointed him as a member of the Race Relations Board in 1970, a national body tasked with the duty to eliminate racial discrimination both in employment and services from British society. His appointment gave East Lancashire Advisory Service huge publicity on a local as well as national level. The Advisory Service started attracting clients from all over England at the weekends. This was also influenced by Mr Malik's appearances on the pioneering BBC Asian news programme, Nai Zindagi Naya Jeevan from 1968 onwards. In 1976, the service was renamed Jinnah Advisory Service to mark the 100th Anniversary of Mohammad Ali Jinnah, whose mission inspired the organisation to serve society. The Advisory Service received strong support from local ethnic leaders and successive members of parliament including; Dan Jones, Peter Pike, Kitty Usher and Gordon Birtwistle.

Below: International visit to Pakistan, wearing pagri. L-R: Mayor Rafique Malik, the Prime Minister of Azad Kashmir Barrister Sultan Mahmood, Peter Pike MP and Haji Javed Akhtar, Minister for Law and Revenue

New members appointed to the Race Relations Board

Mark Bonham Carter, who had been chairman of the Race Relations Board since its formation, left the Board at the beginning of the year to become chairman of the Community Relations Commission. The move left the Board without a permanent chairman and Sir Roy Wilson, QC, agreed to become acting-chairman until Sir Geoffrey Wilson takes up his appointment in the autumn.

There were also changes in the membership of the Board. Mr M. U. Rahman and Mr H. C. Hampton retired and their places were taken by Miss Elizabeth Steel (*below left*) a Liverpool solicitor who served for two years on the Board's committee in the north-west, and Mr Rafiq Malik (*right*) a Burnley schoolteacher who has lived in England for five years.

Miss Elizabeth Steel

Mr Rafiq Malik

In the early '70s the Pakistan Association Burnley got affiliated to the UK Immigration Advisory Service (UKIAS) and Mr Malik was elected its Executive Committee Member. The UKIAS established its offices and appointed staff in all the regions of Britain. They dealt with all the Immigration matters mainly from the Black and Asian workers. Their nearest Office to Burnley was situated in Manchester, the regional hub for the North West of England.

There was a huge increase in unemployment in the early '70s. The government initiated a Special Temporary Employment Programme (STEP) led by the then Manpower Services Commission (MSC), the predecessor of the Department of Work and Pensions (DWP). In May 1976, Mr Malik had been elected as the first Pakistani Councillor to Burnley Borough Council and he played a major role in establishing several STEP Projects, some mainly for the benefit of the Asian Community in partnership with the Council. The Council acted as its PAYE agents. These projects were managed by the late Mr Norman Gregson, a school teacher, the late Mrs Florence Green, the local postmistress, the late Mr Mohammad Yaqub, the first local Asian school teacher, and Mr Malik, who was also a local school teacher and a Borough Councillor.

Above: Rafique Malik appointed as a member of the main Race Relations Board by the Home Secretary Reginald Maudling in 1970

Right: Jinnah and the police working together. L-R: David Barnes (Chair Daneshouse Residents Association), Sher Ali Miah (Board member), Saeed Chaudhry (Manager), Clive Fathergil (Superintendent), Abdul Aziz Chaudhry and Rafique Malik

Above: Sitting, Abdul Sattar and Rafique Malik, standing Mohammad Sharif, Sikandar Khan and Sarwar Beg

Right: Fazal Qayyum Khan, Manager of the Jinnah Community Project, with Jinnah co-workers including Pat Bennett and Abdul Sattar in 1991

From its inception Mr Malik has been Honorary Director of Jinnah Advisory Service. Since 1976 the organisation has had the following managers:

- Mr Munsifdar Mirza 1978-1980
- Mr Fazal Qayyum Khan 1980-1986
- Cllr Saeed Chaudhry 1994-1996
- Mr Abdul Sattar 1996-present

Mr Abdul Sattar has been managing the Advisory Service voluntarily with assistance from other volunteers since 1996.

At one stage in the late '70s Jinnah had 81 people working for it on seven different projects and the late Mr Norman Gregson was appointed full-time paid General Manager of these projects. The projects were Burnley Better Homes (41); Jinnah Advisory Centre (4); Youth Training (10); Sports & Recreation (4); Home School Liaison (1); Translators/Interpreters (1); Keep Stoneyholme/Daneshouse Tidy (4); Pre-school Play Groups (8) and Management (8).

They ran two play groups, one from the St James Parish Hall in Stoneyholme and the other from Burnley Lane Baptist Church, Colne Road in Daneshouse. The Colne Road play group continued to provide services until 1994 and was then handed over to the Burnley Lane Baptist Church Trustees. During the 18 years Jinnah ran it, it was funded by the Manpower Services Commission, Burnley Borough Council and BBC Children in Need Fund.

The Pakistan Women's Association Burnley and various Mayors of Burnley also raised funds for the Colne Road play group because it had 75% children from indigenous working class families and 25% from Asian working class families. These fundraising activities brought all communities together and improved community relations. Jinnah was not only busy in project work; they also took a lot of other steps to improve community relations in Burnley. They organised dinners for the residents of old people's homes at Christmas. They held other functions i.e. celebrating Eid Festivals, Pakistan Independence Days, raising funds for disasters i.e. for victims of floods in East Pakistan and wars between India and Pakistan. In 1983, they changed their constitution and name to the Jinnah Community Development Trust and got themselves registered as a charity with the Charity Commission as an umbrella organisation and Local Development Agency.

By that time, Pakistani heritage people had established several single-purpose groups. They became affiliated to the Trust because they had been supported by the Trust. The following groups were actively providing services supported by the Trust:

- Pakistan Women's Association Burnley
- The Urdu Society Burnley
- Burnley Islamic Trust
- Daneshouse over-50s Association/Luncheon Club
- Burnley and Pendle Asian Youth
- Jinnah Diamond Youth Club
- Burnley Council of Mosques

Pakistani Women's Association helped women to come out of their homes, learn English, take part in social and religious functions as well as go out as a group to visit sea-side resorts, zoos, safari parks etc. The Trust ran English for Speakers of Other Languages (ESOL) classes in partnership with the Pakistani Women's Association. This activity is continuing to date.

Above: PWA's Urdu Class rehearsing to celebrate Pakistan Independence Day, teachers standing. L-R: Surayya Rafiq, Nasreen Malik and Zarin Saleem

Right: Mayor, Frank Bailey, and Mayoress attend the Fundraising Dinner organised by the Pakistan Women's Association for the Burnley Lane Play Group run by Jinnah Community Development Trust, from Colne Road Baptist Church, Burnley

The Urdu Society organises Poetry Recitals annually and invites internationally renowned poets like Professor Anwar Masood from Pakistan whose poetry, mainly satire, is enjoyed equally by young and old. He comes and stays in Burnley as the Society's guest and travels to other towns in the UK to chair the Poetry Recitals at the invitation of the literary and cultural societies in those towns. The Society had the honour of being host to the great Rebel Poet, the late Habib Jalib who read poetry for three hours without a break in the Bingo Hall which is now Abu Bakr Mosque.

Above: A poetry recital organised by the Urdu Society - Rebel Poet Habib Jalib read his poetry for 3 hours non-stop. L-R: The late Yousaf Moghul, the late Masood Ahmed Mirza, Rafique Malik and Abdul Aziz Chaudhry on stage

Daneshouse Luncheon Club is the main meeting point for the over-50s. They hold luncheons/ dinners every month with over 30 members attending. They also visit zoos, safari parks, seaside resorts etc and take members on walks to keep fit.

Jinnah Diamond Youth Club has over 100 members. They meet every Thursday. Mostly it is run by volunteers with occasional funding from Lancashire County Council and the University of Central Lancashire (UCLan). UCLan also provides them volunteers to oversee the activities at the Club.

Burnley and Pendle Asian Youth Council helped the young Pakistanis to form various cricket and soccer clubs and join various leagues. Their work enhanced equality and diversity amongst the youth in Burnley and Pendle. They regularly held annual tournaments and Awards Evenings for the young people where they enjoyed meals, listened to after dinner speakers and strengthened networking. Their activities not only provided sports for young people, they also enhanced understanding amongst all cultures present in both towns.

Burnley Islamic Trust was started by the Pakistan Association Burnley in the late '60s. Its Trustees included both Shias and Sunnis. Its founding Trustees were: the late Mr Mohammad Yaqub; the late Fida Hussain Bokhari and Mian Abdul Waheed, Mian Afzal Khalid; Ghulam Nabi Chowdhary and Mr Mohammad Rafique Malik. It started from 102 Rectory Road and moved up to 4 Brougham Street, the old Majestic Bingo Hall. They also own St James Parish Hall which Jinnah rents from the Centre. The Burnley Council of Mosques, an umbrella organisation of eight Burnley mosques was started as a project by the Jinnah Development Trust. We assisted at all stages from the start to its completion i.e. membership, writing up of the Constitution, holding the Inaugural Annual General Meeting, registration as a charity, applying for funding to work on better community relations and joining Burnley Building Bridges to further improve community relations in the town.

The original Trust members prepared an exit strategy and persuaded young Pakistani professionals to join the Trust first as individual members and later elected them to the Board. The young leadership changed its constitution and decided to prepare Articles and Memorandum of the Association and registered as a company with Companies House on 2nd October 2006 and named it the Jinnah Development Trust Ltd.

I became a member over 10 years ago together with several other second generation young people, mainly professionals. Since 2002, there have always been 6 out of 12 Board Members who are young. I was elected Chair of the Trust last year for 2 years. I followed 2 other young chairs of the Board.

We are an infrastructure as well as service provider charity and company. We assisted our affiliated organisations to access funding and provided them assistance in strengthening their governance, administration and financial systems. Six of them have been able to access over £60,000 in the last 5 years.

'Our Work, Our Lives, Our Town' our current project is, probably, the first-ever HLF-funded history project undertaken by a Pakistani heritage organisation in East Lancashire.

We are grateful to the Heritage Lottery Fund for their financial support and to the HLF and Burnley Council officers for their guidance to complete the project.

It would be remiss of me if I didn't put my thanks on record to:

- Mr Mohammad Rafique Malik who has been working on it as a volunteer, in fact this project was his brain-child.

- Ms Sobia Malik, the Project Co-ordinator and Editor of this book who has gone above and beyond the call of duty. Without her persistence and commitment this project would not have succeeded.

- And finally, the contributors, the Board, and the Steering Group for the Project whose invaluable guidance and support made it all possible.

Above: Audience at the Annual General Meeting of Jinnah Development Trust

Left: Rafique Malik (Chair) and the late Florence Green (Secretary Racial Equality Council) present trophies at an Annual Sports Tournament, organised by Burnley and Pendle Asian Youth Council (B & PAYC)

Safdar Baig Mirza
Chairman, Jinnah Development Trust Ltd
August 2013

Chapter 1 - Public sector

Civic

Mohammad Rafique Malik

My name is Mohammad Rafique Malik. I was born in Gujrat, Pakistan. Gujrat is right in the middle of Islamabad and Lahore, and it was a village called Kamla where I was born, with 100 or so houses in the village. I have quite interesting, fond memories of that time; village life was very simple with open fields and a lot of fresh vegetables and fruits. We had a river, part river (stream we called it but it is four times wider than a river in England) near our village and in summer when it rained on the mountains it was quite full and very fast moving. We used to enjoy swimming in it. It was enjoyable when it left big, sort of mini lakes in its area after the fast flooding had gone and we regularly used to swim there. It was dangerous, sometimes children who couldn't control themselves, they were swept away and some of them lost their lives. But also lives were saved sometimes. I remember dragging a gentleman out who was twice my size and, because of the water he was unconscious, so I dragged him out and brought him to the side of the stream. I saw people running along the banks of the stream because they were following him and seeing if they could spot him and catch him. Luckily he escaped. I think I would have been 13 or 14 years old then, quite young.

I was born in 1937. My mother was a housewife. My father, when I was born, he had a small shop, a village shop. It was a very small house we lived in; we had the shop in one corner. We had very rudimentary things; matches, oil, kerosene oil, some sugar, raw sugar, and other stuff like that. And people came and bought it. But afterwards, he left the shop and he went to work for the railways some 40 - 50 miles away from home. I went to school in a village near our village, a couple of miles from our house. That was a primary school. The secondary school I went to was in a small town, Lalamusa, which was three miles from our village. We used to walk to school every morning and walk back in the afternoon. That's where I did my matriculation, which is equivalent to GCSEs in this country. I wanted a job in Pakistan, so soon after doing my GCSEs I became a teacher in the same school. I was there

for six or seven years. I was studying as a mature student in the evenings. I graduated from Punjab University as an external student. After teaching for another two years I went to a teachers training college where I did my Bachelor's Degree in Education.

I came to England in 1965. I did sponsor my parents for a visit here in 1978 but they didn't like living here. They stayed for eight or nine months and then went back. They didn't like terraced houses and especially first floor bedrooms because they were not used to them. They were used to open courtyards and open sunlight or

Above: Mohammad Rafique Malik, the first Pakistani heritage Councillor in Burnley elected in 1976

Below: Rafique Malik, the first Pakistani heritage Mayor of Burnley

ON THE EVE OF
FAREWELL PARTY in Honour of MOHD. RAFIQ MALIK B.A., B.ED "HEADMASTER"
ISLAMIA HIGH SCHOOL, Dhoria. Gujrat

CHAIRS :- R.M.INAYAT   AHMAD KHAN   M. FIDA HUSSAIN   M. RAFIQ MALIK (Headmaster)
L. TO RIGHT   P.T.I.   F.A;C.T   B.A;B.ED   B.A; B.ED
            M. AFZAL BUTT   A. REHMAN QASMI   CH. FAZAL DAD
            F.A   H.A;O.T   S.V.
STANDING:- M.FAROOQ AHMAD   AZAM SHEIKH   CH. RAHM DAD   CH. RAFI AHMAD   S.M.SIDDIQ
            F.A;C.T   MATRIC   MATRIC;J.V   B.A   MATRIC
            CH. GHULAM SARWAR   CH. GHULAM MOHAMMAD.   CH. AFTAB AHMAD   M. FAIZ AHMAD
            MATRIC.S.V.   F.A.   F.A   F.A
BACK   ABDUL AZIZ (Peon)   TAJ DIN (Chawokidar)   RASHID AHMAD (Sweeper)

Above: Rafique Malik at the farewell Party at Islamia High School, Dhoria, in the middle garlanded, with other teachers and staff in March 1965

moonlight. Here, it looked very desolate to them. So they decided to go back. It was very cold, very cold. I think that was one of the reasons why they didn't like it here because they came in September and they went back in May. So they saw the English winter. To be quite honest, I also came just for five years. I was head teacher of a high school in Pakistan and I had a dream that I would get some money from somewhere, earn it and build a school in my village as there was no school there. So, some of my friends had come to England and that's how I applied for a work permit, which I was granted. I resigned from that job and came here. I actually went to Halifax but my two colleagues who had also been teaching in the same school in Pakistan, they had moved from Halifax to Burnley and found jobs with Mullard's, in Simonstone, the TV tube manufacturers. So I arrived in Halifax

but the same night my colleagues collected me and brought me back to Burnley. Since then I haven't moved anywhere else, apart from a year in Bradford when I was studying for my post-graduate certificate in education. When I came here, I was asked by the then Director of Education in Burnley, the late Mr Beeston, to go and observe teachers at Rosegrove Secondary School so I went there for a week. I could understand the teachers but I couldn't understand the children! So I went back to him and I said, "Mr Beeston, I can't teach there. This is my problem; I can't understand what the children say." And he told me that Leeds University was running a course for overseas teachers and graduates at a teacher training college in Bradford, and they first spend three months in intensive spoken-English teaching and then you graduate in Education. So I applied for it, got a grant, went there and completed my Post-graduate Certificate in Education and then started teaching in Burnley on the 1st January 1969.

I think the problem was that I'd never heard children speaking English. I had heard mature people speaking English but the children spoke a bit of slang and a bit of dialect. It was difficult to comprehend them. It did me a lot of good going to the college where in three months they gave us a good grounding in pronunciation especially where our pronunciation was different from the people here. We did a lot of practice. The two letters, 'V' and 'W', you have to pronounce them differently, whereas in our language there is just one, 'W'. We did a lot of training. We had some Bangladeshi teachers who couldn't enunciate vah, which they always pronounced as bah. So the teachers already had a list of the letters which we couldn't pronounce and they gave us a lot of practice in them. It was very good, very helpful.

Before I go to my life here, there is just one thing I want to say. I was perhaps the youngest head teacher in Pakistan. I wasn't even 26 when I was appointed head teacher of a high school where we had over 700 boys. It was a boys' secondary school, and 30-odd teachers. I think most of the teachers were older than I was. It was very interesting to head a school. I did bring about a lot of change; I brought in some good teachers wherever I could spot them and raised the

standard and image of the school. But coming here, I got a job at the Mullard factory. I worked there for over two years as a repair person. People made those TV tubes and they used to come to me and another (English) gentleman and we looked at them. We put them on a bench and connected them with the electrics to see if there was any mark or scratch or anything wrong with the electrical equipment. And if there was, we put them on a trolley. If they were okay, we let them go on the belt and then the next batch of people did whatever they were supposed to do with the parts. It was… it was quite a contrast, yes. I think I adapted well but it wasn't easy. I remember, I can't forget, sometimes when the process broke down and there were no tubes on the belt, we had nothing to do. If we had nothing to do my colleague used to go to the toilet or somewhere and I would sit on the chair and read a newspaper. Once, a foreman came and he said, "Oh, you have nothing to do, can you sweep this floor?" Nowadays, I'm a different person, my attitude is different to work, but back then I couldn't accept it so I said, "That's not my job." And he said, "Well you have no job, so clean this," and he himself started cleaning and he said, "Just clean this area." And I said, "I'm going to the medical room." I went there and literally cried, literally cried. It was the sudden change in my status perhaps, from head teacher of a high school to being asked to sweep the floor. Previously, I'd have had two or three people who worked for me

Below: The Mayor, Rafique Malik sitting surrounded by his family in the Mayor's Parlour in 2000. Front L-R: Shahid, Mayoress, Nasreen Malik, Rifat, Sobia, Alia and Zahid carrying his baby daughter Leila. Back L-R: Jahanzaib, Zeeshan, Shehryar

Above: The Mayoral Party ready to go to the Council Chamber

Below: Rafique Malik, the Scout Master in the centre, standing with boy scouts in Pakistan in 1959

to do this. A silly thing to be upset about but I found it difficult.

Perhaps that helped me to go back to teaching! I went to Margaret MacMillan College, Bradford where they had about 1,000 teachers. Most of them were young people coming from colleges with their 'A'-Levels and they also had some mature students. So there were 40-odd mature students from the Indian sub-continent and they taught us English for three months as I explained before. After that they split us into two branches, two sections. One section comprised ten of us; I was one of the ten people who they thought could do the post-graduate certificate in education. The other 30 they said could only do qualified teacher status. So we spent a year there and it changed my attitude to life, and my understanding of the systems here. For the first two or three months, the lecturers (I thought and most of us thought) were wasting their time, they weren't teaching. So I said to them, "You are not teaching us at all, we want to learn." And then they said, "Well, we are glad that you have said it, we are not supposed to teach you; we're supposed to teach you how to learn. So if you want to learn, you ask us questions. What do you want to learn?" I said, "You should have told us that if we want to go to the library, the library is in this part of the town

and if we want to go and buy some books, the bookshops are in that part of town." And they said, "Well that's not how we educate children here. It's not pouring knowledge from a big bottle into a small bottle, we teach you to learn how to know anything and that's how you should go and teach the children."

The education system in the Indian sub-continent is, as one of the lecturers said, pouring knowledge from a big bottle into a small bottle. The teachers tell you things, you go on and you learn about them in books, you learn them by heart, you learn them by rote, but without really understanding. I have no hesitation in admitting that I taught for eight years and I was head teacher for two years,

20

but I didn't know exactly what area meant until I went to the training college. One of our lecturers, he spent two or three lessons asking us questions; "Look at this surface, feel it, what do you feel?" And we would say, "It's cold, it's hard, it's plain." And then he would give us some cardboard pieces, "Now these are different surfaces and you tell us which one is big and which one is small and then which one is--, how big is it?" And then he put some beads out and asked us if we could grade the beads and count how many beads were bigger than the others. Eventually, he used the word area; the area of this cardboard is twice the area of that cardboard, and so on and so forth. I fully understood then what area meant. Although we had learnt by rote that if it is a square, one side multiplied by the other side will give you the area and if it is a triangle, the base multiplied by the perpendicular height of it and divided by two will give you its area. We had learnt the formula to work out the area but we didn't really understand what 'area' was. So here the concepts were explained logically and very, very nicely - that was real learning.

As I said, I came here for five years to earn money and set up a school and go back home. But then my wife joined me seven months after I came here and we started a family and then several other families came. We became a sort of community. Then I changed my mind, I said, "Well, I want to go back and help the community in Pakistan, however, there is a Pakistani community here too. This is our village, so I can get my children educated here because education is a very important thing in life but I can also help the community in Pakistan." So we set up an association, we called it the Pakistan Association and we started helping. Because a lot of people couldn't read or write English, we helped them to fill in their forms from temporary offices in different houses where single people lived. There weren't many families then. Eventually we grew and grew. At that stage we thought that we need a place of worship where our children could go and we bought 102 Rectory Road. It was a house which was not joined on the right or the left. On one side there was a side street and Holme Road was on the other side, so we got planning permission for it. Then we bought the house behind it and expanded the mosque as it were. Children started going there, people started praying there but then it was considered too small and some people bought North Street Church. That was converted into a mosque and now we have eight or nine mosques, so religion

has played a very dominant role. We have been critical of the Imams we brought from Pakistan because they didn't know the life here; they were still talking about things which happened 200 years ago and what have you. Then it was felt that we needed Imams who could speak the language, who understood what life was like in this country. I'm very happy that we have two or three Imams who have been born, brought up and educated here, and they have been trained as Imams in this country so they understand the life, the issues and the lifestyles and now they are opening up, especially after Rushdie where it really shook the Muslim community.

We set up the Lancashire Council of Mosques; I was elected as secretary in 1990 and for ten years I was the secretary then I retired when I became Mayor of Burnley. So religion has played a very major part and it has progressed from religion being practised in the community or society, which was perhaps 100 years behind the society in England. We are still trying to overcome the difficulties but the good thing is that when I was Mayor, the Bishop of Burnley, the new bishop who is still Bishop of Burnley, Bishop John came and I invited him to the Mayor's parlour. We talked about setting up a sort of partnership of mosques and churches so that we could understand and celebrate what is common and work on it to give a positive note, a positive aspect of religion to the community as a whole. I'm very pleased that it has grown from strength to strength and it is doing its best to bring all the faith and non-faith communities together

in different activities, celebrations of festivals; of Christmas or Easter or Harvest Festival or Eid, and people from different faith groups visit each other's places of worship. So it's quite fascinating to think that what we want to see happening in the whole world, is happening in Burnley and in several other towns in England, but especially in Burnley because that's what we are concerned about primarily.

Initially, we bought the building in Rectory Road and then we bought this Majestic Bingo building that we're in now; before that it was a

£30,000 to build some indoor school rooms and improve the whole building quite a lot. So this shows what could happen if the Muslim communities up and down the country follow this example and have faith in young people, those who have been educated here (and most of them are very sound, level-headed people), people who want to live and enjoy life according to their own faith and religion without harming anybody, without antagonising anybody and who continue trying to reach out. During Ramadan fasting time, they have a communal sort of fasting programme where everybody joins in and they bring food from home and they eat. So a lot of progress in the positive sense is being seen to be made.

Responsibility is important to me. In 1975, my younger brother got married and our MP then was Dan Jones and he was addressing the ceremony and he said, "It was time that we had an Asian councillor and I would have no hesitation in saying," he embarrassed me, "that Rafique will be the best person to fulfil that responsibility." So next year they selected me to stand for election; there were three people standing from each party in each ward. The whole of Burnley

cinema hall. The owner wanted to sell it. He was an Irish gentleman. We went to meet him at his daughter's house, which was in this area on the other side of Crow Wood Farm. He said we could have it, "If you can pay me £4,000 a year." We bought it for £32,000 and we paid for it in eight years. Now it's a very nice mosque; it has been improved quite a lot. One thing that I would be very pleased to mention is that last year I was able to persuade the first generation trustees to retire and relinquish the trusteeships of the Trust. We drafted a new constitution and a lot of young people have come onto the management committee. Within six months they have raised

went to the elections in 1976 and although the election was on Thursday, I couldn't go to the vote counting because it was on Friday. My brother-in-law went in my place because I had taken Thursday off from school and you could only take one day off school for political reasons or civic duties as it were, so he took Friday off. The counting was at Barden High School because there were more votes to be counted and the Town Hall wasn't big enough. When Brian Whittle, who was the presiding officer and chief executive then, announced the result, I got elected. The whole hall went quiet and some of the people made some noises of disbelief, like it was something surprising, an Asian gentleman being elected; the first Asian councillor of Burnley. Then from '76 onwards I spent 30 years on the Council, except for two years when I was not elected but after two years I was re-elected. It was not until 2000 that my turn came to become Mayor, because the Burnley system is that the most senior councillor is elected as Mayor. So I was elected Mayor in May 2000.

I think, to be quite honest, I had heard from my parents and their peers that when British people

English better than they expected, they were very pleased and they brought their complaints to me and they were really appreciative if anything was resolved which they were unhappy about, or they wanted to be resolved. I got tremendous support from the community, both the Pakistani community and the local people as they were then. It was humbling. My mind flashed back; a boy in a small village, a far off village in Pakistan, coming here to work and then being elected mayor of the town. Quite a journey from my recollection of swimming in the river in the

Below: Reginald Maudling, the Home Secretary appointed Rafique Malik as a Member of the National Race Relations Board in 1970

New members appointed to the Race Relations Board

Mark Bonham Carter, who had been chairman of the Race Relations Board since its formation, left the Board at the beginning of the year to become chairman of the Community Relations Commission. The move left the Board without a permanent chairman and Sir Roy Wilson, Q.C, agreed to become acting-chairman until Sir Geoffrey Wilson takes up his appointment in the autumn.

There were also changes in the membership of the Board. Mr M. U. Rahman and Mr H. C. Hampton retired and their places were taken by Miss Elizabeth Steel (*below left*) a Liverpool solicitor who served for two years on the Board's committee in the north-west, and Mr Rafiq Malik (*right*) a Burnley school-teacher who has lived in England for five years.

Miss Elizabeth Steel

Mr Rafiq Malik

were in India they were very fair; there were fewer burglaries, and administration was very good and everything. I'd also read a lot about English people exploiting Asian communities in Africa and Australia and what have you. For the first time I felt that no, all we have heard is not true. They would not discriminate against you if you are of Pakistani origin or black or Asian because there were only a couple of hundred Pakistanis in the area when I was elected, so a great majority of the people who elected me - they were white. When they came to me because I could speak

village - a complete change and completely humbling. But my belief is that if you work hard God rewards you. If you work honestly, if you work hard, if you are sincere, God puts thoughts in people's minds and they support you and He opens doors for you. During my Mayoral year, I went in to different schools and organisations, voluntary organisations, and saw the amount of work which is being done for the community - for disabled children, for elderly people, for young people - it's immense. It dawned on me that we think that we as a Council are doing a lot but a lot of voluntary groups are doing perhaps more than the Council is doing, and they are raising funds voluntarily. It was very, very interesting and fulfilling. It made me humbler than I was, that here they are, people who are not themselves millionaires, working class people, but who give their time and raise funds. They help disabled people, they take them on holidays, they take them to the Vatican to see the Pope; it's a substantial amount of sacrifice being made by ordinary people. And I think we all should. If some people are not as fortunate as we are then it is our duty, moral duty, or human duty that we should try to do our best so that nobody feels neglected or nobody feels that they are deprived, they enjoy it as much as the others do.

I've lived a very, very busy life! I've heard there's only one life and one should do one's best. Way back in 1968, the government set up a Race Relations Board. It was actually set up in 1965 but it had very few powers. But in 1968, there was a good piece of legislation. The late Mark Bonham Carter, who was later elevated to the House of Lords, he was chairman and he came to Manchester and invited me because at that time I was chairman of the Federation of Pakistani Associations all over the UK, and he must have read about me in the papers. So he met me and then he invited me to become a member of the Race Relations Board way back in 1969. For seven or eight years I was a member of the Race Relations Board, which had a major impact on changing the attitudes of people. I had the honour of working with him, and later on with Sir Geoffrey Wilson who was the Principal Cabinet Secretary and when he retired from that post he replaced Lord Bonham Carter. I worked for seven or eight or years on the national scene and I was going to their offices every other Thursday to have meetings to decide about different cases of discrimination that were investigated by officers, and they brought their reports of evidence and everything to us and we sort of adjudicated. Later on, I was a primary school teacher but the then Director of Education made me a permanent supply teacher and I was based at Barden High School where I remained until 1984 when I left education. In the same period, I was also vice chairman of the local Racial Equality Council which covered Burnley and Pendle and I remained there for 20 years until I was appointed director of the Blackburn Racial Equality Council, where I had the honour of working with Jack Straw MP who has had many ministries in his career. So my major piece of

work outside my employment was racial equality and community relations. This is something which I'm very pleased with, and proud of; that I have had major encounters with people who had rigid ideas and tried to persuade them that we are all created by God and we should try to respect each other, we should try to be polite to one another, we should have differences but not fall out with one another. Forget the differences; try to celebrate what we have in common and the positive aspects of life. I feel that we will be a far better world if we look at the positive side of the things instead of the negative; instead of always trying to pick up on differences, or disagreeing and getting into conflicts and using weapons. I'm glad my first son did his PhD in physics but he totally rejected the study of atomic energy. He was so 'anti', he said it could destroy mankind, it's a dangerous sort of material. So I think if I can be happy for anything, I don't want to say proud of anything because I haven't done enough, but if I can say something which made me happy about myself then it is my work in the community relations field, bringing different people within the Pakistani community and outside the Pakistani community together. Living in a wider world I have come to the conclusion that people will be what they want to be. If you want people to change then give them some positive reasons why they should change or give them some hope. If they want to, they will. There is no room for coercion. I read in the Qur'an that a religious person should not force anybody to become Muslim, just leave people to make their own decisions in their way if they want to. So coming from that sort of background it was fascinating seeing it far more practised in England where you have people from many different backgrounds; you have Catholics, you have Jews, you have Muslims, you have Hindus, you have Sikhs, and apart from a few complaints which might occur in different towns, I think people are living very peacefully and very happily compared to any country in the world. That is something I think several other people, thousands of other people, including myself, have contributed to. That we are the same, God has created us all, He has given us vast amounts of treasures; we should enjoy them, we should exploit them, we should share them, and we should explore them instead of fighting amongst ourselves or fighting against one another.

Perhaps if I had another life I would do it in a different way and in a better way! Well, I have a different experience from many Pakistanis because my great-great-grandfather migrated from Kashmir. When the British sold Kashmir to Sikh Raja for 50,000 Rupees, which I can earn in a week now, my ancestors had to migrate from there to Punjab which is an area of Pakistan now. So I had that sort of thing in my veins, migrating from one place to another. I remember quite vividly that when I was a young person, people were still coming from Kashmir and their children were learning their language after school; it was very different from the language of Punjab and they were trying to retain their language and retain their culture. We did the same thing when we came here. My wife and other ladies set up classes for our children. They used to go to school during the day, in the evening they would go to the mosque, and then at the weekends they would go to Urdu classes to learn their language. Some of it has been included in the curriculum of schools now. Schools teach Urdu or Hindi or Bengali where there is a demand. But that's what we were doing. We have a saying in our language, actually it's not in our language it's in Persian, "Everything that goes into a salt mine becomes salt." So having come into England we have learned quite a lot of new things, English things, and we can easily see them (our children) going for fish and chips and similarly, adventurous people - English people, going for hot curry and rice and chicken masala. So it's interesting. But I think it should be - because of advanced technology and mobility, people can go from here to Pakistan in seven hours, whereas before, they went from one end of Pakistan to the other in seven or eight hours, so the world has shrunk into a sort of global village. People are changing, their attitudes are changing, their ways of living are changing and we are in a melting pot.

I said earlier on that I was a committed educationalist and learner and I wanted my children to get the best education; I did mention it. I mean one of the selfish reasons for staying here was not just to help the Pakistani community here but also to get the best education for my children. I knew back in Pakistan that only very rich people could send their children to be educated in England. I thought, "I'm here, why shouldn't I exploit this facility?" All my children, I'm pleased that they have got a university education at least. One of them is a doctor, one of them is a solicitor and one of them runs his own company (he has a PhD). One of my rising stars was elected an MP. He was the first new generation, first generation MP and he was the first Muslim minister in the western world. So

if, leaving myself apart, if I could be very proud of anything, that is my son's rise in the civic field in the politics of the country. This is a great satisfaction to me, that at least all my children have had a university education for which I count myself very lucky.

Below: The Mayor, Rafique Malik placing a wreath at the War Memorial in Towneley Park

I didn't have any time to inspire them but I think it was self-starting, observation. There is in education a theory of learning by suggestion, children learn by what they see their parents doing. A lot of children smile like their parents, mother or father, but they spend more time with their mothers. I think that's where they got that sort of inspiration. I would like to say that this building we're in now, the mosque, was a derelict building six or seven years ago. We bought it and during the last five years we have made it a sort of centre of the community for all sorts of activities, where it is used all the time by the people in the community. I think it has played a major role in bringing the community together and in exchanging views with one another. I'm very grateful to the mosque for continuing to provide support and supporting the community use. We bought it when we sold the old mosque on Rectory Road to the Council, for clearance. We bought this building but it was in a derelict condition with a wrought iron, central heating system that had large pipes, so we ripped it all out. There was a period when we removed all this and added double-glazed windows and refurbished the toilets and kitchen; everything was done over the last five years. You couldn't enter it five years ago; it really was a derelict building.

Finally, I have no home elsewhere. Burnley is my home. Although I am 75, I still enjoy living here actively.

Civic

Mohammad Najib

Above: Mohammad Najib raised the largest amount of funds for his Mayor's Charity, to buy two scanners, to detect mouth and throat cancer

Below: Mohammad Najib, the Mayor of Burnley, 2006

My name is Mohammad Najib and I was born in a Pakistani village, Kotli Allah Yar, in the district Jhelum, which is 70 miles away from Islamabad. When I was the mayor of Burnley, in my maiden speech I mentioned my school situation because of my disability. I couldn't walk, and the school was a fair way from my village and my elder sisters, one by one, used to carry me to school and bring me back by carrying me in their arms – 3 miles there and three miles back. That is how I completed my primary education. Then I started high school which was 3 miles away from my village. At that time, by the grace of God, I had acquired the strength to start walking. I went to school for five years and I always walked there and back. I completed my basic education in school in 1969 and then I started higher education at college in Jhelum. After that time I completed my BA degree over there and then I went for further education. Actually, I was in Lahore going to the Law College and somehow, I was passing a teachers' training college. So I went in and decided to go for teacher training rather than go into law and I completed my teachers' training degree in 1975.

After the completion of the teachers' training degree I should have started teaching in a school but somehow I got a job in a government organisation, in the registration department organised by the central government. I worked there for two years and then came to this country in 1978 where my wife was waiting for me. She was already living here and we got married in 1978. She had a house in Burnley and so we started living in Gordon Street in Stoneyholme, Burnley. I have always found it to be a nice area and a nice town and started developing myself, very slowly and steadily in Burnley. I went for a job in this small factory called Mitchell's Plastics in Burnley and we went to find out, really, if the job was available and the foreman over there asked me, "Do you want to start work now?" I said, "Yeah, I will do it" and I started working the same night. I worked the night shift, 12 hours a night and completed two years over there and then I was made redundant. It

was actually very fortunate that; I think it was a turning point in my life because I applied for a job at Jinnah Community Development Trust and I was appointed as a community development officer and I worked here for two years. I think that's when I learned more about community work, how to deal with people and understand more about the town. During that work I was interested in going into business. I bought a shop and I made the shop different. I put together my store, improved it and started building it up steadily and then I bought another store and by that time I was owner of two stores, so on the inside I was quite satisfied. At that time I thought I should contribute to society as well. I should do something for the community and society and that's the time when I became a member of the Labour Party and their Panel of Candidates, and fought my first election but I was defeated. In the second year I stood for Queensgate Ward and was easily elected, I was there as a councillor until 2007.

incident but it was very important to me, and she said, "Yesterday I voted for you and I'm glad you won, and I'm proud I voted for you." I think that is the thing for me. It is love and affection from the community who I work for. Everybody had their own style of working as an elected

for 18 years I represented that ward. I think that is the unforgettable thing, and the reward, you have been given by the community. I felt that as I belonged to the Asian community, I should contribute so that the local indigenous community would remember that we are a part

of the community and I wanted to build that confidence in the indigenous community. I wanted there to be a good understanding and I will always believe, even though at one stage seven British National Party councillors got elected in Burnley, that Burnley is a good town and not a racist town. It is the best town to live in, and luckily I was around to contribute to some of that situation. It is very clear to me, because I was involved with regular people from going door-to-door and street to street, that the people were not racist. Outsiders came in and took advantage of the disturbances in Burnley and they helped seven BNP councillors in getting elected. There was another political element at that time because the Burnley Labour Party dominated the whole town and there was no powerful opposition to them, and people wanted some type of opposition. Not everybody likes one party and they need an alternative, and at that time there was no other strong opposition party so when the BNP candidates stood, people overwhelmingly voted for them. That is why I believe strongly that Burnley was not a racist town, it never was and I don't think it will ever be in the future. That was totally a protest vote. You can see it, over the years, when it happens. It's died down, they started losing their seats and it proved my point. Only one of the seven is left on the council.

representative. My style was to go door-to-door and speak to people because I knew who lived there and I especially targeted older people first and went to them in my spare time asking, "Is there anything I can do for you?" and they were surprised thinking, what sort of service will he provide? When I was first re-elected there were no Asian people to vote for me. They were English people, it was a predominantly white English ward that voted for me and they always voted for me. One or two elections I lost, but

I think the whole of my career in politics was at the right time in my life - when I was elected as a mayor of the borough, and it is a wonderful thing for a person to have things given to them, to become first citizen of the town. I still feel I should have done more for my town, but I will always be grateful to the people of Burnley, especially the people of my ward where I was elected.

It is a very basic thing, my religion says, "Where do you live, that's your home." That is the basic teaching of our religion and I was quite aware of that teaching and that's why I started working. Islam also says that regardless of whether your next door neighbour is Muslim or non-Muslim, he is your neighbour and you respect him and all the people are your brothers and sisters, take care of them and respect them. I can remember when my next door neighbour was moving; he was an English person. We were crying and he was crying as well because we were so happy with him and proud that he was our neighbour, and it was the same way for him. That is the influence of our religion on me. When I was mayor, we took a delegation to Pakistan but before that, I made a friendship link between my home town, Jhelum, and Burnley and it was a wonderful thing to do. Obviously, there were seven BNP councillors and I was told that they might oppose it and that there could be unrest in the community about the proposal. Well the officers said they would speak to them about it. I said, "If you don't mind, I will speak to our political groups about it." I called the BNP leader into the mayor's parlour and spoke to her and she said, "It's a wonderful thing. There's nothing wrong with that, we can understand each other, we can talk, we can know about their culture, build awareness, it's a wonderful thing. We have no objection." Similarly with the Conservatives, and Liberal Democrats; they all agreed and we got a resolution passed by Burnley Council and even though the British National Party didn't vote for that proposal, they didn't vote against it either. So I was able to achieve that friendship between Burnley, which is my home, and my first home town, Jhelum, that friendship link. So we took the delegation there. The chairman of Lancashire County Council was included in the delegation. We went to different places, different towns. We went to Islamabad and there were people carrying British flags and Pakistani flags. I think what we achieved at that time is more than any ambassador could; to bring the relationship closer between the two countries and the two communities and the two cultures. It was a wonderful thing. I'll never forget it. I went with other key community leaders, including Mr Malik. There was media coverage as well from DM Digital, they were covering the whole

tour from here to Pakistan and there was also a photographer from the Evening Telegraph. We went everywhere and were overwhelmingly accepted. That was the best part of my mayoral year, it was wonderful.

In 1990, I was appointed as a Justice of the Peace in Burnley and it was an amazing experience. It was a wonderful piece of community work, and I really enjoyed participating in the British justice system, which is excellent, the best justice system in the world. It works regardless of anyone's class; it's based on merit, and I'm proud to have been doing that work for over 22 years. I said I'd become a member of the

Below: Chair Lancashire County Council, Terry Burns; the Mayor of Burnley, Mohammad Najib; Rafique Malik, former Mayor of Burnley; Chaudhry Tahir Zaman, Chair Peoples Party Gujrat; Nadeem Asghar, Chair Tehsil Council Kharian on the stage at a large reception in the village Jaurah organised by Naseer Zaman from Nelson, Chair of the Union Council

Labour Party to work for the community, well it's a similar thing. Because I was involved with the Jinnah organisation and at that time I was also involved in the Community Relations Council, they proposed my name to become a Justice of the Peace. It's been a really enjoyable 22 years in community work, and it's a wonderful community and I've met a lot of nice people in Burnley. Excellent, I remember those years. I think anybody who lives in Burnley and whose roots are in Pakistan, I strongly believe they feel Burnley is their home. I can only give you the one example of mine, and it's a true example whenever I go to Pakistan, I love to go and when I come back to Britain and my aeroplane lands at Heathrow or Manchester, I just feel I've come home. That's my feeling and I'm proud that I made Burnley my home. It is the home of my children and my other relatives. I'd like to carry on with the community work. We still do

Above: Chair of Lancashire County Council, Terry Burns; Mayor of Burnley, Mohammad Najib; and former Mayor of Burnley, Rafique Malik at a large reception organised by the Chair of Tehsil Council Kharian, Nadeem Asghar Kaira at Lalamusa

community work together, we volunteer at the Jinnah centre from Monday to Thursday, for 3 or 4 hours, and we specialise in welfare rights for people who want us to represent them, and any other thing we can do for them. We do have a literary society with poetry recitals and other events and we are always here. I love it. I go to the gym and do some community work, that's my hobby at the moment. I'm proud of my town.

There is an incident I will never forget, which was in early 1988; it was perhaps the end of May, the last week of May. I was newly elected at that time, my first time on Burnley Council and my cousin died in Pakistan suddenly and I rushed to Pakistan. I came back after five days. I used to have a small shop at that time; I had all the shops takings there to put into the bank. I went to the bank and the amount was written in the paying-in book, and I had a change bag as well, with it, and some cash notes. It was quite a big amount in those days, in 1988, over £3,000 including the change – and I was going into the Yorkshire Bank in Burnley, in Hargreaves Street. I was driving a van and when I came out of the van, I was a bit tired. That was a cool morning and it was breezy, and a bit windy. Somehow I lost the grip on the money bag, which was tied by a rubber band, and the money slipped out and spread all over the street. I thought, I've lost all that money, and people were rushing about after the money. Some people came out of offices, people stopped their cars and they were rushing towards the notes, and I was amazed when the people started to bring the money back to me. I was so confused; I started putting the money in the change bag, which was a closed bag, and I thought, what I get back will at least be something, which is better than nothing. I went back home rather than going to the bank, to find out how much I had lost and it was amazing to find that whatever I had written on the paying in book, all the money was there, not a single note was missing. I think that is the greatest example of character in any nation to be able to do that. I think some people would kill for money but I was amazed by the

www.burnleytoday.co.uk Tel. 01282 426161

NEWS

Mohammad is sworn in as new town mayor

FAMILY AFFAIR: Burnley's new Mayor and Mayoress with their sons Muddassir, Adil and Hamayed, daughter Arooj, daughters-in-law Iram and Samina, the mayor's sisters Shah Begum and Raza Bibi and the grandchildren Muazma, Iqra and Hassan.
A170605/5b

BY MARGARET PARSONS   Roger Frost and his sister, Mrs Pauline Frost-Hardwick, at the traditional mayor making   brother Mohammad Rashid who died

local people, how they behaved and how they helped me. I'll never forget that.

Mr Malik was mayor before me; he was the first Asian mayor in Burnley. Every mayor chooses a charity to support and I chose a charity that was in my mind, long before I became the mayor. In the early '60s, my brother came to the UK and he lived in Burnley. From a very young age he suffered from mouth cancer and he died. There are still quite a large number of patients with throat and mouth cancer so I wanted to discuss it with the Health Authority, to see if there was anything I could help with; to buy something for the NHS which is not already available for local people. The mayor's secretary arranged a meeting with the Health Authority and the doctor in charge of the relevant department and we had a discussion. He showed me something very interesting. He said, "There is a scanner type of thing we have and two types of machines in the UK, which have been sent from America as a model and they show from a very early stage if the patient is suffering from mouth cancer or throat cancer. It gives a picture on a screen that is so clear that the consultant only takes a few seconds to diagnose it." I said, I'll go for it. He also mentioned that if we got that, we would be the first hospital, Burnley General Hospital, the first in the country to have that scanner. So I said

definitely I would go for it but the price was very high. He said one scanner costs around £30,000, and I said I would definitely go for it. Obviously my wife, who was the mayoress then, worked with the committee that was helping at that time but I held different events to organise it. It's not only that my brother died from mouth cancer, I didn't want any mouth cancer deaths in Burnley due to a lack of diagnosis. That was one reason. The other reason was because of that charity, I wanted to bring a closer relationship between the two communities and I wanted to enhance the relationship between the communities. That was my dream, showing that we are shoulder-to-shoulder as a local community, that we are concerned with the local health of the local people and we care about them. I'm glad that in the history of Burnley mayoral periods, my charity was the highest earner, I believe. I'm not sure, but I'm aware that we raised the highest amount ever raised in Burnley. It was around £60,000. The consultant was delighted that instead of one, we were going to buy two scanners. This is a small instance but very important to me. For example, an English child came to me to hand over some money for my charity. How he raised it, it's amazing; he had a bouncy castle in his garden and he was charging his young friends for using it and he raised some money and gave it to me. Similarly, there was a

Above: Chair of Lancashire County Council, Terry Burns, and Mayor of Burnley, Mohammad Najib, presenting a Burnley Crest as a gift to the British High Commissioner, Robert Brinkley and Mrs Brinkley at the British High Commision in Islamabad

family in Nelson, an Asian family, the children saved up from their pocket money and they came to me and handed over that money. That is the spirit I think that has come out through my charity and I'm delighted. I'm able to serve Burnley and make it unique in the country – they have the scanners and there is a reduction in deaths from mouth cancer.

As we are looking at the history of Burnley residents with roots in Pakistan, I think it is worth mentioning that I stood in elections for Lancashire County Council in 1993 and I was overwhelmingly elected in Burnley Central East division. I was the first British Pakistani who was elected to Lancashire County Council and it was a great privilege for me, and gratifying that I had made history. I'm one of those people who came to Burnley from Pakistan and made a contribution to our society. Through Lancashire County Council's various committees, I made my contribution. I was chairman of the Education Equal Opportunity Committee and I worked on several other committees and helped the local people through my role at Lancashire County Council.

Civic

Shahid Malik

My name is Shahid Malik. I was born at Bank Hall Hospital, an old mining hospital, which like the many pits of Burnley in the last century, sadly no longer exists. Unlike my siblings and I, my parents were born in Pakistan and came to Burnley in the swinging '60s where they worked initially on Burnley's many assembly lines. They were part of a mass exodus of people from Commonwealth countries who came to the UK to ease the huge labour shortages and to help build Britain. My father's ambition, having gained a Bachelor of Arts degree in Pakistan, was to gain a Bachelor of Education degree here in the UK, and to teach in this country before returning to Pakistan. However, like the best laid plans of mice and men……. And the rest is history!

Over time, both my parents moved from blue-collar jobs to white, with a particular focus on education and public service. For my dad it was a natural progression as he had been the head teacher of a school in Gujrat, one of Pakistan's major industrial cities. It was a role I know he reluctantly left to come to the UK. At 27 years old, he was probably the youngest head teacher in Pakistan at the 1,000 plus Dhoria boys' high school. My mum also worked in education, as a school liaison officer and got involved with teaching and civic life. She later became a Justice of the Peace (Magistrate) in Burnley. My dad became a Councillor in 1976 (retiring 30 years later in 2006) and he and my mum were Mayor and Mayoress of Burnley in 2000. They were both very involved in the local community and trying to help, support and move things forward. I think they came because my mum's brother initially came here. Now, why he chose Burnley - the Lord knows. But I think he was the magnet that drew my dad to Burnley and then over time, all of us (seven kids in total) were born in Burnley.

Above: Shahid Malik is the first British born muslim MP (2005-2010) and the first muslim Minister in Europe

Left: Stoneyholme Junior School pupil 1975

Below: Shahid Malik MP speaks to the media, outside 10 Downing Street, after a meeting with the Prime Minister, Tony Blair, following the London 7/7 terror attacks. Flanked by Parliamentarians, including the Leader of the Opposition, Michael Howard, as well as muslim leaders in 2005

Right: The then Secretary of State for Northern Ireland, the late Mo Mowlam MP, appoints Shahid Malik as an Equality Commissioner for Northern Ireland as part of the implimentation of the Good Friday Peace Agreement in 1999. He was the only person appointed to the role from Great Britain

I went to Stoneyholme Infant and Junior Schools and then onto Barden High School and thereafter to the Sixth Form in Kiddrow Lane, Habergham Sixth Form, as it was then known. I wanted to be a professional snooker player, but my parents 'convinced' me that doing some 'A'-Levels and then getting a University degree was a wise move.

In terms of my career, I feel that I've really been blessed to carry out roles, national and international, which have been incredibly worthwhile and satisfying. I've been able to reach heights that as a child I would never have believed possible - often becoming the first or youngest person in those roles. However, if there is one thing of which I am absolutely sure, it is that all those achievements were only possible because I was able to stand on the shoulders of giants – the first generation British Pakistanis, people like my mum and dad and many others who came here as immigrants and built a foundation and platform that allowed all those who followed to realize their potential and achieve their dreams. The things that the first generation had to endure, the sacrifices that they made, and their relative achievements, despite the often acutely challenging circumstances, helped to mould and inspire so many others down the years.

Because I understand where I came from, one of the things I find most rewarding is speaking to young people from working class backgrounds to help lift their aspirations. I want them to believe that they can achieve despite their economic background and despite the often-limiting aspirations others may have for them.

I've been very fortunate in life, not least because

of the family I was born into and the public service ethos that was instilled into all of us at an early age. As a result most of the things that I have done in my life have been linked to helping change society for the better. In my early years perhaps the most significant and satisfying national role I had was as an Equality Commissioner for Northern Ireland as part of the Good Friday Peace Agreement. It was particularly special because I was appointed through open competition by the late Mo Mowlam MP – the then Secretary of State for Northern Ireland, and a truly unique woman. To play a tiny part in the huge forward path for Northern Ireland was deeply humbling.

You've asked which roles I am most proud of, well there have been numerous such roles, from being the youngest chief executive in the country, managing a £150m development fund in London, to being the first elected Muslim to become a Minister, not just in the UK but the entire Western world. Though these may be significant roles in themselves, the real significance was the direct and indirect impact of those roles. Having been able to improve the quality of life of people living in deprived neighbourhoods in various parts of the UK has been tremendously satisfying. However, changing lives for the better is only second to saving lives. I remember, as International Development Minister, I approved and allocated some £90 million for a project in Pakistan which focused on maternal and new-born health, and that, masha'Allah, has saved the lives of some 35,000 women and over 300,000 children who would have died unnecessarily. I'm proud to have held such a privileged role. Had I not been a Minister, then I wouldn't have

played any role in saving those lives in Pakistan or anywhere else for that matter.

As Britons, we're privileged that we live in one of the richest countries on earth and as such I believe we have a responsibility to those less fortunate than us. I'm extremely proud of my country, and when I said that I allocated £90m – well, it's this great country that allocated the money and saved those lives. It's the core values of this country that provides the desire and passion to help other countries in the way that we do, and I think we're a beacon today across the globe and especially because our 'giving' is not tied or political but based on poverty and need. Of course £90 million or 300,000 children are just figures. You can only really understand this giving if you witnesses our anti-poverty initiatives in action; whether that be in Africa, Bangladesh, Pakistan, India, Nepal, Vietnam, Yemen or

Indonesia - there are so many countries that you could go to witness the impact of our decisions on aid.

Bangladesh is a good example. I went to the capital Dhaka to a slum called Mirpur. In this slum we had allocated some funding to a non-governmental organisation (NGO), a local NGO that was working jointly with, if you will, a Western NGO. Together they just got three flush toilets, and there was a lot of celebrating going on. In our country you would think three flush toilets, what's the big deal? Actually it was a big deal for them. But when you think there were over 140 people that would share those three flush toilets, and in this country there are homes that have three or more toilets, it gives you a sense of perspective. I think quite often we moan without putting things in a global context and I think if we did then we'd moan a lot less.

Whilst in Bangladesh, that same visit, I met a girl who I think was nine years old perhaps, and because of an NGO that we'd funded she was now being released from her workplace to spend a few hours every other day or so on education. She worked five hours a day every day and she earned as little as a penny an hour for her embroidery work. But when I spoke to her not only was she more confident about herself but also she now had great aspirations for her children who were going to become doctors and engineers – and that is the power of education in liberating the human spirit and the human potential.

Of course there are dozens of examples I could give from providing basic nets treated with insecticide that save millions of lives from malaria, to providing basic retro-viral drugs to push the life expectancy in some countries, in sub-Saharan Africa, to above the sub-40 years old level that previously existed. As a country we can rightly be proud of our role in changing lives and saving lives across the world – that is the "Great" in Great Britain.

Can young people really make a difference? I have seen time and again how young people can get involved and make major strategic and practical contributions. Young people are generally idealists who also want to change the world for the better. I think today they're well motivated and much more positive than at any time in recent history. One of the initiatives that we launched while I was International Development Minister was a youth volunteering programme that allowed young people to make a contribution in the developing world and then come back to the UK to talk about their experience thus making a difference abroad and at home.

I've been speaking a lot of the challenges in the developing world but of course we have many in our so-called developed world. There's still so much to do in terms of bringing communities together. There are too many divisions within communities, based on religion, race, stupidity, ignorance, class, and so on. And the solutions can be simple; so much can be done by diverse groups just coming together, mixing and thus creating understanding. I thank God that the Burnley that I was born in is no longer - it was a violent Burnley, it was a racist Burnley. That isn't the Burnley of today. Burnley today has sharply changed - its much warmer and much more accepting place.

How has this change come about? Time, education, the internet, TV, integration, food, music and schools have cumulatively created this positive change. It's a far cry from the days I went to school. Junior school was heaven but at secondary school was a living hell with the phenomenon of so-called 'Paki-bashing', which meant daily violence. Sadly, and if I can put this diplomatically, many of the then teachers weren't "brilliant" but thankfully today teachers are. The education system has changed and that's primarily because of government and politicians introducing standards, different expectations, increased accountability and a changing world. I think we're in a much, much, healthier place today but I don't want to be naïve either - there are still lots of challenges and racism and things like that are still alive. It's not just one way; I mean this evil works in every conceivable way. Racism isn't about white on black, it can be black on white, it can be brown on black, or brown on white, and it's very complex. I would unequivocally state that racism in any of its forms is completely unacceptable. We're all here today and we're here to stay so we have to find ways of making our society work for all its citizens.

I am happy to speak about my belief in politics making a difference and I will give you a really micro example and then something just slightly larger scale. As an MP I remember coming into the office on a Friday in Dewsbury; I'd been in

Below: Signing a historic 10-year Aid Deal between the UK and Yemen (the first of its kind in the Middle East) with the Prime Minister and Deputy Prime Minister of Yemen in 2007

Parliament all week, and there was a woman waiting for me with some flowers and chocolates. She had a baby in one arm and she had a young toddler with her as well. She gave me this unexpected hug. Basically she's somebody who had had a debt for a long time; the bank interest on that debt had been such that she hadn't been able to pay it off. She was a single mother and she was suffering. I was able to intervene, to speak to the bank and to threaten them in a very diplomatic way and the end result was that they wiped out her debt. Now, her face that I saw then was the kind of face that if you've had a bad week, you would still feel you're in the right job and you should continue. That's on a very micro, individual case level. I can't remember her exact words, "Thanks so much, Mr Malik, now come here," a big hug type of thing. To be honest there's hundreds of examples like that. But I think on a wider scale, across the town, helping to save schools and post offices – being able to have that kind of positive impact means a lot.

If you're in that privileged position of being an MP, then I believe you have to fight with all your might for your constituents. It was this belief and desire to go the extra mile, above and beyond the call of duty that ensured we succeeded often where no-one else had previously. Writing a 35 page report and a 17 page report to save two post offices may seem extreme for an MP, but by doing so we became the only constituency in the country that was able to save two post offices.

Similarly, fighting for two schools that were targeted for closure despite being excellent schools was an outrage and so I fought both the conservatives when they controlled the council and then my own party, Labour, because they continued with the closure programme. Leading the campaign I became the first ever MP to directly give evidence to the Schools Adjudicator, which resulted in saving the schools – a great triumph for my constituents and for our young folk.
The courage to fight, even if it's against your own party, in the interests of the greater good is something that came from my parents – it's something they instilled at an early stage and I'm pleased they did.

The Dewsbury community was completely over the moon at the outcomes. They had resigned themselves to the fact that the schools were closing because every political party supported the closure. As for the post offices, the perceived wisdom was that they were bound to close

because no MP had ever been able to prevent such closures. But by mounting good campaigns and putting together good evidential reports in the end we defeated the might of the Local Council, the Education Authority and Post Office Counters Limited. When we got the result, everybody felt part of it, and they were.

To be honest, at the offset the odds on succeeding in saving the post offices or schools was probably four in a hundred, but we still did it.

Above: Speaking at a rally against the BNP following the election of a BNP councillor in Burnley in 2003

Below: On poppy duty as patron of the British Legion in Dewsbury

These weren't easy campaigns because I was fighting my own Party, but we still achieved success. But there have been other campaigns where I've fought against the will and wishes of the local community and those are very difficult because you know you're losing voters. In one area in Dewsbury, I was supporting the school's application to have five-a-side football pitches developed and the whole community in that area was completely opposed to it. But I stood with the school because I felt that resources for young people were more important and I had campaigned on the issue during the elections. In the end I did the right thing. We got the money for the sports facilities for the kids and for young people, and they're still there today. Interestingly, none of the complaints and fears of local people came into being.

The one thing I've learnt is that there are no easy wins, and unfortunately somebody is always going to be upset. The alternative is never to get involved in anything that may create opposition, and to be candid there are some MPs who adopt such a "neutrality" strategy but that's not me.
This sense of wanting to help other people to do good, to be a citizen of not only your town, your city, your country, but the world I think all that developed during my childhood at home.

I got an incredible sense of satisfaction for example in some of the peacekeeping and conflict work that I did in places like Nepal. They'd had civil

war for a decade; thousands of people had been killed, and then I was kind of plonked in there. I was speaking to the Prime Minister, to the Maoist leader, to the seven parties' leadership on a continuous basis. I was making phone calls from the UK at 3:00 in the morning to fit in with their timetables in Kathmandu and elsewhere to make sure that people, I suppose, stayed on-track. I think we're lucky that in Nepal, for example, the biggest aid programme is UK-led and of course we've got a superb relationship with Nepal going back over decades due to the Gurkhas. I was fortunate to be able to have that kind of position of trust, and play this broker role and to be part of helping push Nepal towards a democratic republic, which it became, and for it to have its first ever democratic elections. My actual role really was to fight poverty but I wanted to do much more than that, which was to deal with this kind of conflict and to help push it forward. Similarly I tried to play a peacekeeping role here in Burnley during the disturbances/rioting in 2001 and I think, again, that came from my desire to want to deal with conflict. Of course during 2001 there were people of all shades and descriptions that were involved in negative activity as well as positive activity.

Kosovo was another fascinating assignment for me. I had been meeting with its leadership prior to it being declared an independent country in order to assess its needs and to offer support via our UK aid programme. I went on to become the first British Minister to visit the world's newest country and as

Below: Departing following talks with Nepalese Prime Minister, Girija Koirala, in a bid to secure peace and elections at the end of 10 years of civil war in Nepal

well as meeting key politicians, I went to the sites of many massacres – some 1,500 Kosovars were killed - which was a very powerful reminder of the evil that exists even today. It reminded me of when I visited Majdanek Nazi death camp in Poland – although the sheer scale and industrial nature of the genocide in Majdanek was something very different with nearly 80,000 people being killed.

How did I first formally get involved in national politics? Probably when I was elected onto Labour's National Executive Committee (NEC) - on my first attempt as an unknown, something that had never really happened before; I was the first non-white person elected. The victory was completely unexpected and I felt honoured because I hadn't been gifted the place, but had been elected by Labour party members in their tens of thousands in England, Scotland, and Wales voting for me. Only 6 of the 33 are actually elected by members across the country, while the others are appointed because they happen to hold positions such as party leader (Prime Minister), Trade Union reps etc. My decision to run for the NEC stemmed from my visit to the Labour Party conference a year earlier where I'd looked at the 33 NEC members in a magazine with their photos and to my amazement they were all white. I was shocked. I just couldn't believe it. And I thought okay, but that can't be right. I put my name forward the next year and managed to get on. You had 200 words to say what you were all about, and what you wanted to do.

I spoke about some things that I was involved in, in Northern Ireland, on regeneration, on race issues in the UK, and it was on the basis of that that I got elected. I remained there for five years unbeaten 'til I stepped down on becoming an MP in 2005.

So there are lots of things like that I'm pleased to have contributed to. All the urban regeneration, anti-poverty work in this country gave me tremendous satisfaction because you know you're changing lives. Okay, it's not like internationally where you're changing lives and saving lives, but you are still changing lives in this country for the better and that makes me feel good inside. I suppose that's the kind of thing that drives me. I got a real thrill from being involved in international development which I first got formally involved with when I became Vice

Chair of UNESCO UK over a decade ago, that was tremendous, my first insight into the world of international development, co-operation and understanding.

Also, being elected as a Member of Parliament – sometimes I've got to pinch myself because I was born in Burnley and grew up in a ward, which at the time had the sixth highest child poverty rate out of 8,814 wards in England and Wales. So growing up in Stoneyholme it's hard to believe sometimes that from that you can go on to do so many things nationally and internationally. But the fact it happened means if one person can do it, who isn't particularly special, and that's me, then anybody can do it as long as they want to enough. Sometimes we're limited by what we believe is achievable, and it's really important for young people, I think, to see people who've achieved and then realize they too can fulfill their own potential. Although I obviously have a great affection for my parents country of origin, Pakistan, I am most proud of being British, English, Lancastrian, an adopted Yorkshireman and of course being from Burnley but in this interconnected and interdependent world in which we live, I don't believe we need limit ourselves and in that sense I also view myself as a citizen of the world.

Below: Shahid Malik MP, with Gordon Brown MP, speaking at a Parliamentary Reception to thank the British Search and Rescue Teams who assisted Pakistan following the devastating earthquake, that cost 75,000 lives in 2005

Chapter 2 - Public sector

Community/Public Service

Sajda Majeed

Above: Sajda Majeed, co-ordinator Daneshouse Healthy Living Centre

My name is Sajda Majeed. I was born here in Burnley in the Edith Watson Ward at Burnley General Hospital in June 1973. My father worked at Smith and Nephews, it's a textile mill. Prior to that he worked at Mullard's which was in Simonstone, and I think they made television screens for Phillips. I'm fairly certain that's what they did. My mum was a housewife but my father was only with us for a short time. I was nine when my dad died. He was only in this country for a short time. I obviously remember some of those nine years. He arrived in the 1960s and worked in Yorkshire and again, I think it was mainly in the textile industry, and mum was a housewife.

It's a bit of a tale; my dad came here first with two brothers. Their father died when really young, so my dad lost his father when I think he was about three. And times were hard, so my grandmother remarried; really there weren't many opportunities where my father was from. A lot of people from that region were the first people to come to England, I believe, in the 1960s. An opportunity arose actually. There's a tale about how when my dad was a young man sitting in a café, there was a guy that had come from England, he'd gone on holiday there and in those days, people used to carry their money around with them. I think he'd come off the aeroplane or something and he'd stopped at that cafe and was on his way to his village and people knew who he was. Anyway, he'd gone off and left this bag which had lots of money in it. My dad had found the bag, I only found this out very recently, and he located the man and gave him the money back. This chap was just so taken aback by his honesty that he then approached him and said, "Well, you know, I live in England," and I think in those days, there were agents that took people abroad because in the UK they were looking for workforces from abroad to work in the textile industry. He approached my dad and said, "You know, if you'd like to go I can arrange that." That's how it came about.

He came here really through an opportunity that arose and then my mum joined him when she got married to him in the late 1960s. I think it was about '69 she got married and I think she came here in '71, to Yorkshire. They settled in Sheffield for a short while, and then they came to Burnley. From what I remember, my dad had some friends in Yorkshire and one of them had family here in Burnley as well. I think there was an opportunity with work, and there were jobs going so Dad decided to move here and obviously Mum moved here as well. My brother was born in '72, they were still in Sheffield then, and then just before I was born (I think it was just a short time before) they moved to Burnley. My dad was very strong in his faith and he got very involved with the mosque community. He was involved with the building of the mosque, the Ghausia Mosque which was originally on Colne Road; there was a group of them that worked on that as well as his work. I think because the mosque was so important to him being involved with that, he made friends and then they just settled really and that kept them here. Obviously work was key at the time, as well as providing for his family here he was working to provide for them abroad as well because Mirpur was a very poor region. It's very affluent now but at the time work was important and key for him that he had a job that could provide for both families really.

I went to school at Barden Infants and then Barden Juniors which was on St Philips' Street. They have knocked down the schools now and built the super school, which is Burnley Campus. I've lots of happy memories really because a lot of the people I went to school with still live in the area and I'm still in touch with them and it's great to see how our kids are now friends. Some of them had also gone to Barden as well. I went to Walshaw High School and I left in 1989.

Well, when I left school I then went to Pakistan and I got married at 16. I came back and I worked at a textile firm and I was the office junior there. I did all the jobs, making the brews, going for the buttie run, all those kind of jobs that I didn't really like! But I think they gave

Above: Sajda Majeed's sons, Owais (11) and Danyaal (5), ready on their first day to go to Secondary and Primary schools respectively

I managed to get a discount and I brought them back. I think through him I learnt a lot about negotiation because he was young; also that if you persevere you can achieve whatever you want. My mum had a huge influence in the way that I've approached work and life in general because when my father died, my mum was on her own. She was only 28. She had five children all under the age of ten. I said she was a housewife but she also worked from home. She sewed clothes to make extra money. The work ethic was always there. For me it was always about what's been instilled in me, not to give up and to go for your goals and achieve. What's been rewarding is if you do something and it makes a difference to a person. After I left Northern Textiles I worked at a training organisation, Future Direction Training, and then I went to work at the Careers Service and I was there for about ten years; I did a lot of work with young people, with 16 to 19 year olds. Then I did some work guiding adults into education. But with the young people, I think that was always rewarding. Helping them find work, giving them the confidence to go for an interview and then when they actually got the job, seeing the big smiles on their faces. I've been very involved with the Chai Centre where I work now and I was involved with that project prior to being employed by them.

It was back in 1999 when a group of us from the area, residents, decided to set up a group to make a difference in the area really. It was Daneshouse Development Trust, Daneshouse Community Economic Development Trust. A group of us came together, like-minded people, all in their 20s at the time, all working as well. We all had our jobs but we just wanted to make a difference to the community that we lived in. I wanted to focus on fitness at the time because when I was looking around for myself there weren't many facilities available that sort of met the cultural needs of women. I had this idea about setting up a fitness facility and that was a project I wanted to work on. With the support of the others I pursued that and from a little idea, what we ended up with was what we have now, which is a Chai Centre which houses the Healthy Living Centre project. I always see that as a very rewarding project because it was an idea that I had, and to be able to take it forward with the support of so many people and professional people, at that level, that had the vision to be able to see that it would work. We had the Primary Care Trust on board and a gentleman called Tim Mansfield who backed us as a community group, and Bradford and

me a good grounding. One of the things that I learnt was the owner there, Bill Gleeve, was a young entrepreneur and I learnt a lot from him and negotiation was one of them. I remember being about 17 and we needed some mugs for the office and he said to me, "Right, can you go and get some mugs from town?" and I said, "That's fine." He said, "Yeah, but I've got a task for you." And I said, "What's that?" He said, "You've got to go and get these mugs but whatever the price is you've got to knock it down." And I was like, "I can't do that." I remember thinking I can't go into Woolworths and ask them to give me a discount. He said, "Don't come back unless you've got a discount." I said, "Right, okay." So off I went and

Northern Housing which is now Accent Housing, and they supported us. We were able to engage with the community and get their feedback and actually put a project in that was over £1 million for the build of the project. We amalgamated with the Children's Centre which was Sure Start at the time, and it was supported by the Primary Care Trust. We were able to have a building that was a community facility and housed the Healthy Living Centre and Sure Start, which is now the Children's Centre.

To see something like that come from a small idea that really, at the time, seemed like it was not going to happen - I remember, the first time I found out the Stage 1 bid had gone through, the Healthy Living project, and I was like, oh God I can't believe this. When the second and final bid went through and it was accepted, I remember I was on a coach trip, because I was working for Sure Start by then. One of my colleagues had phoned me up from the Development Trust and said, "You know, I've got some great news, we've been accepted and the bid's gone through and we've got the funding for the Healthy Living Centre." I was like, wow! She said, "Let me have your words, let me have your first words, I want to know what you're thinking." I remember saying to her, I said, "What it's made me realise is that when you actually have a dream if you're willing to focus on work you can be anyone and you can achieve." That's how I saw it for myself, that I'm just an average person that lives in Daneshouse, lived here all my life, but actually if you focus and you're determined and you get the people behind you to support you, you can achieve anything. That's what I try to instil in my kids now, that actually that is an example – the Chai Centre – of how a community can come together, have an idea and take it forward. For me that is a real achievement because I see people going in there, they all feel ownership of it because they've all

had a part in it, because they've been consulted. They've had ideas that have been put into that building. We looked into all sorts, even the layout of the building so that it was culturally sensitive to the needs of the community. For us it was always going to be key that it wasn't just for the Daneshouse and Stoneyholme community, it was for the wider community. We saw it as a project that would bring people across Burnley together, which it did. We had exchanges with South West Burnley and we did some work where the Asian women from Daneshouse went to South West Burnley, Howard Street, and vice versa. We were able to get rid of some of those myths around don't go into such an area, it's a no-go area and actually it's just like any other area. Today it's testament that we have people from all over, not just Burnley, Nelson and Pendle; we've had people as far as Rawtenstall and Haslingden that come to use the facilities. I find that just so rewarding because a lot of those people that access that gym wouldn't be accessing that kind of facility, because there aren't many facilities here that are for women only and men only. Over time, what I've learnt from speaking to people, it's not just Asian women, there's a lot of white women that prefer to go to single gender sessions rather than a mixed gym. It's great to see that the Chai Centre, it's such a fantastic facility because it has a gym and has a cafe. We have a women's health suite so we have a female doctor on site once or twice a week, and a female nurse. It's a very secure area where women can go and access that facility. We have midwife facilities, health visitors and there's a sensory room; there's also a nursery on site and there's a crèche facility. It just goes on and on. It's a fantastic facility. But again, I think if it hadn't been for the support of what was the Primary Care Trust at the time and then the Primary Care Group continuing to support it, I don't think we'd be in that position now because we've had those services behind us, supporting us, and we've been able to take it forward.

I draw on my faith a lot because for me, it's very important that while we're here, we make a difference. Obviously there are the rules about Islam and reading your prayers and reading the Qur'an, the basics. But then there's the wider bit again, my mum's always taught us to be kind to people, you're answerable for your actions and you'll be answerable in the life hereafter, so be good to your neighbours, be good to the people around you and make a difference, for the better. As I was growing up my mum reinforced in us the need to be kind to our neighbours, to

Left: Sajda welcomed the Mayor and the Mayoress of Burnley, Mohammad and Shamim Najib to the Chai Centre

Below: Sajda Majeed, the Programme Manager and Tim Mansfield, Head of Multi-Agency Development Group enjoying the news of the Daneshouse Healthy Living Centre bid making the final list

Above: Sajda Majeed with her friend Fara Sharif at 'the consultation with the Community' workshop to make a bid for the Daneshouse Healthy Living Centre

interact with them. I have really fond memories of when I was growing up; we had this Irish lady who's since passed away, her name was Brenda. Every Christmas, we used to celebrate Christmas because she'd invite us to her house so we'd put all the Christmas decorations up, trim the tree. Then she'd cook a halal meal and every Christmas we'd be at her house on Christmas and Boxing Day. A lot of those memories, I only remember slightly from when my dad was alive, but after my dad passed away, she always made that effort. Now looking back I think some of it might have been to actually give my mum a bit of time out because my mum was on her own here, well we had no family. My mum didn't have any brothers, sisters, cousins, no one here, she was on her own. It was through the support of friends that were around her that she was able to bring us up and also neighbours and friends that helped. For me my growing up has never been just about being in this Asian environment, it's very much been like we celebrated Christmas with her. When it was Lent, we always celebrated. On Eid she'd come to our house. Those things are really important I think, as Muslims, for us to instil in our kids and just, humanity in general, to be kind to people, to make sure that they're okay.

The other chore we always had was in the winter, when we had really bad snow my mum would always make us go and knock on the doors of all the elderly. We had quite a lot of old people that lived on our street so every winter we'd have to

go and knock on their doors. She'd give us all a house each, she'd say, "You go to such and such a house, now go and knock and see if they're all right, see if they need anything from the shop and if they do, then go and get them something from the shop." It was a good thing that was instilled in me because that is very important to me and I try to instil that in my children – that you should always be kind to your neighbours. Because one of the things that's key for us, is that what they say is that when you die and you're going to be held to account, there are many things you're going to be held to account for and one of the key things will be how you've treated your neighbour and your neighbours will be asked how were you treated? It's very important that as Muslims we keep our neighbours happy, we treat them with kindness and for me that always sticks in my head. The other bit I think, with my faith, has always been about how you represent yourself as a Muslim and that you come across as someone that's obviously good, kind and in a positive light, because people learn from that. So for me, when I'm invited, whether it's to a wedding or a funeral or a gathering, I try to make the time to go and if I do go, I go with that intention, because intentions are very important. I'm going as a Muslim because I think it's important that people know that just because our culture's different and in some aspects it might be difficult to socialise, but at times when it's important and particularly in times of sadness, I always think that it's important to be representative and to be there and offer support. So my faith is very important to me.

What really opened my eyes was when I was involved with a mediation project called Building Good Relationships that was run in Burnley and came about through issues around community cohesion. We worked with Northern Ireland and Mediation Northern Ireland who have obviously their own issues. They came here and they did a lot of work where they brought people from across the borough together. It was a three year project, and that opened my eyes in a way that I probably would've never been exposed to. There were 50 individuals including people from the British National Party and people in a sort of official capacity from Burnley Borough Council, as well as different organisations and people from the community. It was about coming together and understanding where people are coming from and why they hold the views that they do. Actually you might not agree with them but it's about recognising that you might be different but you can still get on. I learned a lot from that whole process. I've learnt a huge amount that actually people are different but if we don't have dialogue and we don't talk to one another, we're never going to understand one another. I was then very fortunate to be part of a delegation from Burnley that went to Northern Ireland and spoke to a conference there about community cohesion and the experiences that we'd had in Burnley. For me to come away from that and to think, wow, we could actually learn so much from other people and actually there are people there that can learn from us. I've learned that people have preconceived ideas but actually, deep down, we're all the same. We've all got the same issues whether it's family, fears that you might have, concerns that you have; you're all striving to do better, but it's how we come together. You can only come together by, I think, being kind to each other, by understanding one another and remaining calm. I think that's what I've learnt over time really and to be true to yourself and not give up. As my mum always says, "Never give up, once you give up that's it, you've lost the battle." That's what I've learnt over time.

I'm proud of the fact that I have a family and my children, that's the major achievement in my life. I have four children that I would say span the decades because my eldest is 18, then I have a ten-year old, a five-year old and a two-year old and, and for me it's been key to bring them up in an environment where they engage across communities and not be isolated. I've tried to select schools for them so that, obviously, they're integrating with people from their own culture but also the wider community and that for me has been key. What I try to always instil in my children is that you have respect for everyone irrespective of their culture and background.

I'd call Burnley home because I've been brought up here. I've lived here all my life. There were times when we went through the unsettling period of the disturbances in 2001. I think that brought its own challenges because you had a community, which was obviously the Asian community, almost questioning that if these things are happening, actually is there still a place for us here? I'm not going to pretend, there was a time when it did upset me because my mum obviously when she first came into this country, she had experiences with a lot of racial abuse because there weren't that many Asian people around, and especially in Yorkshire. She always said to me, you might think you're English, but

your colour's always going to be a barrier. That's what she used to say to me. But that was from her own experiences, which is another tale, because she lived in India then in 1967 her family went over to Pakistan and they had their own experiences. It made her realise that although she was in India until she was 12, when the divide came it was clear that she was never going to be accepted in Indian Kashmir and that they had to

Above: Sajda Majeed standing in her office at the Chai Centre

Below: Sajda Majeed's daughters, Aisha (2) and Aminah (5), dressed up to go to their grandma to say Eid Mubarak in 2012

Right: Sajda Majeed speaking to a group of Chai Centre users

Below: Sajda Majeed's son, Owais, meeting the Queen, at the Weavers' Triangle, as Prince's Trust Young Ambassador in May 2012

that aren't going to understand, but only through love and kindness, because I always believe that will always conquer, and it's only through that you can get people to understand. Now I think, no, Burnley's my home and my children definitely see it as their home. They have an ancestral home, which is obviously in Kashmir where their family are from, which I like them to go to see and experience and see the way people live there, but for them Burnley will always be their home and it'll always be my home. I just hope that it continues like that because I'd like to instil in my kids that you need to input into society to make it better, and that we are part of this society and that's why we try to input into it so we're part of the bigger picture and we'll make it better for the whole community.

go over to Pakistan. When she used to say that to me, it used to upset me a bit. Then when the riots happened in 2001, I did start questioning myself a bit about where I sit with this, how you are perceived, can you ever be part of Great Britain? But you know what I've realised over time is, there's always going to be a small minority

Community/Public Service

Shufkat Razaq

Above: Shufkat Razaq, First Pakistani Heritage Chair of Burnley Local Strategic Partnership (LSP) 2005-08

My name is Shufkat Razaq, I was born in Burnley on the 22nd of February 1975. My mum was a housewife, like many of the mothers of our generation. My father worked in the local mills, textiles mainly, when he first came here and later on he became self-employed. He had a stall on the market. He has stayed pretty much self-employed since then. I think they settled in Burnley because of family. They had members of the family here already. My dad's elder brother, with one or two other relatives, was here.

I went to Towneley High School in Burnley. When I left school, I went to college for about three or four months to do 'A' levels in Law, Business Studies and Sociology. Then I dropped out of college and I started working over in Nelson, at Lomeshaye Industrial Estate; I packed chocolates - that was my first job.

Now I'm a partner involved in the running of two businesses. We've got a consultancy business which works with local authorities, police, probation, and various government departments. Then we've also got a recycling business. I've had decent jobs so I've earned a decent amount of money. But what's more important I think, is that whilst I've been able to earn a decent amount of money, I've also been able to do something which has been really rewarding because I've been able to work at helping others. So I've got paid for helping others and I've got the pleasure of working and helping others.

It's been really interesting in the sense that I feel a lot older than I am. I probably look it as well. I feel a lot older than I actually am because I've been very, very fortunate to be able to do things which I think some people probably sort of achieve over a lifetime. I chaired Burnley's Local Strategic Partnership. I was the chief executive of Burnley Enterprise Trust as well, and that was all at the age of 30. So I managed to do that - I was lucky enough to be able to do that by the age of 30, not just sort of job titles but the actual work as well. Working in partnership with the council, with the police, with the health service and

others, we managed to secure the St Peter's Centre which is down on Church Street. We managed to secure funding for various other initiatives in the town as well. I was involved on Burnley College governing board when we secured the site which the new college is built on. I was part of a sub-group that was meeting with the council and with others to try and secure that site. That was really rewarding, really, when we managed to do that and the college was built. Obviously, a lot of the hard work was done by the principal on a day-to-day basis, but there was a group of us who were able to help him and support him in making sure we got that site and that the funding came through, and the organisations that mattered supported us as well. So we managed to do that. We also managed to do quite a lot of other things, or put things in place which have helped other initiatives take place, for example, the Todmorden Curve, which will provide direct access to Manchester by rail. I was involved in the Local Strategic Partnerships (LSP) when that was started off and now that's beginning to happen. The Knowledge Park, which has been talked about, that's starting to happen. As an Enterprise Trust, we managed to help a lot of people into work and start a lot of new businesses. Some of them are very, very successful; some of them have gone on to become multi-million pound businesses as well. In something like 3 or 4 years, I think we created a thousand jobs. We started about 600 to 700 businesses, so that's a lot of work that we've managed to do. Before I was at the Enterprise Trust, I was at Business Link and before that I worked very closely with some businessmen in Blackburn to set up the Asian Business Federation. That was very successful back in 2001. It's still going now. We managed to recruit 300 members to the Federation in a space of nine months when the target was to get 300 in 3 years. There are a lot of things in that sense which I've been able to contribute towards and work with others. None of it has been done by me on my own, obviously, but I've been able to work with others as a good team player. I've learnt from others and achieved a lot with them.

My parents are from a farming community in Pakistan and I think what I feel most proud of is that I also come from what you call a deprived community. But I don't feel that we're really deprived in terms of our ability, in terms of our commitment, in terms of our enthusiasm as a community. So I feel really proud of being part of a community that's come here, and settled here, and has contributed as well. We've got some really good examples of people who've put something back into this town, into this area, into this country. I feel really proud that I've been able to contribute as well as many other people have. I also feel proud of the fact that I've been able to help others rather than just help myself. I'm proud of who we are and where we are. This is home for us. I wouldn't say we've done more than our fair share, because you can never do more than your fair share. There isn't such a thing, but I certainly think that we've really punched above our weight as a community, and as individuals as well.

In the last six years I certainly feel that my faith is the cornerstone of everything that I do. It's absolutely critical and crucial to how I conduct myself as an individual with others. Certainly faith has played a big part.

Burnley is home, home is where you actually live. Obviously our ancestors are from Pakistan. My father was born in British India, it wasn't Pakistan then, but my parents obviously have a very, very strong link with Pakistan. We do have a strong link to the village back where my parents were born, where our ancestors lived. But home is Burnley because this is where we live. We do go for holidays to Pakistan, we try to go every year for two, three weeks. The link remains because it's where our parents are from, where our ancestors are from. But home is Burnley, so when you do land at rainy Manchester, coming back from wherever you've been to, it's a very strong feeling of coming back home.

I think my parents would be proud of the fact that they came to a foreign land, an alien land; they couldn't speak a word of English. They didn't know the culture, they didn't know the environment. They had a few family members here and the fact that they've been able to settle here, work here, build their homes and bring up their children here and fulfil their duties and responsibilities, they'll be proud of those facts. I think they'll also be proud of the fact that no matter who they've come in touch with here, they've always had good relationships. They really had very few difficulties with anybody, whether they were Pakistani or whether they were our English neighbours. They always had a good relationship with everybody. So they'll be proud of the fact that they have been able to live and work here as citizens of Burnley, like anybody else.

A factor that shaped and changed my life in Burnley includes the disturbances in 2001 as it highlighted something for me. I always took it for granted before that, okay there were always some people who did not get on with each other. I went to Towneley High school; there were only about 50 Asians out of 900 students there and amongst my friends living on our street, many were English friends. Whilst we were Pakistani others were English, we didn't really see a difference. But I think the 2001 disturbances highlighted the fact that people do see each other differently, at least some people do, and because of that difference there is tension. That was like a wake-up call. I took it for granted that everything was fine and everybody got on. Yes, you did get the odd, occasional (very rarely though) racist sort of remark, both ways; white on Asian and Asian on white, but generally speaking things were good. 2001, although I don't think it was specifically to do with race, that's my opinion, and it is shared by others as well, did still highlight an issue in the aftermath, we can't take it for granted that everybody gets on with everybody, and everybody's happy with things the way they are. So that was a turning point. That's when I started getting involved – that's when I really got involved in Jinnah Development Trust which I chaired for six years, and got involved in other things as well. I thought to myself, it isn't just about you earning a living; it's also about you trying to contribute something back as well. That was a turning point, I would say, 2001. I think that if it hadn't happened, we probably just would have gone along, doing what we normally did and not really being bothered about anybody else. I think, to an extent.

Community/Public Service

Fara Sharif

My name is Fara Sharif. I was born in Pakistan but came here when I was a few months old. I was born in January 1971. My dad was a bus driver and my mum was a housewife. When my dad came to England he started off in the weaving mills like everybody else. They used to do back-to-back shifts, leaving my mum home all the time, poor thing, all on her own with nobody to support her. Then later on he became a bus conductor, and then a bus driver.

My dad came in the 1960s and then my mum followed just a few days later. My dad went to Bradford first as most people did at that time and then they moved to Nelson. My mum actually came to Nelson and she remembers all the different houses we had because we had moved around. She went back to Pakistan because there was just nobody here; the networks just weren't here but then she came back again. She was always on her own because my dad was at work.

Above: Fara Sharif is mother of three children, successfully completed her Master Degree in Community Leadership, from the University of Central Lancashire (UCLan), Burnley Campus in 2013

Below: Fara Sharif's late father, Mohammad Sharif, in Bus Driver's Uniform

In total there were about four Pakistani families in Nelson at the time when she was there. And to go out on your own, it was virtually a no-no on a Saturday and Sunday. Sunday especially; it was their visiting day, because that was a day off so they'd go round visiting people, but apart from

that she didn't get any other contact with anybody else. But my dad got the job at the Burnley and Pendle Bus Company, so that's why we came here, plus his best friend also moved here.

We ended up going to Pakistan for two years, with

my last two years of primary school remaining, because my mum wasn't well; she hadn't been well and the doctors couldn't find out what was wrong with her. They said it was depression but then my dad thought, we'll go to Pakistan, see if she gets any better. We stayed there for two years but eventually we came back. Mum was still ill; it was TB that nobody had picked up, so when we came back she had x-rays and they found it. But she'd had it for that many years that her lungs were totally covered and it's a miracle that she recovered from it. I went to Towneley High School. When I left school I went to college. I did extra GCSEs because I needed those to do my 'A' levels. I went on to do 'A' levels in English Literature, Psychology and Law. I did that for another two years and then I was going to go to university but I didn't go because my dad died. That's what changed my life. I became the head of the family as the eldest child and because my mum was ill, like I said. So it was just that fact that I couldn't go to university, that wasn't an option any more. I started working at a dental surgery. I was a dental receptionist and a dental nurse; and just looking after my brothers and sisters. I've been mother to my brothers and sisters as well. I got married very quickly after my dad died. I was 19 when my dad died and just a couple of months later, I turned 20 and that's when I got married. I had my first child, and I left work for a year or so. I went back to college to do a course and from that I started working at Jinnah Development Trust as an administrator. All my experience came from Jinnah. From Jinnah I moved on to Sure Start in Nelson, and that's where I've been for ten years now. I went as a Community Development Worker but now I'm an Outreach Worker. We do family support and most of the cases that I deal with are concerned with child protection. Obviously it's low level child protection and it could just be emotional support for a family that you do. So it's family support running the groups to support parents. We go out and do visits, provide family support in the houses as well. It can be stressful and it can be emotionally draining but when you see that family in crisis and then you see them when they've moved on, that's what makes it so enjoyable. Sometimes it is really, really hard – some of the things that happen to those families. You go home and you are still thinking about them. They're down there, and then you build them up gradually to independence and that's what really does motivate you to do the job that you do. Like one of the families that I've been working with, I've worked with her for over five years really, on and off; she keeps coming back. The other day she actually went out and got herself a bus pass. She came back and told me; I was so proud of her because that's the first thing that she's actually gone out and done on her own. The most rewarding work for me is helping the community. It's when you see that person who's struggled but, by you just helping them that little bit, it makes a huge difference to their lives.

When I became head of the family, if somebody said "boo" to me I'd cry. That's the type of person I was. I didn't have any self-esteem whatsoever, nothing, and to go from what I was then to what I am now; people that knew me when I was younger, smaller, notice the difference. I didn't have any self-esteem but being pushed into that role and getting on with things, I think

that's what made me so resilient. Regardless of what problems you have at home, when you go to work, that is work and you have to do it. So, juggling everything, I think it's ingrained in women and I think we embrace it in our attitude of just go ahead and do things. And that's the only way to get on with life, isn't it? You have to. So that's my motivation.

Me and my friend Sajda started an initiative off. There was some Healthy Living Centre funding going around and Sajda said, "Why don't we do this?" So we organised a meeting at Jinnah with all the lead agencies like Burnley Borough Council and PCT. First of all, it was just a little meeting and then from that we organised a bigger day with all the lead agencies

Above: Fara Sharif holding her Master Degree in Community Leadership at the University of Central Lancashire (UCLan), Burnley Campus in 2013

Above: Fara Sharif (in white) with her friend Sajda Majeed, the pair of them spearheaded the campaign for Daneshouse Healthy Living Centre over a couple of years

at Daneshouse Community Centre and with Burnley Borough Council, the PCT and all various agencies that worked within the area. From that it grew and that's why the Chai Centre is here today, because of that initial day that we organised, everything just blossomed from there. If it wasn't for that initiative, the Chai Centre wouldn't exist so the Healthy Living Centre is one of the achievements that I am proud of. We saw the project right through, to it being an actual building and then a couple of years ago I resigned from the management board because of my other commitments. I'm a governor as well – at one of the nurseries – and with other family commitments there's only so much time that we've got that we can give, but that is one thing that I'm really, really proud of.

Everything you do, there are obstacles. You have obstacles from your community and you have obstacles from partner agencies making life difficult for you as well. Jinnah, as an organisation, has been running for years and they have made a huge difference to the lives of people, whether people agree or not, they have. I mean, the motivational Playbus was started by Jinnah and the Advice Centre at Daneshouse which has since moved to town; they were started off by Jinnah. So for the first people that came here, Jinnah was a very, very important place. It was where they found answers for everything and it was somewhere where they could go, whatever the problem, whatever they needed, they could go to Jinnah and Jinnah would either sort it out or find the answer for them. So that's how important Jinnah was and still is for the community.

That is my story. Well, because I didn't go to university and it was my dad's dream that we all got educated and that's what he wanted, I've just recently finished my MA in Community Leadership and I was motivated by the fact that

I still wanted to get an education. Yes, it's 20 years later but I have managed to do it. It was really difficult, really difficult, because as a mum and working as well, I was juggling everything, working till three o'clock in the morning just doing research, doing my dissertation; three months to complete it is not enough. But I had to do it, so yes, that's one achievement I'm really proud of and I did it for my dad. When I went to college, within our family not many girls went to university. To send your daughter to university was a really, really big thing, and even to college, or even to learn to drive. Because within our family, I was the first person to go to college, the first person to learn to drive, everybody had a go at my dad for it. It was just said that girls didn't need to be educated. But my dad was educated himself so his way of thinking was no, they do need to be educated and they need to move on in society; how else are they going to function within this community? He wanted better for us. Now everybody has that opportunity. There are still people out there that do have restrictions but not what we had at that time. It was, "Oh, what will the community think?" All the time it was, "What will the community think?" When I went to college, always in the back of my mind I had that knowledge that my dad had trusted me to go to college and I needed to keep that in mind for any actions that I did, you had to respect your parents for giving you that opportunity. Even to send me to university, this was a huge thing for him as well. He had to stand up to his family really. I mean at that time you didn't make telephone calls to Pakistan; it was just letters. So somebody from Pakistan told my granddad, and he actually wrote a letter to my dad, "Why are you educating your daughter?" I remember that to this day, my dad was so furious, so furious. He said, "Why, do these people not understand? Education is what you need for these children, not restrictions." So I'm glad that I got those opportunities.

My eldest son is going to university and my daughter's at Burnley College – she wants to go on to do midwifery. I want them to take those opportunities. Like I've said to them, if there's an opportunity, take it, whatever type it is, you need those life experiences to make you a more grounded person. I suppose life's been a struggle because, at a young age, I was thrust into being head of the family and I didn't have a clue. But I think that's just made me a better person, and a calmer person. I deal with whatever's thrown at me and I don't get flustered or angry or whatever. I look at a situation and deal with it as best I can.

Of course my faith also gives me peace and it gives me that sense of satisfaction. Especially at night when I sit down on my prayer mat, it's my time of reflection and I reflect on what's happened during the day. I suppose it's my spiritual counselling and that's what I use it for and also it's a basis for my life. I won't make Islam strict to the point that the children just totally go away from it. There's so much leniency, especially at work. When you go to work and you don't have time to read prayers, you can come and read them at home. Allah, He understands that as a working parent there are certain restrictions, so even for the children, if you pile too much onto them, they're just going to move further and further away from it. So we try to do it in little bits and just make them understand that whatever they do has an action, has consequences - how has that affected them, what would Allah think? And things like that. It makes them realise how fortunate we are. I remember once my son had given £50 to the phone-in charities for Pakistani flood victims. The next day we were travelling, and our tyre blew on the motorway, travelling at 70 miles an hour. I don't know how we survived that. Even the AA person said that to us, "I really, really do not know how you survived this," the tyre blowout was so bad. But it was my son who said, "I know how we survived that. It was angels who picked us up and brought us to the side safely because I paid £50, £10 for each of us." So now we've got a little box and every morning, even if they only put a penny in, it's for their protection. It's instilling those values from home in them and making them think.

I think wherever you grow up, that is home. Even when you're travelling within Britain, you come to the sign that says Burnley and you think, oh, yes, I'm home. So it's that connection, that feeling that you have with Burnley and it holds so many memories as well. I've got quite a wide variety of friends from different cultures, Burnley is what binds us together and that's why it's home.

Below: Fara Sharif at her younger brother Asim's Degree Ceremony, with her husband, children, brother and mother in 2004

Community/Public Service

Khalida Sharif

Above: Khalida Sharif, a family community worker, is endeavouring to bridge the generation and culture gap to support family cohesion

Below Left: Khalida Sharif at Barden Infants School in 1979

My name's Khalida Sharif. I was born in Burnley on May the 20th 1976. My father was a bus driver and my mother was a housewife. My father came in the early '60s and worked in the cotton mills and then went on to become a bus driver. My mother joined him a few years later on. I went to Barden Infants and Barden Juniors and then I went to Towneley High School. I went to college to study; I wanted to be a nurse. But I soon changed my mind and thought to myself, no, business is the way to go. I wanted to do something with marketing because it's something that I really enjoyed. So that's what I did. I was supposed to go on to university but took a year out and never went back because there were other doors and avenues that opened up for me.

In particular, recently, I've been doing community work. All the years have been about helping young women and young girls with issues such as marriage, domestic violence and obviously, other issues within the household, which needed to be addressed. I think the thanks you get from the mothers and the children - there's nothing like it. Money can't buy that. I am who I am because of the blessings and du'a (personal prayer) that they

give to me. For me the satisfaction lies in seeing those smiles on their faces, knowing the fact they've been in a situation that they've perceived as hell and they've come out of that hell and now they're living their lives how they should; in a happy kind of environment where the children don't have to suffer, the mother doesn't have to suffer. There's interaction there, there's love and genuine care instead.

I was working for another organisation and we were based in the community centre. Women were forever coming in crying; saying what was going on in the home with their mothers-in-law and their fathers-in-law or their husbands. Within the community, things happen. They used to come in and we used to sit them down, have a chit chat and say, "Why don't you do this, why don't you do that," try to kind of be an advocate for them and try to point them in the right direction. That's where it started from because I thought to myself, hang on, there are young girls coming saying, "Aunty, will you please come home and speak to our parents, we want to go to university but they want us to get married." And I used to think, do you know what, maybe I should. That's where it started, the first case I worked on. I went in and spoke to the parents because otherwise this girl would have left home. But it worked out for the best because you've got to balance it out, do they want the girl to go and never come back, or is there a compromise? That's how it kind of started off, with mediation between the parents and the ladies and the mothers-in-law and daughters-in-law. They felt they couldn't speak to anybody else so they came to us; it was mediation that used to take place really. It worked, and it worked well. I remember the girl saying to me if it didn't work she would leave home. I thought to myself, how would I feel, how would my mum feel if that was me, what would I want if I was in this situation? I know people always go on about spoon-feeding but I feel that we need that sometimes. We need somebody to hold our hands and then just to gently let go. That's exactly what I did. I just kind of said to her, "Would you mind me speaking

to your parents?" And she said no. I went and I spoke to her mum, explained the situation. It kind of threw her. I said to her, "Aunty, what would you prefer? For your daughter to go and never come back? At the end of the day she is your izzat - she's your honour." And we kind of

started a dialogue there, and there were issues from both sides which we patted out and the rest was history. I always do it for Him above. I just feel that karma always comes around. If I do something good for somebody else then I'm sure it will come back to me.

From there it kind of evolved into something great and big. We sat down, we had a meeting with the parents and other community people that were involved and said to them, "Look, we've got an issue here. This should've been addressed a very long time ago. But for whatever reason it wasn't." We then got together and decided to apply for funding and go for organisation status, which we achieved. It was all to do with working with mothers and daughters and mediation, and then we went on to domestic violence because we were getting loads of cases coming through. We felt that sometimes within the Asian heritage it's trivial things which, if you sit down and you speak about them, you can actually save that marriage and that's exactly what we did. And that is exactly what we want to continue to do.

One of the young girls who came to us was married, obviously from Pakistan, fairly young, and had children at a young age. She was having issues within the household. I don't really want to go too much into it. She just needed somebody to talk to about these issues, were they normal, what's going on? She came in, had a word with us, and it was something trivial, something that could be sorted out. So we said to her, "Would you want us to get involved and speak to your mother-in-law?" At first she was reluctant, and I don't really blame her, things can be blown out of proportion. However she thought about it, and she said, "Yes, why not?" I went down, and had a word with her and it was something and nothing, where the girl wanted to attend classes but the mother-in-law didn't want to take care of the children, and she thought she was being quite funny with her but she wasn't. It was just that she couldn't cope with the child, that's what it was. You know, she was ready to, "I can't cope with this and I want to move out." It was something very trivial.

If we need to move people out of the houses, without a doubt we will do that, when lives are in danger. But not with something as trivial as that, you can sort it out and you can save a marriage.

The issues are going on everywhere and it's time that we spoke out about them and we addressed these issues. If we don't face facts, we're the ones that are going to lose out. People got to know about our work, I think it was by word of mouth. Because somebody who'd come to me had their problems sorted, the aunties at school would say to such and such a person, why don't you go to Khalida, she may be able to help? And it just snowballs from there. I'm not going to name names, however, there was one particular case, the woman had come from down south. Her husband had probably carried out an honour killing in Pakistan. He'd done time there I think as a minor. He went to Pakistan, got married to this young girl, very beautiful, very attractive, and brought her over. She was pregnant with her first child and then the abuse started.

I'm quite surprised by the fact that the parents didn't know what was going on, nobody said anything. The poor girl found out on her wedding night and he said to her, it wasn't me, it was somebody else, it was an uncle. She came to England, that's when the abuse started. He literally threw her out. So she had her first baby, she had fallen pregnant straight away; he threw her out on the street. It seemed that nobody would help her. Nobody. Everything was against her. Somehow they got her here, there's always somebody that you know within the villages, so somebody, a family friend of hers helped her. They went to a solicitor for help and he kind of referred them over to me. She had nothing. She had no money. But somehow by God's mercy we, (myself and another counsellor) really pushed

for her, to find help for her. She went into a refuge. She got her status. Her English was so poor, but for you to meet her now and see how far she's come, you'd be amazed. She speaks fluent English, she's sorted herself out, she's now going to remarry, and she's got two beautiful girls. That in itself is a success story because she had nothing, she had nobody. Her confidence was right down there. She was sure that he would find her. But to look at her now, she's a completely different person. To me, that is a success story for her. Her achievement. It's something that she should be proud of. There are so many experiences that I could go on forever.

Things are changing slowly, in a positive manner. It's just about us going out there and really selling ourselves, talking to people in a respectful way. If you show respect you will get respect back. I'm a great believer in that. It doesn't matter whether you dress in your jeans or your Shalwar Kameez, that doesn't matter. What matters is self-respect. Those people respect you back for it. I remember I was walking down town once and an uncle just stopped me and said to me, "Are you Khalida?" I said, "Yes." "I heard you on the radio, can I say you're doing a fantastic job." I thought to myself, my God; that really threw me, I thought wow, somebody complimenting, well, a man complimenting us, we're doing something fantastic. The radio interview was just to promote the organisation and what we do and if you want help we're there and we don't care what anybody says to us, we don't care what anyone throws at us, we're there, we're there for you.

Above: Khalida Sharif with baby brother Abid and elder sister Fara, in 1980

Well, it's open to all really but predominantly it is the Asian heritage women that we need to help more. They are the ones that need that push and their confidence building. I think everyone struggles, initially, but I think we've got a really good relationship with all the statutory and voluntary organisations. I mean the police, the Home Office, all the refuges, other counsellors and the Council themselves. So we've had a lot of help from a lot of people. I also think it's through hard work, through dialogue. We have an open dialogue, and then you get people coming in wanting to speak to you, wanting to know, wanting to help. I think that's really important.

I've seen a huge change right across all communities; whether it's Bangladeshi, Pakistani, I've seen this huge change, people are going out there and educating their daughters more than they used to. That is something I've realised and they're really pushing themselves, wanting to really educate their daughters and asking them to make something of themselves. That is a huge change in the way they are, the way they integrate into the community, there's a huge change within the last seven years. It's not a small change, it's a huge change. It puts a smile on my face because I think we're doing something right. Not me personally, but everybody else around us, we're all doing something right for that change to occur. Our mindsets must be changing for the better really. Islam says that you can be who you want but with modesty. Nobody's stopping you from educating yourself, you must educate yourself, and it's for yourself. That is your passport really, isn't it? If something happens tomorrow you've got your education to rely on.

For me it's not just a religion, it's a way of life. From day one we've been taught that your teachers aren't your teachers, they're like your parents. I remember my father saying that if we were told off by the school, dad would say, "You mustn't say anything bad about the teachers, they're your mum and dad." I can remember mum saying that, "That's your mum and dad, that is how you respect them." I remember when I was a child, I went into the school once; this is really funny actually, I said to my teacher, "My mum said to me you're like my mum and dad." I don't think they quite grasped the concept, but that was the truth of it. It's Allah who has made me who I am, it's why I want to contribute to society, it makes you a better person. I feel that it's not just about here; it's about the hereafter for me and whether I'm a good person to others, not that

I'm perfect, nobody's ever perfect, I just feel that for me it's spiritual, it's a spiritual journey that I'm on and that is a part of my fulfilment. I came here with nothing; I take nothing with me, no money, no house, nothing. But I know what I am going to take, and that is going to be people's thoughts.

I think Muslim girls really think they've grasped Islam and the culture and their British heritage; I think they grasp it quite well. We're second generation, some of these people are third generation and the way they're juggling things, I think it's fantastic. They've not lost their heritage or their religion, but they have now taken up this identity, which is a British identity and I think they're balancing it quite well actually. In terms of home for me, I'm Burnley born and bred! For me, Burnley is Vegas! Oh definitely.

Chapter 4 - Public sector

Education

Wajid Khan

Above: Cllr Wajid Khan is the first Pakistani heritage senior lecutrer at the University of Central Lancashire (UCLan)

My name is Wajid Khan. I was born in Burnley in 1979. My mother was a housewife and my father used to work in the old Smith & Nephew factory as a weaver, and thereafter he went on to become a taxi driver. My father came to the UK in 1967 from Pakistan. It was a common thing to do. It was a trend from the early '60s. It was also a popular route to economic prosperity, a better way of life. They moved to Burnley because the other emigrants from our village who'd arrived in the UK had all settled here in Burnley.

I went to Heasandford County Primary school then Habergham High School and I went on to study at the Habergham Sixth Form Centre with some minor education at Burnley College. When I finished college I did the typical biology, chemistry, maths, quite influenced by my parents at the time towards one particular direction. I went on to have a radical change of mind and went into law. I studied law at the University of Central Lancashire, completed three years law there, did the barrister course at the College of Law in Holborn and completed that. I didn't like future life as a barrister so I came back to do my Master in European Law. Whilst I was doing my Master in European Law, I had a

sudden interest in social cohesion arising out of disturbances in Burnley. So I undertook many projects working with young people, looking at sectarianism in Northern Ireland and we looked at the problems in the northern towns, Bradford, Burnley and Oldham. We designed and delivered and evaluated quite a few projects. One of them won a national award; in 2004 I was voted Council for England National Volunteer of the Year, which was nice really.

I completed my Masters and then I got accepted on a legal consultancy contract in the European Commission. At the time my father was ill, hospitalised. He'd had kidney problems and the condition meant that I had to change my life plans so I stayed here. That was the first challenge

Below: Receiving a national award in social and community cohesion

Left: Childhood picture

but it was a really good blessing in a way to spend some time with my father, because I'd recently gone away to London, been here and there and not spent much time with him, so I think it was a blessing in disguise. Just a week or two before I was due to set off to work in Europe; I had a call from the University on the back of the national award I'd achieved. It was great publicity for the University, and generally, to have a national award project under their belt. I developed quite a lot of experience around social cohesion projects and on the back of that, they wanted me to take a role working as a Millennium Volunteer's Co-

Right: Meeting Ed Miliband,
leader of the Labour Party

Right: Meeting Ed Miliband,
leader of the Labour Party

and the rest of the community leaders, and I used to be fascinated by the issues they used to have to deal with. Then there was a rise of BNP councillors in Burnley in short succession. That was a kind of incentive for me to get up and think, this is the time to challenge the BNP and expose them for what they really stand for. I'm quite glad that after all my time in politics we've only got one BNP councillor left in the borough, which I think is good for everybody in Burnley, to eradicate all forms of extremism, including the extreme right wing which is quite dangerous for the long term prosperity of the borough.

I'm back here in Burnley now. Politics is a fantastic lifelong experience to be involved in. It's nice to see people and just walk into Asda one day and get a can of coke and somebody will say, "I need something sorting out in my back yard" and, This is not right. You know, it's really good to see the satisfaction of just seeing that you can make a difference to people's lives. I think that message, in terms of an academic context within my teaching, especially in relation to cultural anthropology; it's about people and how to make people's lives better. I try to, not pontificate, but I try to project that out to students and for them to make a big, strong, positive impact in their communities. Recently, I've just come back from doing some work and research in Moscow and am now working with The Ministry of Social Development, which is comparing and contrasting over there with voluntary community organisations over here in the UK. But in terms of this project that Jinnah Trust undertook; I'm glad they undertook this project, it's a fantastic concept and I think it's something that has needed to be done for a long time. My heritage is Gujrat, Pakistan; it has a very strong place in my heart. It's my roots and I often visit Pakistan, Gujrat, and I've managed to build some very strong institutional links between the University of Central Lancashire and the University of Gujrat in Pakistan, where I've pioneered a MOU - a Memorandum of Understanding - at the University so we're doing some collaborative work together. In May this year, I'm taking myself and a group of students over there to deliver a global youth leadership conference. We'll be working with young people over there because half the population is young people, so there are a lot of charities for them and we want to replicate our work in Moscow, California, Stanford and at Gujrat University. We've also done a lot of collaborative research, not on communities but on nanotechnology, in

ordinator to co-ordinate volunteering activities on behalf of the university in a particular region, that was East Lancashire. I started that job and from there we decided to run a university certificate for volunteers. These volunteers were amazing, had so many talents and they were really skilled, but after they did the volunteering what was next for them? So we thought we'd develop an academic certificate; it was called the University Certificate in Volunteering and Community Action. Once they did that, completed that, where next? We ended up writing a degree course which was underpinned by volunteering, called BA Community Leadership. I developed this BA Community Leadership academic programme with students coming from all over the region primarily, and later on we had students come from all over the country. That's still running now, which is good. I later went on to develop a Masters in Community Leadership, which was really aimed at professionals and senior managers, and people who are already community leaders, just wanted to professionalise and be provided with a theoretical context to working with the community. This is also running now.

In my life as an academic, I ended up getting involved in politics as well as working at the University as a senior lecturer. I started as a Lecturer, and then became course leader and now I'm a senior lecturer in cultural anthropologies, my earlier expertise, which is very closely linked to this project in particular. I ended up in politics and as a young lad, I used to watch Mr Malik

particular, with a professor here at the University. So Gujrat University and UCLAN are very strongly tied together and the cementing of this relationship is very important for me personally because although my father lives over in Gujrat, Pakistan, he spends a lot of time here, but when he goes over to visit Gujrat he spends a lot of time in the local village. So it's a great comparison of rural village life in Pakistan where you're totally cut off from the world and all you've got is a natural habitat; and a very active lifestyle here in Burnley, Lancashire, where you wake up in the morning at about eight and may not be home 'til 12 midnight or 1.00 am sometimes because you're working full time and then you've taken responsibility to act as an advocate for the community and serve the community. The community is fantastic because there's no set pattern or formula to work in communities. You can get a phone call at 1:00 in the morning and at times, I've unfortunately had phone calls at 4:00 in the morning when someone's died and you've got to organise the Muslim funeral, Janazah. You're working with coroners to get the death certificates, working with registrars to get the appropriate documentation for them to bury, or transport the body over to their native country, Pakistan or Bangladesh. No one day is the same. It's very challenging. It can, at times, be gruesome because you're seeing people at all kinds of hours. You're expected to be there, available at all kinds of silly hours in the morning and there's no rest really, because your weekends are occupied. But it's fantastic because at the end of the day what underpins my thinking is that from a religious perspective, and for me, politics - it's your way of life and it makes you a better person, and if you can make a difference to someone's life, and I believe you can do something with your hands, do it. I'm one of the lucky people in the world, probably, because I'm living my passion both with politics and also with academia, so it's fantastic really.

One thing I say to people is that travel, if you get the opportunity in life, travel because first of all it broadens your horizons. There's a very educational context to travelling because you're visiting new places, you're meeting new people, and you're meeting people with a range of issues, a range of challenges in life and a unique dimension to dealing with those issues. So for me personally, I've learnt just by going around. I've been to many different countries through my work because one of my other roles is as an executive director for an organisation called Volunteurope, which is about sitting on an international board and advising various organisations how to promote active citizenship and volunteering in their respective regions and countries in the world.

Burnley has excelled, but what you've got to look back on and remember is that as youngsters, as third generation, second generation, you need to look back and actually give testimony to all

Above: Speaking to Prince Charles at the Prince's Trust Event, Towneley Hall, Burnley in 2010

the first generation that came over here. Because they had to deal with the most difficult challenge of their lives; to come into a new country, to be alone with very little English and hear how they've struggled, how they've been exemplary, and that's leadership for you. And that's real leadership in practice, for them to come over and

Right: Celebrating a family event

Below: Meeting the Queen at University of Central Lancashire (UCLan), Burnley Campus

settle here, to work hard and raise their families and then educate their children. I think, for me, for looking at applied leadership as a corrective community, whether it is Bangladesh, India, Pakistan; whichever country you come from - Eastern Europe, the Polish community coming over. That takes a lot of guts, determination and motivation and for us growing up, we've had it quite easy if you compare and contrast our upbringing to what they had to undergo when they came over in their teens. I think a lot of the first generation lost their teenage years working to send money back to Pakistan, Bangladesh, India, for them to have the good life over there and bring up their families. We need to learn, as British born Pakistanis, we need to look back and learn and think, if looking at history and heritage is forgotten and you're writing your reports and books, the contribution is very difficult to quantify.

I think my faith (I'm a Muslim) is a very important identity in my life. I think people often look on Islam as being battered a lot in the last few years with Islamaphobia, and people having their own interpretation of Islam. I think the key to being a Muslim is to be able to reflect. You've got your five fundamental pillars of Islam but to me, as a person, it's very important because it makes me reflect at the end of the day to think, what have I done today? What were my actions today? What haven't I done? What should I have done? So my own self-assessment and reflection would be to step back and just realise how things are going, and when you have the time to reflect, and you make it a priority to reflect, you can

understand, you can summarise and analyse and strategise for the future based on your reflection.

I call Burnley home because my heart, my life, my friendships, my deal with Burnley, is through my blood because when I go away there are certain times when I think I've been travelling, let's go back home. It's time for home, I'm ready for home. I mean, I go away and represent Burnley; it's a very proud moment for me. I'm not one to say I'm from Manchester. I'd say I'm from Burnley. And when they don't know where Burnley is I say it's near Manchester. So it's a very strong identity, we've all got multiple identities. Burnley is home for me but Pakistan, and Gujrat in particular, forms part of my roots. You never forget, you should always remember that and I think it's important to contribute towards a part of the world which has been part of you and your mother and father. Also, I think when you love your parents so much you kind of want to, in one way or another, no matter who they are. But everything about them, their identity, you try to capture that identity and relate to that and communicate with that. And have a relationship with that identity because that in a way is yours, thinking of them and relishing them in a way and missing them. I think Martin Luther King said that no matter how young, weak, old or ill you are, you can all lead great lives because we can all serve, and as long as you can have this element of serving people and not wanting anything back in return, just doing something because you think it's the right thing to do, I think we can make Burnley and the world a better place.

Education

Safdar Baig Mirza

My name is Safdar Baig; I was born in Gujrat, which is a district in the north of Punjab province in Pakistan, on the 6th of May 1973. My mum was a housewife and she's always been a housewife. My father was an engineer. I went to school in a twin city with Islamabad, called Rawalpindi. I went to college to further my education. In my educational career I have been quite successful in terms of qualifications; I was ranked first in my school and fourth in the whole of the region among 22,000 students when I finished my school qualifications. Then I had a choice to make between medicine and engineering but I wanted to follow my father's footsteps as an engineer so I chose engineering and I went to college to do some 'A'-Level equivalent qualifications. Luckily, this time I did better than I did at school and I was ranked second in the whole board for the Rawalpindi region. I went to what they call the Cambridge of Pakistan, the University of Lahore. I did my degree in engineering there. Luckily, I got a first class in engineering so I was offered a job but at that time I was ready to move to England and I came here.

I, and other students I had known in Pakistan and India, classed the UK and America as lands

of opportunities; however, there were some misconceptions about these countries. I had a view in my mind that I would go to England and straight away I would find a decent job in engineering, and that's it, my career will be sorted. But that was not the case. I mean, when I came here I applied to around 200 different organisations and companies and I was only offered two interviews and they were both in London. I was struggling to travel at that time, I couldn't travel; I couldn't go to interviews so basically I couldn't get into a job in engineering. Three months down the line when I came here, when I was not working at all, I managed to find a job at Asda. So I filled shelves for about six months. Then I got my first job teaching engineering at Nelson and Colne College, which was only four hours a week on a part-time basis. But I could see incentives in that because they offered me a teaching course at Nelson and Colne College, which I did to further my education. But my number of teaching hours increased and within about six to eight months I was teaching for about 18 hours a week. At the end of that year I had a qualification as well; I was teaching at Nelson and Colne College as more or less a full-time lecturer. But then when I had done that job for about 18 months, I went into one of these conferences where I met with a lady who offered me some teaching in schools, and she found a placement for me at Ivy Bank High School in Burnley. I was offered a year's contract at Ivy Bank High School with a contract that would also help me to get into a graduate programme as well.

At the end of my Post Graduate Certificate in Education (PGCE) for schools, I had a qualification to teach all ranges and all abilities among schools and colleges. From Ivy Bank I moved into Mansfield High School in Brierfield, and that was an interesting time, for two and a half years. I was quite glad that I moved to Mansfield High School as a newly qualified teacher and as soon as I finished my first year, I was offered a job to be the second in the department for mathematics, which I happily accepted. I struggled initially but my head of

Above: Safdar Baig Mirza is an Engineering Graduate from Pakistan, smiling for his picture in Jinnah Centre, where he is Chair of the organisation

Below: With his wife, Ishrat Mirza, in Pakistan in 1996, as newlyweds

Above: Safdar Baig Mirza outside Park High School Pendle where he is a Maths teacher

Below: Safdar Baig Mirza welcoming the guests and members to Jinnah AGM, sitting next to him is Barrister Amjad Malik, the guest speaker

faculty was quite supportive. I was responsible for Key Stage 4 results as well. For somebody who had never been to school in this country and had been teaching in schools for less than two years getting that kind of position I thought that was kind of an achievement for me. I think it also showed their faith and their trust in my abilities.

I considered the responsibility; I mean, it wasn't fair on kids to actually not deliver them outstanding lessons, and then expect other colleagues to be outstanding. I thought, it's not right that I'm expecting my colleagues to deliver outstanding teaching if I couldn't manage it myself. This was one of the reasons. Secondly, I always wanted to inspire students in the classroom, rather than doing a lot of paperwork or collating their results or preparing schemes of work away from my classroom. So I think it's all down to inspiration. I wanted to inspire the youngsters and I realised when I was at Mansfield that it had about 55 to 60% Asian heritage kids and I knew that a number of pupils saw me as a role model. I wanted to deliver really good teaching to them so that if any of them, any of these pupils followed in my footsteps; they would know exactly what would be expected of them.

Every single day in teaching is a memorable day. Because the buzz you get when you teach kids and when they learn from you, I don't think you can get that from any other job. I'm 39 now and I still remember my teachers, and we always say that nobody forgets a good teacher. Personally speaking, when I was at Mansfield there were about 55 to 60% Muslim students who actually struggled to find their feet within school in terms of religion. I had to fight with the management in the school to get a prayer room for them and I had to fight with the school management to have a regular Juma'ah prayer in school. The school found the benefit of this because it really, really calmed students down. In terms of teaching, I teach almost every day; kids produce results, they move on. Some of them are in really, really good professions. A couple of students managed to finish their medicine degrees - you're supposed to see your students doing well in their lives. I was always questioned by these students, so why didn't you do medicine? I always said to them that I probably needed to teach you, because if I have done medicine I probably wouldn't have been here. It's all down to engineering, which actually sort of eased my route into maths teaching. If I had been a doctor I probably wouldn't have been in a classroom.

If you could differentiate between where I was born, where I was brought up; that world and this Western world, I think one of the major differences would be education. I was lucky because my father was highly educated and he inspired me. He used to say that the easiest way to succeed in your life is to attain better education because education can change societies. That's one of the quickest ways you can move your society up in a certain number of years. I was always of the opinion that the quickest way to improve society was to educate them.

When I came from Pakistan, that's in late December 1998, I was getting bored at home, writing applications to these companies. After that, I had plenty of time to do other things. I was then introduced to Mr Malik; I think it was my fifth or sixth day after I came to Britain. Mr Malik said to me, "If you have time why don't you come and do something for Jinnah?" And I think I was in the Jinnah Development Trust's office on the tenth day of my arrival. Then I started coming more regularly doing little management kind of things. I wanted to know more about how a voluntary organisation was run and I think Jinnah Development Trust helped me a lot and taught me how you help people in the community, especially the people who are not advantaged in terms of education. I was quite surprised; the first form I filled in was for somebody who has been living in this country for 35 years, that was on the tenth or eleventh day of my arrival. And that was another reason why I appreciated education.

I did not look back after that. Jinnah was a sort of link between Pakistan and Britain for me, so I started spending more and more time at Jinnah and at the same time I was going to college as well to sort of polish my English, which at that time wasn't good enough. I was told that to do well at any level I need to improve my English.

When I went to college I found other opportunities. I started doing some volunteer work in a classroom with somebody who was, I think, head of maths at that time. He realised that my mathematical abilities were, if not better, at least level with him. He sort of offered me a volunteer job in his classroom, so I was working as a second teacher with him. I think that was key. And this is why, just like Mr Malik, I always encourage Asian youngsters, in fact all youngsters, to volunteer because that is so helpful. When I look back, I wouldn't have been a teacher if I hadn't done those three months as a volunteer teacher. Because those three months actually gave me an insight into teaching, a teacher's role, and those three months and that experience actually helped me to find my first college job at Nelson and Colne College.

I'm Chair of Jinnah now. The board has shown trust in me and put me in this position. I personally feel that there are some other people who are more deserving of this role, but I'm very grateful to the Jinnah Board, and people who work for Jinnah who've actually shown their trust in me. I can see the potential; see what more Jinnah can do. I will go back on to the same thing, volunteering. I need to bring more people on board so that they can volunteer and they can push Jinnah forward together because Jinnah has done so much for people. You look at the history of Jinnah for these people, for all the community in Burnley, the Pakistani community in Burnley,

the Bangladeshi community in Burnley; the local people of Burnley. I mean, Jinnah has done so much for the local people in Burnley.

If you think about religion, all faiths and without any discrimination, they all teach you about respect and respecting people, respecting communities, respecting cultures. Being a Muslim, I know that Islam teaches you to live with other communities in harmony and in a peaceful manner. Our kids, they've got that, they've got that inside of them as Muslims. So I feel that faith can be a very, very good connection for groups. We did some community partnership work after those 2001 serious disturbances in Burnley; there were several organisations which were formed and one of them was Building Bridges, and when I looked at the objectives of that organisation I said, wow, that probably is what this country needs, bringing different faiths together. And we enjoyed being together; with Christians and other religions as well with Islam; people getting together, these imams and these priests hugging each other. It's lovely, it's

Above left: Safdar Baig Mirza receiving Volunteer of the Year Award at Lancs BME Awards ceremony

Above: On holiday in Spain with his wife, Ishrat Mirza

Below left: On holiday in Spain with his cousin, Shahid

fantastic and I thought, I wish I could take that into the community as well. And there were so many people from Christian communities who used to come and visit mosques, and their misconceptions about Muslims and about Asian Pakistanis or Bangladeshis, those misconceptions literally vanished. Some of them made comments like we now know that you're genuine people, you are genuinely nice people. It's just that sometimes the language barrier and this religious barrier, and sometimes the media don't play their roles properly, so that meant all these factors actually divided communities. Faith can play an integral role in bringing communities, people, together; keeping them calm. Whether you go into a church or into a mosque, you will find people very, very calm and they will be down to earth. I know that when you talk about Islamic education, Islam does persuade you to go out and see people, meet them, greet them and invite them towards you. But I think as a society it's our responsibility to do what you can do for the community. And, like I said before, when you differentiate between two societies, an educated and an illiterate society, that's the difference, and these are the differences you find. There are millions of people in Britain who are volunteering at this moment, you won't find as many volunteers in less developed or less educated countries. These are the people who actually are the backbone of a civilised society, these volunteers.

The longer I live in this country, the more I believe that it is a land of opportunities but what you've got to do is, you've got to work hard. But I feel that if you work hard you get a reward. I'm quite optimistic that this society will move on and move on as an integrated society. Because people are trying to understand each other and like I said before, education is the key.

I have lived in Burnley for almost 15 years with my family. All my children were born here, so was their mother. Burnley is home. Like I said before, you never forget a good teacher and sometimes you don't forget the sayings of good teachers. And one of my Islamic Studies teachers when I was in school, he said to me, you've got to travel for two reasons; educational and financial, and never look back. For a Muslim, there's no homeland. Wherever you go that's your home and you've got to invest yourself here. So, when I moved to this country I came with this perception, that I'm going to a new home and I've got to invest myself there. I've always invested

in this society. I'm proud that I did it because 14 years down the line I'm actually seeing that I made the right decision. We do what we can do for Pakistan, we do what we can do for Pakistani people, but I think your first priority is the society where you live and I think you've got a more important role to play in it. What we've got to do is, rather than sit back and think about Pakistan, I think it's important that we're actually active in this society because our future generations are going to live here. They are probably not going to go back, so what you need to do is, you need to invest in their future and you need to invest it here. That's what I think and Mr Malik agrees with that.

Chapter 5 - Public sector

Health

Dr Ahsanul Haq

Above: Dr Ahsanul Haq is the first Pakistani heritage Consultant based at Preston Royal Infirmary

My name is Ahsanul Haq. I was born in Halifax in 1968. My dad worked in the cotton and weaving industry. He came over to England in 1961; there was a huge core of Pakistanis who came over when he first came to England. He lived in houses with other people. My dad never had any intention of actually staying in England. If you speak to him he says, look I was going to be here for three or four years, make enough money to send back home and pay for a shop, and that was when he was going to go back. But then he got settled, got married and my mum came over in '67 and I was born in '68 and at the time he was working in a mill in Halifax.

My family are from Azad Kashmir, a little village not far from the border with India. We moved over to Nelson when I was about three or four years old and then I think in about 1975 we moved to Burnley. Initially I went to St John's Primary School on Colne Road, which was my infant school. From there I went to Barden High School that was between 1980 and 1985. Between 1985 and 1987 I was at Burnley College. I went on to study medicine at St John's College in Cambridge between 1987 and 1992, that's when I qualified as a doctor.

I qualified in '92 and my intention was always to be a surgeon so the way surgical training was, well 20 years ago now, I did one house job in Newcastle, I did my second house job in Cambridge and then I did three or four different jobs to get the FRCS which is the Fellowship of the Royal College of Surgeons. I became a FRCS in 1996, then I became a registrar in surgery until about '98. I went into a higher surgical training scheme in urology which is a sub-speciality in surgery that concentrates on surgery of the kidneys, bladder and the prostate. That was between 1998 and 2004. In 2003, I got the FRCS Urol which is the highest surgical qualification in urology and in 2004 I became a consultant surgeon. All my training was down south. Once I'd qualified, I did some training in Sheffield but the majority was back in East Anglia and that's where my children were born. I trained in

London as well but the plan was always to come back home. The other major milestone in my life in '95 was I got married. My wife is from Bury originally, and her family are still there, as are my parents. So the plan always was for us to come back. A job came up in Preston and I've been there since May 2004, and been a consultant surgeon there for eight years now.

I think growing up in Burnley in the early '80s, if you were academically good, and I was, medicine was the only real career that I knew about. The only doctor I knew was our GP and a doctor in the Asian community was always held in very high esteem. I did my 'O' levels and scored grade A in all of my 'O' levels and then went on to do my 'A' levels, again I got grade A in all of them. I think there wasn't going to be anything else apart from medicine for me to do. I didn't really know about any other careers to be honest with you. I was fairly focused, blinkered you might call it, but focused on doing medicine, I always was. Medicine is a bit of an apprenticeship really, once you're going through medical school, it's a layered approach. You build your foundation in pre-clinical, then you go on to clinical medicine and it was slightly odd because I did my clinical training in East Anglia and it's not exactly the most cosmopolitan place in the world, going to places like Peterborough. Actually Peterborough's not bad but Bury St Edmunds and Ipswich and Norwich… I'll just say it was interesting, but, what was it somebody once said - Experiences make you the person you are and I thought it was a very rich experience again when I was in East Anglia.

It was difficult growing up in Burnley in the '80s I must say, with the best will in the world, I mean there was a degree of racism when I grew up. I

Below: Dr Ahsanul Haq as a child in his mother's arms with his father, sister and elder brother circa 1970

was the only Pakistani in the top three streams at school. I tell my kids and they just don't believe me because they're at Lancaster Grammar School, life's different for them. But life in Burnley 30 years ago was very different to what it is now; things are much more cosmopolitan now. It was difficult; you go to an all-boys school and Barden School was an all-boys school, and there was a mixture of people in the school. There were kids from good families and kids from not so good families. Being the only Pakistani kid in the top stream and also being a swot, which I am, I'm happy to admit I'm a swot, always have been a swot, and I've always been very hard working. At a boys' school you tend to get gentle ribbing, you don't mind, but getting sort of fairly severe abuse sometimes, there was a bit more than banter really. I used to get that quite a lot and I just developed a bit of a thick skin really.

Do what the Americans say; don't get even, get successful. The interesting thing was all the kids in my class, apart from me as I've said, they were all white, and I had a bunch of white friends and some of them I'm still in contact with now. The Asian kids didn't like that actually. I mean, on the one hand they were quite proud of the fact that I was a Pakistani and I was doing well and I was also head boy. But on the other hand they didn't really like me mixing with the white kids, but I had to mix with the white kids because I had nobody else to speak to in my class. So it was a bit of a dichotomy really, it was difficult. I had two sets of friends and never the twain shall meet. I'd be with my English friends in my class, my English white friends; I'd say I'm just as English as them, but in the school yard I'd spend my time with my Pakistani friends and it was fine. As I say, it was a difficult way to grow up but I say you

are what your experiences make you, but I don't like to think that I was hindered in any way. I don't have any baggage associated with it; I just got on with it. To me it's always been a stepping stone, I did well at school and I had to get into college. I had to do well at college and once you get to medical school it's the same, you're at the bottom rung of a different ladder and you make your way up.

The work ethic came from my upbringing. At home I had a typical Pakistani British upbringing in Burnley; my dad was educated to a fairly low level; my mum wasn't educated at all. My mum still has difficulty speaking English and so you'd come home and you'd speak a different language at home and I suppose it's come from my parents really. When my dad came from Pakistan he had five pounds in his pocket and he came to this country, couldn't speak the language, and he then made enough money to make himself relatively wealthy compared to where he came from. So if you look at it as far as being successful is concerned, some would say I'm successful because I'm a consultant surgeon, I have a busy practice - I'm known nationally and internationally for some of the things that I do. But then if I compare myself to what my dad's done, I don't know maybe have I achieved that much, I'm not sure? We'll have to see. You'll have to ask my dad, although he's very proud of me he would never say, but if you could compare where's he's come from, from where he was born and where he grew up to where he is now and where his kids are I think he's probably done better than me. My dad had eight kids, he wasn't educated, he worked in a factory and then he got ill-health in his sort of late 50s and I think it was a struggle, when we were kids. When I was at school my dad wasn't working, I used to have free school meals, it's something my kids laugh about but I said to them look that's what it was. I wasn't ashamed of it and I said you shouldn't be ashamed of that, you haven't to be ashamed of what you are or where you've come from because you are what your experiences make you.

I've got a specialist interest in the management of patients with urinary incontinence and I teach locally and nationally. I actually teach at the Royal College of Surgeons for London now and Edinburgh and when I start off my lectures I usually say you wouldn't believe, I'm a working class boy from Burnley and here I am teaching at the Royal College. I'm fairly high up as far as education is concerned. Educating not just

medical students and junior doctors but also other surgeons and internationally I've been invited on to panels. I've given interviews. I actually gave an interview once to the Arab News Network, I was invited on because somebody had heard me give a lecture somewhere and it was beamed out to something like 50 million Arabs - quite daunting actually, I didn't realise until afterwards. It was a three–hour live programme and they interviewed me for an hour. After that people were ringing up from all over the world asking questions, that was quite an interesting experience. I do get asked to go and operate abroad and teach abroad. I mean, it's difficult to fit it all in to the busy practice that I've got.

My dedication is also about being restless I suppose, not being content to just be as you are, trying to better yourself – right I've become a consultant now I need to do other things. I mean my career, as a consultant, (I was a consultant at 35) means I've got another 30 years of work. You can't just do the same thing; you've got to better yourself and by bettering yourself and learning new techniques your patients benefit from it as well. Well, I've not found the cure for cancer yet. I don't start off on January 1st thinking, by the end of this year I will do this. What I try and tend to do is I keep myself up to date with the new medical treatments. I try and learn at least one new operation a year and then with that come other things basically.

My career goal when I first started at medical school was actually to be a plastic surgeon. Obviously very glamorous until I actually did a plastics job and I didn't enjoy it at all. I just didn't; it didn't really appeal to me. I quite like the re-constructive side and the cancer side but I didn't really like the cosmetic side, it wasn't the sort of work I wanted to do for the rest of my life. It's an odd thing to become a Urologist, it's not exactly the most glamorous job. My wife still tells me off actually, because when she met me I was a plastic surgeon and she liked the idea of being married to a plastic surgeon but I just didn't enjoy it, I just didn't want to do it. When I did my first Urology job, which was at Addenbrookes in Cambridge. I worked for this fantastic surgeon. He was second generation Irish, a lovely man, and I'd never done any surgery but just looking at him I thought, I want to be like him and that's why I did Urology in the end.

I still remember his whole demeanour, he was just fantastic with the patients, he was well respected and I just thought - one day if I'm half the man he is I'll have done alright, but I don't think I am yet. When you're growing up in life you see these role models and you want to emulate them and he was my professional role model. I suppose the people you mix with, my parents, my wife and my kids, they shape me. Well, my parents are constantly telling me off, so is my wife, and my kids too I suppose! But seriously, you want to do as well as you can to make your parents happy, I mean my parents have had no understanding whatsoever about what I've done in my life. As far as they were concerned, I had to study. I could never go to them for any sort of careers advice because they just wouldn't know. Obviously my wife understands more because she's educated as well, so I can bounce ideas off her, and then you want to be the best dad you can for your kids. My kids; they just see Dad really. I tell them you have no idea what I do, as far as they are concerned, I just come home after a hard day's work and sort of slump in front of the TV and then I'll go up to my office and do a bit of work. My son wants to do medicine so hopefully, when he gets into medical school he'll have a little bit more of an idea about what I do but I don't think they understand now.

I think it's all about setting an example and it's a real shame when you see families where the parents don't work. My kids have got the work ethic because I've got the work ethic, they see me leaving for work every single day, they see me coming home tired, they see me working at home and they see their mum doing exactly the same thing so they know. We impress on the children that if you are going to get anywhere in life you've got to work. It's all very good looking at role models like footballers and so-called celebrities, but that's the minority. If you want to do well in life, you're going to have to work; and then I mix with people who are doctors and professionals as well and they see these people who are similar to ourselves and I think my kids appreciate that if they are going to get anywhere in their lives they are going to have to work.

Looking back, you could probably say over that time I've done things that have saved people's lives. But when you see hundreds of patients a week and thousands a year, it's difficult to be able to say, well that particular thing is the one I'm really proud of. I can remember the day I became a doctor, which was a lovely day. I can remember the day I got married, that was a lovely day as well; I mean, I remember the birth of my children – there are these specific highlights in your life.

But if you look at it professionally, it all becomes a little bit of a blur unfortunately because you do so much on a daily basis. Although I still remember the first operation when I took my first appendix out - I was quite proud of that. But I'd say I do much more complex, much more difficult operations now but I tell my trainees, once you've done one operation and it's done well, you can't expect a round of applause because you've got another one to do afterwards. That's over, you've done your job, you've done it properly, you've just got to get on and do the next one, it's not a case of expecting gratitude and applause every time you do something, you've just got to get on and do it.

I'm a Muslim and I've got a strong faith, I must admit I don't pray five times a day as often as I would like to. When things are difficult you do fall back on your faith there's no denying that. My parents always had a fairly strong faith and it's got stronger as they've got older and religion becomes much more of a major facet of their lives and I've tried to instil that in my children as well.

I'm English, I was born in England, I grew up in England and although my memories of Burnley aren't the nicest memories, it is my home, and my parents are still here. I would pass the Norman Tebbit test if England played Pakistan at cricket, I would support England. When the national anthem comes on I stand up and I sing and I put my hand on my heart, I'm English. If I was in Pakistan I'd probably be working in a shop or tending a field. I am here, I'm a consultant surgeon, I studied at Cambridge University, and I have reaped all the benefits I have because I'm from England and I'm English.

I suppose if you want to do well in life you can't do anything by half measures. I just used to lock myself in my room and study. I'm lucky that I had enough intelligence that when I did study, I did well in my exams and I could go further. My advice to anybody growing up in Burnley, or any other sort of place like Burnley, would be to try and make the most of what you are and just work hard and if you work hard you'll be fine. I've still got nephews and nieces here in Burnley who are at school now. Burnley's a much better place to grow up, it's much more cosmopolitan, and people accept people much more. Also, it's a fantastic place to be a Muslim because the people who teach in the mosques are much better and they make you understand your religion much more. When we went to mosque it was just reciting the Qur'an whereas my kids understand what they're reading and they teach me - which is wonderful.

Health

Dr Misfar Hassan

My name is Misfar Hassan. I was born in Rawalpindi in Pakistan in 1956. My father was a businessman and my mother was a teacher. I came to Britain in the year 2000. I was living in Nottingham and we were doing preliminary exams, by profession I'm a doctor and so is my wife, and we were just doing the basic qualification exams. After the exams, we got our first jobs here in Burnley, so I'm thankful to Burnley that they offered us a new life in the UK. That's how we landed in Burnley.

I have had lots of very good experiences in Burnley. I would divide these experiences up into those with my own community here, with the British population here, my professional work and my work in politics. To start with, I was with the community from back home as I was working on an issue which has caused lots of problems for Pakistan and that is the issue of Kashmir. Basically, my parents migrated from Srinagar in 1947, they were forced to flee their homeland and they never went back so I was involved in the politics of my family members. One of my uncles was a front line leader in Kashmir politics. He was the first elected President of the Pakistan side of Kashmir, called Azad Jammu Kashmir and prior to that he worked with Mr Mohammed Ali Jinnah from 1944 to 1947 as his private secretary. During the period he stayed with Mr Jinnah, he became a family member. Ms Fatima Jinnah adopted him as a son and she took care of him quite a lot.

His name was K H Khursheed, he died in an accident in 1988 and that was quite a traumatic shock for me. Prior to that I wasn't involved in practical politics but his death changed my course and way of life. He formed a party called the Jammu Kashmir Liberation League and he stood for the political and peaceful resolution of the Kashmir issue. I have studied him since his death, not before; he was my uncle but I was never involved in his

politics during his lifetime. Later on I collected all the information I needed, and met his friends all over the world, from Azad Kashmir to New York; I have travelled a lot projecting this issue. That brought me into politics; I was working as a GP in Pakistan so I had to divide my time between my profession and between the national cause I had taken up. Working in Kashmir politics brought me to make my first visit to the UK in 1997. In 1998 I was working as the party secretary general in Pakistan. I had a lot of interaction with the diplomatic community in Islamabad including the diplomatic representative of the United States, the United Kingdom and the European Union so they organised a trip for us to visit the UK and meet some officials here in the Foreign Office. We had a good meeting in 1998 and we briefed them on our point of view. Then we went to the European Union in Brussels. We had a meeting in Paris with Foreign Office officials. Then we went to the United States of America. We were just spreading our message; this is what the issue is and this is what the people of Kashmir want. Basically they want their right to self-determination, they want to live peacefully with their neighbouring countries but they want the right to exist as they wish.

Above: Dr Misfar Hassan is also a Lancashire County Councillor from Burnley

Below: Dr Misfar Hassan with his wife and daughters

In 2000, I actually joined Nottingham University as a postgraduate student to study public health and my motive behind that was to gain some international experience of education, and secondly, I wanted to get some experience of public health because that would help me move around to certain areas where I could project my political cause as well as my professional issues. During that stay of one year as a postgraduate student, my kids were with me. I had three daughters so they started to go to school here in the UK and that schooling made all the difference. They didn't want to go back to Pakistan so that changed my objectives further and I just got my professional exams done then myself and my wife joined the NHS. She works in Obstetrics and Gynaecology here in Burnley General Hospital and is working for the Trust but I'm based in Accrington working with children who present with behavioural and emotional difficulties.

In the initial 4 to 5 years of my stay in Burnley I was not involved in local issues or local political issues. Then a group of friends who knew me from back home and knew my background as well invited me to join the Labour party, and Ms Kitty Usher was MP at that time. I met her, and my friends actually persuaded me to join the Labour party and it was in 2010 that Liberal Democrat County Councillor Bennett passed away so a group of friends here from Stoneyholme and Daneshouse persuaded me to stand for election. Actually I was not prepared to stand at that point in time but I will come later on to why I was not prepared.

So in 2010, I went into the election and incidentally, through hard work and through the help of my friends, I beat my opponent by a large majority although I was not known to many in Burnley, there were only a few I was interacting with. I'm thankful to the people of Burnley but particularly my main supporters from Daneshouse and Stoneyholme. They supported me without even knowing me just because they had heard of me by word of mouth; they turned out and they voted for me and I'm really grateful to them, and to the group of friends who persuaded me to join the Labour Party because I now realise how important it is to be part of the mainstream politics in the UK. We live in the United Kingdom so we need to interact with the local communities. Within the communities there are people from India, people from Bangladesh, from Pakistan, from Africa, there are all sorts

of people you come across. I think living in a multicultural society you need to have good working relationships in spite of all your personal differences or different belief systems. That should not be a hurdle in my opinion to have a good working relationship, and particularly with the white communities which are the majority population. I'm thankful to them as well because they have accepted me here in Burnley with open hearts and arms and I have been welcomed in the Labour party as well so I'm also thankful to them. I have also got very good feedback from the Labour Party. I was doing my campaign and there were a few incidents where people didn't like a person of Asian background coming in and asking for votes from the main population. It's a natural reaction. To be honest if someone from the United Kingdom went over to Pakistan and asked for votes I would have the same feelings – Oh, you are an immigrant but still, I kept that aside. I respected their views and I just asked for their help and their votes so I think that also paid off and because in my job in family therapy, I have trained for two years working with families. I understand the basic rationale behind all the interactions and that paid off a lot in my election campaign when I discussed that with them. White people particularly, when I work in my capacity as a child psychiatrist with family issues, I know the problems they are facing. On the door step, I come across a lot of issues and problems being discussed so I was quite comfortable when one of my senior colleagues in the Burnley Labour Party, Mr Pike, gave me feedback to say that he had not seen any man before interacting as I have done with the main population. It gives me a very good working relationship with people. I think this is an ideal sort of way forward; to work with all the communities, respecting their views and projecting your own views, so you give respect and you get respect. It's the basic formulation of my life.

On the professional side, the field I'm working in is child psychiatry and unfortunately, in Pakistan, we haven't developed that field and we didn't have much training or knew how it worked. So since 2006 I've been working in child psychiatry, which is a fascinating branch of medicine with regard to children; how they develop, how they think. It's an amazing subject to be honest and I work with children from the age of 4 to 5 years up to 16 years of age, and there are certain problems that can be treated. Once we start them on treatment then we have to follow them up to the age of sixteen. We see how these young boys and girls are presenting difficulties, how they transform into very well-behaved, presentable people. If they don't get treatment their lives fall apart and it's quite an amazing experience learning how the mind develops and how the mind thinks. It is unfortunate that the communities of South Asian background are not accessing these health services. The dilemma attached to mental health issues means there are big, big difficulties at the moment and probably not having the knowledge about these things is an issue. I think the main problem is that people don't think in a positive way about mental health. The concept of mental health overseas in India, Pakistan, and Bangladesh is that you've got some sort of spirit that's taken over your body and you can't be treated, or you have to go to some religious scholar to get rid of it. We respect that, we encourage them to go and seek help from them as well but we would like to say, that these people need educating about mental health. They need to seek other opinions. They should continue their cultural practices but they should seek help from the available services as well. For example, if a child has a difficulty like Attention Deficit Hyperactivity Disorder (ADHD), if he or she doesn't get help in time, their trajectory of life changes, right from 11 to 12 years on, they can get into difficulties within the education system because they drop out of education. They don't gain any qualifications, they may get into drugs or drink abuse, they may get involved with the justice system and their lives are basically ruined. If they seek help, their trajectory can change, they can go to university, and help is available. I would urge the community to seek information and get help. It is available free of cost and it is for the benefit of future generations. The other thing I would like to mention here is that I am involved in a research project at the moment in collaboration with the University of Manchester as well as with the Lancashire Care Trust and what we are doing is, we are looking at the effect of post-natal depression. Mothers who give birth to babies go through a very stressful time and in that period of time they may get depressed, they may feel lower in mood, and that depression of mood - how it affects the newborn baby - is another amazing field we are looking at, at the moment.

There is a lot of research done in the mainstream

Below: Dr Misfar Hassan was awarded a MBBS Degree from the University of Balochistan in Quetta, Pakistan

white population on this issue but we don't have any data or any available information that could tell us how children born to South Asian region mothers are affected and what are the difficulties. In this process, I think they are doing a favour for future generations of communities who are from these backgrounds. Frist of all, we are trying to educate the mothers and the families about mental health issues, and how to tackle them, how to overcome difficulties, how to seek help and where to find the help available, and it's all free of cost. Secondly, if the mother is feeling depressed and she gets appropriate help it will help the newborn baby, because available evidence suggests that if the mother is depressed the baby could be presenting as a teenager with

behavioural difficulties in the future and you see lots of these cases but we don't know why it is being presented like that. If they get help during the last 3 months of their pregnancy and during the post-natal period, that will have a positive impact on the children's behaviour and we will see a decline in behavioural difficulties within the population. What we are doing at the moment is we are preparing a treatment - an intervention which will have controversial therapies for the mothers and women who will be delivering this intervention and who will be of the same culture/background. The mothers and therapists understand each other's feelings and cultures and how other people think but again, we need some co-operation and help from the community. They'll have to come forward so

that we can generate a database. That database can work out what will be best for people of this background. I would like to appeal to families living in East Lancashire particularly as my area of work is in East Lancashire, right from Pendle up to Blackburn. I was just doing some interviews in Blackburn so as we don't have a database at the moment, if families come forward that would help the people who do this research and in the future they would benefit from the baseline information that is done in 2012; in 2024 it could show how things are and in 2050, how things would be. Another fact is that the families from South Asian origin are the most rapidly multiplying nations. At the moment we are about 10-12% of the total and it has been projected that by 2051 this population percentage will increase up to 20% of the total, so in that context, if our families are living on the sideline not joining in, not benefitting from the main system, then their lives would become more complex and difficult. I think everyone needs to look at that and review their own practices and look at their belief systems and seek help. If they don't, they won't understand the system, they need to contact someone to seek help and get information; lots of information is available and we would also be working within the community to provide information if people are willing to seek help.

I want to explain why this is important to me as an individual. So basically, my ambition is to help the generations who would be coming after say 50 years. I will be publishing a couple of papers and explaining how I've gone through these difficult times for 4 to 5 months. I did a lot of travelling to put these teams together. We did not have any idea of how the process works or how the mothers are referred to in order to protect them. I had to work a lot on that issue; I had to liaise with women from the mental health team, with health visitors, with the midwives, with the community, with the religious leaders and my personal friends, so we have been going through this process for the last 4 to 5 months. Now we have set up some focus groups and I invited the community leaders, the basic thing is that we want to improve lives. My ambition to pass on information to benefit others can be described in two parts; one is genetic - genes inherited from the family and the other is environmental so when you go into an environment, how do you react to that environment. These two things go together, particularly when you have a window of opportunity to do something useful.

I have studied some qualities of leadership and vision; having foresight is the first quality and you only develop it when you are thinking around developing your own knowledge base and you are studying the lives of people who have gone through and changed parts of history. You can trace it back to Muslims in the beginning of Islam. I studied the life of Prophet Muhammad, peace and blessing be upon him, the way he presented his character - that is amazing. I feel so enlightened by the way of life led - such as his personal life before declaring his prophethood, he was a very pious person. He was always truthful, he would never tell a lie so if you left something with him and asked for him to keep your money for a while - he would and he would not take anything from it or add anything to it, so he was called 'Sadiq' and 'Ameen'. 'Sadiq' means the person who tells the truth and "Ameen" means the person who keeps your belongings in his custody safe for you until you take them back. Then, he was in business and he was very, very clear and very, very truthful and honest and this is what he taught for 40 years. He would never sell a thing if it had a defect but these days, these practices are not very obvious and people try to mix things around and this is unfortunate. To be honest, it shows you the present belief systems, and how dishonest people are becoming. Then the Prophet declared his prophethood and before that declaration, he asked people of Makkah to come around and asked them, if I say there's a big army coming to attack you from behind this hill, would you believe it? They said they would believe it because they had faith in him as he never tells lies, when he declared his prophethood, the attitude of people changed and the best thing I have read about him was that he never retaliated or responded negatively. People did lots of bad things to him. There was a woman who used to throw rubbish on him when he crossed the street and it was an everyday routine. One day, the Prophet Muhammad, peace and blessings be upon him, was passing the street but the woman didn't throw anything. So he was a bit curious; he went in and asked her "Are you okay? Because you didn't do that today" and she was so impressed that she embraced Islam. This sort of character is just too forward, you cannot display

those things because we are human beings, and he was a messenger of Allah so there's a big difference but at least we should try to practise whatever we can with our own weak belief system.

I have had great satisfaction working with children and young people. We can see when life is going downhill for them. Once we see them coming back up and getting into a good place, when the parent feels happy, that gives me lots of satisfaction, to have done something for the benefit of someone. This is why the real world has been created in my opinion. I feel sad when people don't understand, particularly my own community. I have been trying to convince them, and I have been trying to communicate with them. They have very, very closed mindsets and the main difficulty that I have felt is that they don't want their community to point the finger because of a mental health stigma. Clearly, we need to rationalise their thinking and I think it's time for them to come forward and take an active part in community projects. I have been trying to get them involved, one way or another, where I feel that they can play a part but still there's lot to do and a long way to go.

As a male person visiting mothers at home it was a really, really challenging job for me because to make people understand why I wanted to do my part of the research, I have to look at the home environment and how the mother is interacting with her baby because that will give us some clues as to why children are behind. Previous research showed children from a South Asian background were one year behind in emotional and physical development compared to their peer groups and that is what led to this project. We are exploring whether maternal emotional well-being causes any difficulties for these children so to get that basic knowledge, we have to see and observe how the mother interacts with her baby and how the

Below: Dr Misfar Hassan addressing a conference on Kashmir in Manchester - Gerald Kaufman MP and the High Commissioner of Pakistan are sitting on the stage

dad is playing his part in the family. The extended family also plays a role in this relationship, particularly the grandma, grandfather, mothers-in-law, fathers in-law; their role is very significant within the family system and I'm now thinking of doing some work with them as well. Although I know quite a few families from the community we need to do some work within a group and discuss these issues with them. They need to realise how it will benefit the third generation. This is what I derive my strength from; I'm doing something with a particular objective and for a particular reason. I don't know if I will succeed in it or not, I will leave that to our Creator. We cannot change everything but at least we leave a thought, maybe sometime in the future someone will come, pick it up from there and carry it forward. This is the hope and this is why I do the work.

My last message is, I would thank the National Health Service, they provided us with a good job opportunity. I have also learnt a lot on the political side. I would like to mention the issue of Kashmir and in the current context, if you look at the difficulties in Syria for example about 6000-plus people have lost their lives and in Kashmir, since 1947, it's about 2 to 3 million people who have lost their lives. Altogether, in the recent episode 100,000 people lost their lives just because they wanted the two governments, India and Pakistan to give them their right to self-determination. I would urge that they give them their rights, which were promised in 1947 through the Security Council; Britain is one of the signatories of the resolution. I'm practising and preaching my beliefs in the Labour party as well, to establish regional peace. And for those countries who are spending lots of money and resources on their defence budgets, to help them overcome those difficulties they need to play their part for the resolution of the Kashmir issue in a peaceful way, like raising the issue of Syria in the United Nations, they need to look at their own practises in the context of the Kashmir issue. Recently, the American Congress has debated a motion on the right to self-determination for the people of Baluchistan, a province of Pakistan and I feel very upset about it. It is a direct intrusion into the internal affairs of the country and they did not have any right to pass such a resolution while the resolution of Kashmir, which Americans are part of, is still waiting for the United Nations to act upon it. They didn't realise they would have to sort it out first before they could go on and into another country's internal

affairs. These world leaders need to reflect on their practices, these practices are promoting extremist activities as well so I think it's time for everyone to reflect on that and look at what they are doing, if we keep discriminatory and selective behaviour then I don't think peace will prevail in the world.

Finally, I would like to thank you very much for inviting me and giving me this opportunity to discuss these issues.

Chapter 6 - Public sector

Judiciary

Susan Hughes

Above: Susan Hughes is Deputy Lieutenant of Lancashire and former Chairperson of Burnley, Pendle and Rossendale Magistrates Bench

My name is Susan Hughes. I was born in Prittlewell in Essex which is close to Southend-on-Sea. It was a Saxon village and Southend became the south end of Prittlewell, hence its name. I was born in 1938. My father was in the advertising business. He was very artistic; he enjoyed painting and drawing so was in the advertising industry all his life. My mother had been a secretary in London, although she'd started out planning to have a career in dancing but then she broke her toe which brought her ambitions sadly to an end. She therefore did secretarial work.

I came to live in Burnley via a circuitous route in a way, including having lived overseas. We came north to Cheshire as my father had a post with ICI Dyestuffs. I met my husband in Cheshire and when he purchased a dental practice in Burnley in 1962, we came to the town in 1963 following our honeymoon. One of the last things my mother said to me when I left Cheshire to come over here, was, "Now you will do voluntary work, won't you?" She had done voluntary work, as had my grandmother, and we had a French ancestor who had founded a Charitable Bureau in Oise in France, so it was very much in the family ethos that I should be involved in the community in that way. I had already done some voluntary work in a children's home when I was 16.

A couple of months after settling in, I went along to what was then the Council for Social Service which became the Council for Voluntary Service. Life has come round full circle because I'm a trustee of that organisation now. I started working with a small group called the Friendly Visiting Committee, which involved visiting the elderly in their homes; these were people who were housebound and who had very few family contacts. In time I became Chairman of the Friendly Visiting Committee. I also volunteered with the Probation Service, and then started work with the Citizens' Advice Bureau because in those days the CAB was a sub-committee of the Council for Voluntary Service. It broke away in the '70s and became an independent organisation.

I started with the CAB in 1964 and altogether I served 40 years with the organisation, firstly as a volunteer, then as a paid deputy manager and finally as chairman of the trustee board in Pendle.

I have almost 50 years of experience of working in the voluntary sector. I became a magistrate in 1976 and was appointed to the Reedley Bench. Reedley Bench joined with Burnley in 1994. I became chairman of Burnley and Pendle in 2000 and that year a merger took place with Rossendale Bench. It then became Burnley, Pendle and Rossendale Bench and I was appointed chairman of the unified Bench.

There were a number of ethnic minority people living in the area and at that time there were only two Black and Minority Ethnic (BME) people on the Bench, and they were both male. As far as I could see there was very little history of nominations from members of the ethnic community. So I set about rectifying this omission. With my colleague who chaired the advisory committee, the committee that interviews candidates for the magistracy, we visited different groups of people, in Stoneyholme, Accrington and in Pendle. Wherever there was a group we could speak to, we would speak to them.

Eighteen months after I had finished as chairman, there was a noticeable difference in the applications as the percentage of appointments of ethnic minority people had certainly increased. It is now four years since I have retired and I recently made enquiries about the current percentages, but I understand that there are not as many people being nominated from the BME communities. That can also of course apply to white people, work being a factor with employers not being as willing to release their employees for voluntary work due to the economic situation.

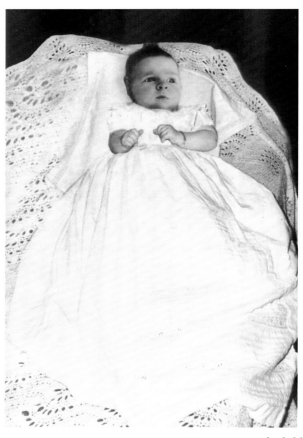

Above: Susan Hughes as a baby

As well as hoping to encourage applications from members of the ethnic communities, I was also keen to heighten awareness by arranging visits to the local mosques and so bench members visited the mosques in Stoneyholme and in Nelson. I was chairman for two years so a mosque visit was planned for each year. These visits were valuable as it gave Bench members an insight into how the Mosques were organised and how the community engages with children through teaching them Arabic and learning the Qur'an. On each occasion we were entertained by the Mosque members.

Once appointments to the Bench from the BME community had been made, the new magistrates were welcomed and soon settled into a role that they may have felt could have eluded them at one time. There was a lot of enthusiasm and I was delighted that my colleague and I had succeeded in ensuring the Bench became more representative of the community. I saw this as inclusion and cohesion and it was a way to connect. We really didn't look back.

There then developed a steady stream of applications from members of the community, which in fact became the icebreaker. Once the ice is broken and people can see that joining the Magistracy is a possibility, that they have an understanding of the language and are willing to work as a team of three people, people will then become confident. In time, BME members joined the Youth and Family Panels so fully participated in all activities expected of them as magistrates.

I like to think I have an understanding of people and their communities. I like people, particularly those from different backgrounds with different creeds and ethnic backgrounds. We're all human beings and all have similar needs. If we're mothers, we all share the same worries and concerns. I greatly believe in the importance of cohesion and was a member of Pendle Cohesion Committee for a long number of years, which was a link with the CAB. I've attended the Face To Faith meetings at St Peter's Church, and through this forum have met people from the different communities coming together, sharing the same problems, and sharing the same joys as well. I was pleased with the BME work my colleague and I did during the years I was chairman and at the end wrote a report intending this to be for my own reference. We had visited many groups of people and had had varying responses so it was important to keep a record for the future. Our work happened to coincide with the disturbances that occurred in Burnley, Bradford and Oldham and as a result, new organisations were born such as Building Bridges that has just celebrated its tenth anniversary. As Lord Clark was asked to chair an enquiry into the disturbances, I sent him my report as I considered it was important for him to know what we as a court were doing for cohesion in the community. As an organisation, we worked in the community, we worked with the community, and we were part of the community, it was therefore important that he knew what we were doing to make efforts to overcome any unforeseen obstacles. He acknowledged my letter and report and replied to say how pleased he was that we were working in this way. The Lord Lieutenant had also heard about the report and wanted to see it, so he also received a copy.

I think many people who came from Pakistan would call Burnley home and I'll say why I feel this is. I'm a Deputy Lieutenant of Lancashire and on a regular basis attend Citizenship Ceremonies. DLs undertake these tasks every six or seven weeks, either at County Hall in Preston or at Burnley Registry Office. The new citizens come from all over the world, but in Burnley they have usually come from the Indian sub-continent. Many have been in this country for some considerable time and have decided to become new citizens. They call this country home as they've been here for a long time - I don't think they would be applying for citizenship unless they felt comfortable living here. They are integrated as much as they wish to be and the UK is where they like to be. Burnley, in particular, is a very friendly place.

I first met Mr Rafique Malik when we were both involved with the Council of Social Service as it was then called, it's now CVS, and were on the hostel committee together. The hostel which was on Palatine Square, provided accommodation for elderly ladies, and it is currently a care home. It originally formed at the end of the war providing accommodation for people from Manchester who had had their homes destroyed during the war and had nowhere to live. As there was a Local Authority involvement, Councillors would be members of the Committee, hence Mr Malik's presence. He was appointed Mayor when I was chairman of the Bench so I was invited to his mayor making. I have also met his son, Shahid Malik. When I completed my tenure as chairman, I started the Primary School Project which I did for 7 years until I retired. This involved informing and liaising with Year 5 or 6 children about the court system and how, if they committed an offence, they could face a punishment. Each autumn, England and Wales would celebrate Inside Justice Week and so I always arranged for a Primary School to visit one of our Courthouses at that time. Prior to their Court visit, a couple of magistrates would see the children in school. This would be an interactive session with the children engaging and giving their views about punishment and crime. The next time we met them was at Court when they would perform a short sketch about the theft of a mobile phone. The children would take the parts of prosecutor, defence solicitor, defendant, court reporters and magistrates. The final time I was involved prior to my retirement was in October 2008. I had invited the High Sheriff, Alan Jolley and his wife along. Shahid Malik, Minister of Justice, heard about this and asked if he could come too. He and the High Sheriff were excellent with the children who asked a range of questions. It was a lovely occasion and I felt very privileged to have the High Sheriff and a Member of Parliament attending at Reedley Court. The children put on a very good show, they were great.

I live in an area where different communities reside and so cohesion is important. Alongside this, fairness is essential with equal treatment and justice for everyone. It's back to being human beings and sharing the same values, it is important to interact with people in a kindly, fair and respectful way.

Below: Susan Hughes Chairperson of Burnley, Pendle and Rossendale Magistrates Bench

Chapter 6 - Public sector

Judiciary

Abid Sharif

Above: Abid Sharif is a bus driver and Justice of the Peace (JP)

My name is Abid Sharif. I was born in Burnley on the 18th of November 1977. My mum was a housewife and dad, when he came here, he worked in the cotton mills and then became a bus driver in later years. They came in the 1960s. Originally my dad went to Bradford where we had an uncle, who has passed away now. I think the work situation down there; there were too many people, not enough factories. So he came here and started work at Smith & Nephew, the first Pakistani guy actually to work in Smith & Nephew. When he came here, the relative sent him on a sort of fact-finding mission and about six months later they all came and they settled here. They moved to Nelson and then from Nelson we moved here to Burnley in the '70s.

I attended Barden High School in Burnley. It has been knocked down now. I went on to college to study motor vehicles. After that I just went on working and did different jobs, factories, bits and bats for market stalls and then went on to become a bus driver. I've been doing it for the past 11 years or so. My first job was a paper round. I was 12 when I started working my first paper round job; then I did various jobs, milk rounds as well. My work consists of driving a bus and, basically the satisfaction you actually get out of that is when you help old ladies on and off a bus, and the 'thank you' you get. That's the most satisfying part of the day to be honest, when you get thanked for doing your job. The basic thank you, that's the biggest achievement of all. You come out and it's nice, it's a good feeling.

Back then we were happy with little things. Everybody was in the same boat at that time. You've got to think of this like, everybody just had less money and they had to balance everything out. It was different then. Nobody cared about the 'my house is better than his house, his house is better than my house' thinking. And if somebody put up wallpaper then everybody used to go and congratulate them. Well, you've got new wallpaper, it's fantastic, it's brilliant. Nowadays it's all changed, everybody's gone ahead; it's just I think people are getting more selfish. They were

good times when we were young. I mean we had extended families and we used to go and visit them and play cricket and stuff like that in the back streets. Nowadays the kids are all over Facebook and so on. The good memories were, going to Blackpool with Dad, basic memories but they were good memories. We were happy with that. Nowadays it's all money, everybody wants expensive gifts and they're still not happy.

I became a bus driver because it's a job. I went and applied at Queensgate and they gave me a job. My dad has passed away but he also used to be a bus driver. When I got the job, you should've seen the smile on my mum's face. It was brilliant because, at the end of the day, my dad did it and now I'm the second generation. She really had tears in her eyes, to be honest. So it was a good thing at the end of the day.

It was a difficult childhood because at times, it seemed that everybody cried racism this and racism that. But when we grew up in Burnley, at the age when the Burnley Suicide Squad – a white football racist group was doing its thing – now that was tough. There was a minority of Asians in Burnley, at least in Nelson they may have had, say, 100 Pakistanis but in Burnley we might only have had 50. You've got to think of this; it was hard for us coming from that minority background. We could go to school and there might only be three or four Pakistanis in the whole school, or 10 or 12, but that's about it. When I used to look at my cousins in Nelson there used to be almost 40 of them, at least they had some lads to hang around with and everything else. And it was very, very hard to grow up in Burnley. But there were nice people here, you just had to find them and get along with them. It's a better place now, more tolerant.

Our generation now, they've got to move forward, they've got to think of Burnley as home, England as home. I understand it, I'm still here today and everybody's asking about me and I'm proud to sit here and say that I'm actually the son of a farmer but now I'm a bus driver, I've integrated

to do with a burning ship. Britain was the burning ship which our parents anchored on and brought it ashore. And it's up to us, our generation, the second generation and the third generation now, to build this ship. Now the next generation needs to say this ship has been built, and they need to sail that ship, and then the world's their oyster. 20 years from now, I want somebody to stand up and say my name is Mohammad or whatever, and today I stand in front of you as a Muslim, as a Pakistani descendant of a farmer or an illiterate man and I stand in front of you as the prime minister of England or the next Albert Einstein. And these young people can do that. But what they don't realise is, they can do this but they should never ever forget where they came from and who put them in that position. It's because of these people that we are here today, speaking English. English people were tolerant but our predecessors used to be laughed at because of their limited English and so they took a lot of racism if you think about it, I think they took a lot for us.

They might have not had education or a certificate to prove what they had but look what they've achieved. With mosques, to try and get somebody to build a mosque here, it was the hardest thing they could do. And they built them, within six months. This Jinnah Centre was done within months. And now, you get onto a project and you've got to do this and do that and it goes on for years and years and at the end of it, all funding runs out. These people, if they run out of funding, they put money, from their own pocket, just to run the project and get it off the ground. When we only had the Jinnah Centre, we used to get people coming from London, they used to think bloody hell, we haven't got this in London. And this one organisation, people all over England, even Scotland, used to come here. My dad used to come home and say I went to the Jinnah Centre, some blokes from Cardiff or

and I'm a Justice of the Peace. And it's a big thing for me; it's a big achievement for me. When I'm working for the judiciary - it's all part of what I am here. Today we've changed the skyline of England. Look at the mosques, the Jinnah Centre's now here and everything. These people have made Asian shops, and takeaways and restaurants. Not just that, now they're going into manufacturing and for example, Joe Bloggs, was from Burnley and his jeans were sold all over the world. So these people actually came, and look where we are today. This is one generation and everybody says they were illiterate. They might have been illiterate but they did something. Either they made a financial contribution towards a good cause or they gave an hour of their time cleaning or doing something or whatever they did, these are the people that actually made this happen. In English, I can't remember the full poem; I read a poem once and it's something

82

Land's End came– that was a big thing. Those people never had this and it is the people of Burnley that made this.

If we can explain to the younger generation by sharing these stories, then they should learn to appreciate it at the end of the day. But if you're going to forget about the first generation yourself and just sit here and say, listen I did this and I did that, then the younger generation are going to be exactly the same, ungrateful, it's disrespectful really. You can only try. You can only try and then it's up to them to make the history books. I remember Barack Obama, when he came to the UK; he addressed the Houses of Parliament in London, and he stood there and said, "I'm here," the grandson or what was it, of a cook on a British ship, "I'm standing here in front of you as a head of state today." And that's fantastic. But obviously his family's told him about that and he's not forgotten who he is. And the same goes for our young people.

I think, the biggest achievement because you know, the trouble is, I was only 13 when my father passed away so there is only a little about my dad's life that I can actually tell you about. My sister could tell you more because, obviously, she's a lot older than me. But personally, I think the proudest thing that he ever thought was the day my sister went to college, because at the end of the day, she was the first generation person from our family that went to college. And he fought hard to let a female go to college because he was educated himself, but he was going against a lot of people, my uncles in Nelson, telling him things – I am most proud of this act by my dad. And when my sister came home with her test certificate after she passed her driving test, these are the two things that I can remember the most and he was happy, really happy about that. It was an achievement for him as a second generation, my sister, a girl doing that. And then people learnt from that and after that said, if his daughter could do it then why shouldn't our daughters? It's an

example he set and a lot of people then used that and most of them started driving and sending their children to college and so on.

You know, the funny thing is you go from here, and you go and you're talking to your mates, "Where are you going?" "I'm going back home." But when you actually get to Pakistan, "Oh where are you going?" "I'm going back home." Right. And then if you just think, you click. You know, when you come off the M65, when you see that sign, when it says Towneley Park and Towneley Gardens, it's fantastic, the best feeling in the world. You think you're home. I know it's different in Pakistan and we go there and try to fit in, but at the end of the day you're always branded as a kind of an outcast. And you come here; I'm born here, bred here but I've got ties in Pakistan. I spent two years in Pakistan when my dad retired from the buses, we went for two years. I've still got uncles there. But it's just one of those things. Here you're safe. We're used to doing things ourselves. I can get up in the morning or even the middle of the night and go to Asda and do my shopping. In Pakistan, everything is stuck, you're in a village but after 6 o'clock, you don't go out, and it's too dark or dangerous. You're so used to jumping in your car, and going off doing things; there, you've got to take somebody with you for safety and it just gets frustrating sometimes. That's all it is basically. But this is home, it's easy for us. I think this is the way we've been brought up and the way our life is, we can just get up and do things ourselves. But England, I mean especially Burnley, I class as home - a brilliant place to be.

Chapter 7 - Public sector

Postal

Hafiz Riaz Khan

Above: Hafiz Riaz Khan worked in the postal service as Assistant Manager at Burnley Sorting Office

Below: Hafiz Riaz Khan is presenting a cheque to the Mayor for his charity fund outside the Mayor's Parlour with other Stoneyholme community representatives

My name is Riaz Khan. I was born in a small village, Waisa, in Pakistan in 1967. My parents initially were farmers, from a farming background. That's what my grandparents did, that's what my uncles do as well. My father came initially in 1970. And then we came, as a family, my mum and my one brother and my sister, in 1976. My father first went to Oxford. There were a few people there from our own village but the majority were in Burnley. Plus, Mr Malik was here as well and he had a good understanding of my father, so my father decided to settle here.

I went to school in Burnley. The majority of my education was in this country. I first went to Stoneyholme Primary School and then went on to Barden High School. When I left Barden School I went to Burnley College and did my 'O'-Levels there. I wanted to further my education but coming from a poor background, my father wanted us to work so I was actively looking for work at that time. After college, I did part time 'A'-Levels, had a job, and got offered about four jobs in one week. First of all, I applied for fire alarm and security alarm installations and then

the same week, I got offered a job at Royal Mail as well. So I took the job at Royal Mail because it was a permanent job. I've been there ever since. That's 25 years I've been there.

It's been a very, very enjoyable experience for me. It's been a very, very good place to work at, they've been very understanding of my religious beliefs, plus it fitted in really, really well with my beliefs for prayers, for Ramadan, for everything that I've ever done. It has always fitted in because my working hours, when I first started, were from 5 o'clock in the morning 'til 12 noon. So at 5 o'clock in the morning, before I even got up for Fajr salah, our morning prayer, I used to be able to pray Fajr - it was perfect in every sense of the word. It's been a very, very enjoyable experience for me. The support I've had from the people I've worked with, from my managers, and the experience of meeting people out in the community, changes your perception of what people are actually like. Before I started working for Royal Mail, our interaction with the indigenous community wasn't that much. I remember it was Christmas time when I started

Above: Hafiz Riaz Khan standing between his manager and the Mayor during a Mayoral visit of the Sorting Office

there and an elderly couple came out of their house, chatted to me and gave me a bottle of champagne. I said thank you very much but I don't drink, but I really appreciate what you said. So they gave me a Christmas card with £5.

Then you got the other extremes as well, which stick out. Stoops Estate - I won't use the language that came out of a five year old's mouth, but it was eye-opening. Yes, very colourful. If that was my own child, he would've got a clip around the earhole, but what can you say? In the workplace, I remember for instance in Ramadan, when we were breaking fast about half past four in the afternoon, if it meant that I would be at work, they would organise my work so that I would also get my break at the time of the fast. So I would get supported that way. They were supportive at other times as well, especially on Fridays, which is a very important day for us Muslims and they would always support me for Friday prayers. Even now, when I finish at 3 o'clock they will say to me, "Yes, Riaz, park your van, make sure it's all locked up, all secure, and by all means go for Jum'ah." So the support has always been there.

It's a family employer. They employ people to keep them employed for life. You have a job for life. That's the reason they do it, so that people stay there. I would say it's like a family community. Everybody gets on with everybody. Shabaz, who works with me, he's totally opposite to me. I'm outgoing, he's very reserved, but he's also very quiet. But he's had the same experience as me. He's also been made most welcome and he's still there as well and he started there before I did.

I've had varied roles. I've done foot deliveries, driving deliveries and worked indoors as well. I've also had a managerial role for eight years. So it's an equal opportunities employer in every sense of

the word. There was a gentleman called Yakoob; he had a managerial role there as well, before I started. There have been times when it has been difficult, especially with the 9/11 attacks. After 9/11 there was a bit of a backlash, but the majority were supportive of me and my beliefs. There were a few people that thought that all Muslims were fanatics, fundamentalists or terrorists. And yet there were others who saw me for who I really am, because they had worked with me and they said, "Riaz's not like that, so why say things which aren't true?"

From my experiences in life, I've learned that it is important to be more tolerant. If we have tolerance, and our religion teaches us that as well, to be tolerant of each other, of differences, of differences of opinion, and that everybody's opinion should count. It's not a case of my opinion is right and yours is wrong, because yours could be right and I could be totally wrong and we should be more tolerant of other people's views, and opinions and religious beliefs.

I see a lot of people who do the same thing as I have done and worked within their beliefs and within their roles and they do the job as it should be done. You see it more and more often now. I think people are more understanding of our beliefs and that's why I think a lot more people are now more open to portray their beliefs as well. Even in our own workplace, people pray openly, pray their salah openly when it's prayer time whereas before, say 15 years before, they wouldn't do.

There's been a change in culture and Muslims themselves have now got more knowledge of Islam. Society itself is more accepting of our religion, of our beliefs, and we are learning more and more as days go on and people are more willing to learn, whereas before it was just what we learnt in the time of my parents and we didn't try and learn any further. And that's all; we only had a little bit of knowledge about Islam. Whereas now, there are books, there are libraries, you can go to the library and get any book you want and it's available for you. So it's a bit of both culture and knowledge.

I don't really see myself as a role model. I've never really seen it that way. I see myself as somebody who if somebody asks me for help or comes to me I would always be there willing to help them in any way I could. I'm proud in all the time I've been there, I'm very proud. My pride is when my moment came when I was actually given the managerial position because working in a workplace where there were about 250 people working with only two Pakistanis, it was a very proud moment for me actually to be able to take that step forward - to take a managerial position. My parents were very, very proud. My dad used to boast when he was around with his friends or family, he would always say, if he was ever asked and he'd say, "Oh my son Riaz, him manager!"

I met somebody yesterday and his father worked for Royal Mail, his grandfather worked for Royal Mail, his great grandfather worked for Royal Mail and so you can see what kind of employer they are. It's just the experience of meeting people, doing a job in all weathers. One of the good things about it is dogs. Well depends, if you like dogs or don't like dogs.

Now I have one son who is seven years old I am looking forward to him getting an education, going to university and basically he wants to become a teacher. Even at this age, he wants to become a teacher. So I will be helping him all I can to achieve his goals insha'Allah. As well as his education, I want him to have his religious education as well.

Most of my life has been spent here. Pakistan is a home to me as well but that's a second home. I go there for holidays; I spend time there with family. But my home is Burnley.

Chapter 8 - Public sector

Prisons

Muzzamal Hussain Ahmed

Above: Muzzamal Hussain Ahmed as a teenager, is the first Pakistani heritage graduate from Al-Azhar University, Egypt. He is now an Imam with the prison service

Right: Muzzamal Hussain Ahmed's first Degree (1st Class) in Al-Ijaazat ul Aaliyah in Arabic and Islamics from Jamia Al-Karam, Islamic Institute, Eaton Hall, Nottingham

My name is Muzzamal Hussain Ahmed. I was born in Burnley on 7th April 1983. When my father, came in the '70s, like most people of Asian background, he started working in factories. My father did go back to Pakistan and got married and came back with my mum. From there he became a bus driver until he retired in the early 1990s. Since then he's been retired, just helping out with the family and enjoying retirement as much as he can. I think most of the people from Pakistan, came from specific areas like Jhelum, Gujrat, the Punjab. Most of the people from Gujrat came to Nelson and Burnley so it was more or less a family choice. That's probably the main factor and the main reason why they decided to move to Burnley.

First, I attended Elm Street nursery school. From there I moved to Barden junior school and then the secondary school I went to was Habergham,

for one year, but then I went to a boarding school in Nottingham called Jamia Al-Karam which is in Eaton, Retford. I did my GCSEs there, so I was there for five years and completed my GCSE qualifications. Then I did my three year scholarship course training to be an Imam, a scholar in Islamic studies. After completing my Islamic scholarship course, I went to Al-Azhar University in Cairo and I studied there for three years. After completing my BA honours in Al-Azhar University, I came back here.

I am an Imam, my main training is to be there to serve the community. My main job, when I came back, was to teach in the mosque and teach the youngsters, because there is a great demand in today's society for the teaching of youngsters about the core Islamic values, and also the Asian values that we come from as well. So what I do find most rewarding is, in essence, teaching the

بسم الله الرحمن الرحيم

جمهورية مصر العربية

جامعة الأزهر

Above: Muzzamal Hussain Ahmed's second BA (Hons) Degree (2:1) in Islamic Theology from Al-Azhar Egypt in Arabic script

next generation, instilling in them the core values which are what Islam is all about. It's also passing on the ilm (knowledge) and also the teachings of one generation onto the next generation. The most rewarding thing I can think of is, in essence, teaching someone else about their faith, about their religion and knowing that hopefully I've made a difference, not just to myself, but to someone else in my community.

I also work as an Imam for the Home Office. So I work with lots of vulnerable people at times. I do work with people who are going through difficult times, people who are thinking of self harm as well, and people who are more or less in the darkest place in their lives. At times, sitting with them, giving them counselling and making a difference, and even giving someone a different option in life, makes them think that there is something more in life for them to do rather than just thinking about the past that they live in. So even making a difference, or even helping someone, or even saving a life - that in itself, as you know within Islam, it does say that if you save a life, you save the whole of humanity and if you take a life, you take the whole of humanity. If you make a difference in someone's life, there's nothing more rewarding, not just being there for yourself but being there for someone else. It is a big difference and it stays with you for the rest of your life.

In Burnley, I would say I spent three or four years teaching youngsters from the age of seven to the age of 15. I think that the time that you spend, the link that you develop between the youngsters, it's a father and child relationship that you develop and you also get to know the youngsters a lot. You get to know the issues and the problems that they're going through. I think to have the opportunity to teach youngsters, not as a father figure, but as a mentor, and also to let them know that there is more to life than just going through the same narrow corridor that their brothers and their fathers have gone through as well, and to let them know they are young, the future is bright, they've got everything to live for and hopefully give them a few tools to use them to make their lives better for themselves and for their families, is a privilege.

Obviously my father has been quite a devout Muslim, my mum's a devout Muslim as well. As I've said, I've studied to become an Imam and a scholar from an early age. The boarding school I went to was an Islamic school as well, so from the age of ten I went to a boarding school which has an Islamic background, and was always doing the five prayers on a regular basis, doing my Islamic scholarship course and going to Al-Azhar for three years. That in itself was an eye opener because I met nationalities from every part of the world, whether Mongolia or South America, you name it, there was every nationality of the world there. It was a great opportunity to understand and appreciate one another and hopefully have a greater understanding of the unity of the world, that it is a global village. I would say that as an Imam, obviously I'm not saying I'm preaching Islam whenever I have an opportunity, but for me Islam is my way of life. It covers every aspect of my life and if I say it isn't then I think I'm in the wrong job then, by being an Imam.

Despite my travels I would definitely call Burnley home because you don't choose where you're born, but the place I call home is where I was born and raised. My parents are from Pakistan and I do not forget my roots, that my parents are from Pakistan, but to be honest I was born and bred in England and Ahmed Deedat who's one of the scholars, said that if you dream and swear in English that means that's your mother tongue as well, so I do dream in English so I would say I am English born and bred. I don't forget my roots, I am Asian as well but I would say that I am obviously hundred percent British, as well as Muslim. I find no contradiction between the two. I find that you can probably be more practising in your faith in England or in Burnley or in the UK than you probably can in some parts of Muslim countries like Pakistan or even in the Arab world as well.

Below: English translation of Muzzamal Hussain Ahmed's BA (Hons) Degree from Al-Azhar University in Cairo

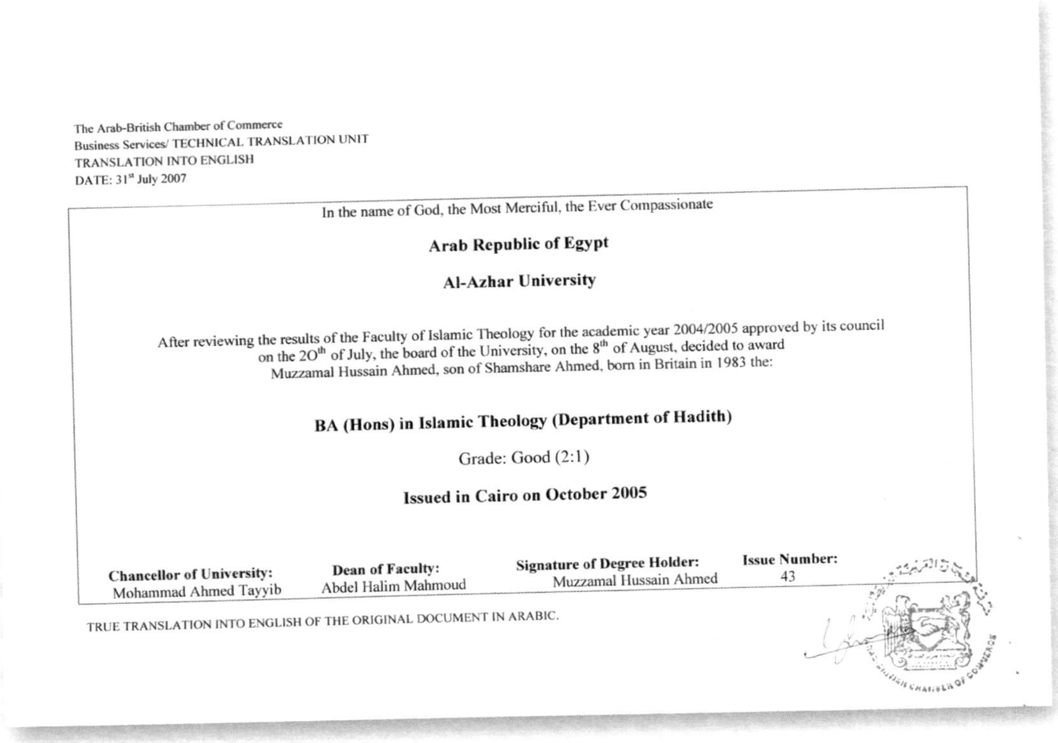

The Arab-British Chamber of Commerce
Business Services/ TECHNICAL TRANSLATION UNIT
TRANSLATION INTO ENGLISH
DATE: 31st July 2007

In the name of God, the Most Merciful, the Ever Compassionate

Arab Republic of Egypt

Al-Azhar University

After reviewing the results of the Faculty of Islamic Theology for the academic year 2004/2005 approved by its council on the 20th of July, the board of the University, on the 8th of August, decided to award Muzzamal Hussain Ahmed, son of Shamshare Ahmed, born in Britain in 1983 the:

BA (Hons) in Islamic Theology (Department of Hadith)

Grade: Good (2:1)

Issued in Cairo on October 2005

Chancellor of University:	**Dean of Faculty:**	**Signature of Degree Holder:**	**Issue Number:**
Mohammad Ahmed Tayyib	Abdel Halim Mahmoud	Muzzamal Hussain Ahmed	43

TRUE TRANSLATION INTO ENGLISH OF THE ORIGINAL DOCUMENT IN ARABIC.

Chapter 9 - Public sector

Race Relations

Abdul Aziz Chaudhry

Above: Abdul Aziz Chaudhry was Director of Burnley and Pendle Racial Equality Council, 1973-1997

Below: Abdul Aziz Chaudhry with the Honorary Officers of the East Lancashire (later called Burnley and Pendle) Racial Equality Council, standing on the left

I was born in Lahore in Pakistan on the 1st of January 1937. I also studied in Lahore. I went to the Islamia College, and after completing my studies there I joined the telecommunication office where I was the secretary of the military meetings before I resigned to come to the United Kingdom. I came to England because it was just a wish to see England. We had heard a lot about it and then I came here. It was an urge to see the rest of the world. I came in April 1962 by air. I had a relative in Blackburn, so originally I went to Blackburn. I was working there in textiles and eventually I joined Community Relations and I became assistant community liaison officer in Blackburn. Then there was a job advertised in Burnley, Pendle and Rossendale; I applied for the community liaison officer job, I got it, so I came to live and settle here in Burnley.

There are many ways of looking at the work I did. Firstly, that which satisfied me. To me, if I had done something which had satisfied other people, it gave me satisfaction and pleasure. And that was in my blood, to help God's people irrespective of their colour, caste, or creed. This applied to every individual and group who I worked with. I think that was the most rewarding thing. When I was able to give satisfaction and pleasure to an individual - believe me, when I went home I slept well because it is the most rewarding thing when you can help, especially the people who are disadvantaged, the people who are usually ignored by others. When I was in office, it was my practice to receive more respectfully the less advantaged people, give them respect and listen to them. The major focus was not to do it for them but to enable them to do it for themselves. Because when you do something for one person, that person may become dependent upon you. I wanted them to be independent, independent of help from other people and be able to

stand on their feet. That was very rewarding and it was very satisfying.

I came to Burnley in 1973; there was one Pakistani Association which was headed by Mr Mohammad Rafique Malik and they did a lot of work. So at that time, in 1973, there were no Pakistani councillors, no school governors, no Justice of the Peace and people were not represented in Social Services or other government departments. Mostly our people were in factories, in transport, and things like that. But then we had to think ahead because our children were receiving education in this country and we wanted to make sure that in time to come, they would not be treated as second class citizens, they would not be discriminated against and there should be equality of opportunity. Eventually this happened. Because if you look at the structure of the Race Relations Organisation, in the beginning it was Community Relations, and the objective was to provide a platform for people of different races to meet each other and

to get to know each other, to discuss, and to be able to live together in an atmosphere of mutual trust and tolerance. But then it was realised that it was not enough. There was a need for equality. So therefore it became the Commission for Racial Equality and the local councils they became Councils for Racial Equality. In Burnley it became known as Burnley and Pendle Racial Equality Council and its office was on Manchester Road, Burnley. So we looked at it and eventually persuaded the Local Authority that they needed to change their practices. Rafique Malik was the first Asian person to be elected as a councillor and it was a breakthrough. After that, so many Asian people came in to the Council, they became mayors when people followed that practice and now it is an established tradition. By the time I left in 1997, representation from the ethnic minorities was in all walks of life. They were magistrates, they were school governors, they were councillors, solicitors, doctors and of course, in the beginning, the spadework which we had done had paid off in the form of having representation in all walks of life. And to me it is satisfying. Sometimes some people say, what have you done for us? I worked for 25½ years in this field of race relations, but an unaware person will be quick to say what have you done for us? We have worked for the coming generations, we have paved the way where people can live honourably, peacefully and have the equality of opportunity in all walks of life. And

that's what has happened. Today you find prayer rooms at the airports, you find prayer rooms in the prisons, and to be very honest with you, I was the first one who raised this question. There are so many examples, which of course I cannot give you, but these are the ones which you can see when you go to the airports, when you go to the prisons, when you go to the police stations; you find that there are facilities because those people were educated, they were well informed and they were advised to provide such facilities.

I was able to have impact in my working life because if you speak with honesty, with dedication, I'm sure then people do understand. When I was in the telecommunication department in Pakistan, I used to control interruptions on the telephone and telegraph lines. The basic instruction to the line staff was to localize the fault so that it does not spread over. I used that experience in community relations. If there was a problem, my advice to my team, and to the rest of the community was, to localize it, do not let it spread, and then rectify it. Now when you say people are very good, they do respect you if you are sincere and they know if you are. There are people who undermine them or undermine their wisdom or judgement, they in fact undermine themselves. It wasn't really difficult to persuade them that their children had a future and they themselves are now British. We made them understand that they are part of this country now, part of this society; they should take interest in the local activities.

There were very few educated Pakistanis at that time. I was talking to those people who had perhaps not gone up to the primary level in Pakistan, and they couldn't speak English, but what they could understand was when something was is in their favour. In 1974, the Dowager Lady Birdwood who was an anti-immigration campaigner and was charged with inciting race hatred, came to Burnley and she marched against the immigrants and against immigration. Now at that time, I had only been here in Burnley for a few months and I had to face this situation where there was going to be a demonstration on the streets of Burnley. There were different schools of thought. People thought that they should also come to demonstrate and we would have more people showing support. My view was not to demonstrate because by demonstrating you are giving them the importance and the attention which they are seeking; ignore them. Well of course there was a difference of opinion, especially with the trade unions. It took me an hour to persuade them not to come to demonstrate. Then I worked alongside the police and I went to see different denominations in Burnley, including Protestants and Roman Catholic. I do remember Father Seal, I think he has died, he was a Roman Catholic Priest and he was very helpful. And in the mosques, the Imams they said prayers for peace in the mosques, they said prayers for peace in the churches, and I asked them to do their shopping in the morning and nobody should be out in the afternoon. I remember in the afternoon, Mrs Green (our secretary), she rang me, she said, "Where are the people?" I said, "Why?" She said, "There's not a single child on the pavement here in Stoneyholme." People stayed inside watching television. They ignored the protestors. There were only six persons out that day and it was a total failure. After that she never dared to come to Burnley. If we had gone to demonstrate, we would have given them publicity and some of our people would have been arrested, tried and appeared in the Courts, and that's what they wanted. So, therefore, the message was clear and there was a good response from the community and that was my first test in the job when I came here in 1973, and the demonstration was a few months after in 1974.

It was a test of my judgement but at the same time, the background work was done. A lot of fieldwork was done; persuasion, talking, and our message was clear that we are peaceful people, we are peace loving people, and we want to live together. It was a very good stance in that sense that even after that, Priests and Imams had been meeting together and there was, I called it a holy alliance, so it was a good way of having dialogues within different faiths. The objective was living together, living in peace. And that was the message, which I gave along with my other colleagues, to the community.

Below: Abdul Aziz Chaudhry (2nd from right) led a delegation to make representations to the Minister for Immigration, at the Home Office, accompanied by Doug Hoyle MP (far left)

It wasn't solely my vision. It was the vision of the Community Relations Council. It was the vision of the 21 members of the Executive Committee. I was a paid officer and my job was to advise them and to carry out the instructions and the decisions that they took in the meetings, which I did on a professional basis. But at the same time yes, I did advise them. They made the decisions and then it became their policy, it became their vision not my vision. So it was co-operative efforts that worked. It was the community as a whole; it was not an individual's show.

I firmly believe, we are British, we are part of British society, and we should play our role. And in certain cases it's lacking, which is very unfortunate. That should not be the case. We should be having regard for our neighbours, and during the month of Ramadan, when we wake up in the early hours of the morning, we should take care so that our neighbours who are not Muslims should not be disturbed, which is Islamic as well, but at the same time it is how you respect your neighbours. So these are important things and in the British daily life we should make contributions. I think it's time now that we think of ourselves as British because the generation after us was born here. They do not know any other country, so therefore it becomes more of their responsibility to be able to discharge such functions with devotion which will contribute to the well-being and prosperity of the society they are members of.

There has been a lot of change in our way of life since the 1960s and we may not always agree but there is a saying, I do not agree with what you say but I will defend your right to say it. I've spent most of my working life in Burnley and though my roots are in Pakistan, Burnley is my home now. My three children were born here and it is my home. I love Burnley, our home, our whole family home. My parents are dead and one brother and one sister live in Pakistan. Now I've six grandchildren and they are all here in Britain. And therefore Burnley is my home. My older son, Saqib, he's married to an English lady, and they have two children. So we're already integrated in many ways and we are a part, an integral part of this society now.

Race Relations

Munsifdar Mirza

Above: Munsifdar Mirza is a retired advocate of Pakistan and Azad Kashmir High Courts

I am Munsifdar Mirza, I was born in a village called Sirla in the district of Bhimber Azad Kashmir on 15th Feb 1937. I was born to a peasant family. My father was Alderman of the village and he lived there mostly. For some of the time, he was in the army and he was also a farmer and he lived on the produce of his farm.

I was in the 4th class when Pakistan came into being. I had left my primary school when we moved to a border village in Pakistan called Mandi Tehsil Kharian in the district of Gujrat. When we returned to Azad Kashmir, I completed my Matriculation examination, that was in 1953 and then I joined the army for a year or so.

I was asked to become a regular informer but I opted for the civil service and I joined the Azad Kashmir Inspector General of Police office I worked there for a year then I moved on to the Civil Secretariat in the Secretary General's office and a year later, in 1958, I was transferred to the personal office of the President of Azad Kashmir and I worked with the President. I joined Sardar Ibrahim, the founder President of Azad Jammu and Kashmir. He was succeeded by K H

Khursheed who had been the private secretary of Quaid-e-Azam Muhammed Ali Jinnah who was also replaced by Khan Abdul Hameed Khan, Chief Justice of Azad Kashmir. By then I had completed my graduation. I had done my Fazil-e-Farsi. I had done my FA and BA and in 1964 I was recommended by the President of Azad Kashmir in a letter to Syed Fayaz Hussain Shah, ex-Chief Justice of Azad Kashmir. He helped me to get admission into Law College in Lahore and I completed my LLB from the University of Punjab in 1966. Then I applied for higher/further education in Britain.

I had an uncle who was in Great Britain, a maternal uncle, the late Said Muhammed. He helped me with Rs 18,000 in Pakistan. I spent Rs 2,000 on clothing etc and Rs 2,000 I paid to Lincoln's Inn and I bought a PIA ticket for Rs 1,700. Nowadays, it is over Rs 50,000 or something like that, it was Rs 1700 when I came in April, 1968. Since I had done my LLB in Pakistan, they equated LLB with Bar-at-Law. Therefore there wasn't much incentive left for me to complete the Bar but anyway I passed a few subjects. I leaned more towards student politics. I was the first Asian to be elected to the Honourable Society of Lincolns Inn way back in 1971. In 1976 I moved to Burnley and joined Mohammad Rafique Malik. He had established a new organisation called the Jinnah Advisory Centre. I was firstly taken as Liaison Officer and then became the Director of Advisory Service. In the year 1981, a post was advertised by the Commission for Racial Equality for Hyndburn and Rossendale. Out of 72 applicants I was chosen as a Community Development Worker. I worked there for a year. In 1983 I went back to Pakistan. I got myself enrolled as a Pleader of the District Court in the same year. Then I was elevated as an Advocate of High Court in 1991. I practised there as an advocate until, th e year 2000. Then I returned to Britain. Since I was involved in student politics at Lincolns Inn, I contributed in the Pakistan political field as well. I was chosen as and remained a Working Committee Member of the Muslim Conference from 1983 to 1993.

Left: Munsifdar Mirza in Pakistan Advocates black gown

Below: Munsifdar Mirza, secretary of the Hon Society of the Inns, standing on the left of Lord Denning, Master of the Rolls with other Honorary Officers in London

Due to certain differences, I left that organisation. In 1995 I joined 'Azad Jammu and Kashmir Liberation League' headed and founded by K H Khursheed as I mentioned earlier, who had been private secretary of Quaid-e-Azam. He led the agenda of the liberation of a separate Azad Jammu and Kashmir that was very attractive and so I joined the League. I served as district president and slowly rose to the rank of vice-president in that organisation. I came back to Britain in the year 2000 and in the year 2002, Malik Abdul Majeed came to Britain to organise the League in the UK. He chose me as a senior vice-president of that organisation. This had been dormant for two to three years and a new convener, Dr Misfar Hassan, was asked to re-organise it. I was convener for the whole of East Lancashire for the last two years for the Azad Jammu and Kashmir Liberation League. When I was in Pakistan, because I had been working in the UK Branch and I had met literary people, there were certain quotations in my mind that I used to discuss with my people and they said, ''You have power in your thoughts, therefore you should write something." I wrote a book "Husn-e-Bay Parwa" or "Awareness of God" in Urdu in the year 1999. That book was presented to the Academy of Azad Kashmir. They awarded me the Presidential

Award for that book. The Prime Minister of Azad Kashmir, Chaudhry Sultan Mahmood, signed and presented it to me. I had written an article discussing the political situation and the leader of Pakistan. I had summed up that Imran Khan was everyone's leader which I said nearly seven years ago. Now all the parties are saying what I said seven years ago. There are my contributions in several newspapers. When I was the General Secretary in Lincoln's Inn, one of the hallmarks was that all Inns jointly arranged a debate on the issue that the people of the Republic of China should be admitted to the United Nations and I was the leader of the house.

I have been a great believer in the UN but unfortunately this great organisation appears to be reverting back to the idea of "Might is Right". Right is might is not being pursued. But I hope that the future world leadership will amend this and they will abide by the charter of the UN. I come from Kashmir and Kashmiri people were promised the 'Right of Self Determination' by this great organisation way back in 1948. Now nearly 64 – 65 years have passed but the promise has not been fulfilled. Every promise has a force behind it and if the principle is violated, the force behind it comes into play and the principle of promise has a divine power behind it. Once you defy the divine principle, divine power comes into play. That's why at present the whole world has been drawn into the jaws of terrorism because they have not helped the small nations to get their 'Right of Self Determination'. I hope that if the principles of democracy are established, enforced and strengthened in future, then the people of Kashmir will get their 'Right of Self Determination'.

Of course, I lived in Burnley in the past and I'm living here now. I consider Burnley as my home. My best memory of Burnley is that I was given the opportunity to serve the local community as the Director of the Jinnah Advisory Service by Mr Mohammad Rafique Malik, he has been a very close friend and I have learnt a lot from him and through that service I came to know many people of Burnley. I'm a political animal; I have been able to preside over various functions in the Burnley area over the years.

Chapter 10 - Public sector

Sport

Afrasiab Anwar

Above: Afrasiab Anwar is co-ordinator of Burnley and Pendle Faith Centre

Below left: Muslims and Christians from Burnley raised £751 for Pendleside Hospice

My name's Afrasiab Anwar. I was born in Gujrat, in Pakistan in 1979. Just from the stories that my dad tells me, he came here and worked in the old cotton mills and, obviously, Burnley was an industrial town. They worked here but spent some time in other countries like Germany and Denmark before they settled here. What tends to happen is, if you move to a country or a different place, you go where there's a community that you know, people that you know, family links. So I think they came, where their friends were or people that they knew, and because there was work here as well.

I went to Heasandford Primary School. At the time it was a bit of a strange decision because Barden Primary School was on my doorstep. I didn't think it was wisdom at the time but now I look back on it and think that my parents were ahead of their time in the way that they were thinking, because at that time Heasandford didn't have a lot of Asian kids at the school and they wanted us to mix with people from different backgrounds. So I was the only Asian boy in my whole year group, and I made a lot of friends. As a result of that I became very open minded and cultured I think. Similarly, instead of sending me to a school predominantly populated by Asians, they sent me to Towneley High School. Again I made lots of friends from the indigenous population which kept me open minded. I then went to college in Accrington; I wasn't allowed to go to Burnley because my parents wanted me to stay away from my friends. I think that was the making of me because it broadened my horizons. As a young person growing up in a

town like Burnley you don't think of it then but later on, looking back, you think the area that you live in is everything and it's the be-all and end-all. Then when you go out of town and you meet new people, you realise there's more out there than just our own little friendship groups that we know in Burnley. I went to university in Leeds. The education side of it is all a bit of blur. I don't remember it. Sometimes I wake up in the middle of the night having a panic, thinking, how on earth did I get through my exams and how did I end up with a degree? But the most important thing I remember about university is living in a house with one lad who was from India, but who was also a Hindu from Leicester. He was born in this country but was from Leicester; a white lad who was a Roman Catholic and a Bengali lad as well, from Sheffield and one other Pakistani lad from Leicester. It was like a melting pot of all these people from right across the country, but secondly, all the different cultures and different religions. The Hindu lad was a Guajarati Indian as well, so he spoke a different language that none of us understood. You learn about other people and about respect and tolerance for other groups; everybody can get on and that's the one thing that I remember.

Then as part of my gap year, I worked at the American Embassy in London as part of a placement there. I worked there for a year. I had a really good year there about two weeks before 9/11. My placement finished and I came back home and then obviously back to Leeds to finish off my degree. That Christmas, after 9/11, I went back to see friends who worked at the American Embassy in London and for me the whole world had just changed. I was able to get in because I worked there and all of a sudden, this massive presence of security people, and everything had been cordoned off. That's when it dawned on me; the situation in terms of being a British Muslim growing up in this country and following things that happened with 9/11 and the disturbances, as a town, in terms of Burnley, our own local history. I realised then the town that I grew up in and the country that I'd grown up in and loved and made

Above: Daneshouse FC and Ghausia Mosque arranged a trip to Manchester Paint Balling, as a reward activity for Hifz Class

Below: Daneshouse FC under-14's team 2011-12

me who I am, that everything was changing, and it was simply because of the religion or the colour of your skin. I'd studied Social Policy and Social Science at university, but then I got a graphic experience of it through those two big events: the 2001 disturbances that we had as a town and secondly 9/11. There were American friends who I'd worked with at the American Embassy, and people from London, and I felt a loss of identity in terms of who I was and what I saw. The one thing for me that stands out that people can't take away from me, is my religion and I wanted to be proud of that. The other thing that people can't take away from me is that I'm from Burnley. I want to be proud because nobody can say to me, "Oh, you're not from Burnley," because I am and they can't say to me, "You're not a Muslim." I want to be someone that I'm proud of and show it in a positive light. Especially in line with those two big events; they had a massive impact on me personally. Certainly in terms of my education and then career wise, I started off as a volunteer, working with kids and organising soccer groups. I worked for Jinnah Development Trust as a frontline youth worker for six months as well as a voluntary youth worker in Stoneyholme and Daneshouse.

I applied for a job as a Sports Development Worker working with ethnic minority communities in Hyndburn. I went for the interview and ended up getting the job, but my manager at the time, she said to me, "It wasn't your degree." What she felt that stood out was the fact that I was doing voluntary work within my own community and that was the thing that they were looking for - someone who goes above and beyond. I think over the past ten years that I've been doing this; I think one of the things that we as an Asian community lack, I think sometimes we don't value volunteering. We're okay if it's volunteering in the mosque because that's God's work, if it's in the mosque or if it's something religious, then it's wonderful, yes, everybody should do it. But I think sometimes as a community we forget that volunteering is, even when you're helping kids and you can change one of their lives, that is God's work as well. That is religious as well, from my point of view. I think, sometimes, people believe that you do things for personal gain or whatever, and what they need to do is put the value and emphasis on volunteering. Volunteering's changed my life because if I hadn't had that I wouldn't have got the job working part time as an Outreach Worker at Hyndburn. Then a job came up in Burnley about a year and a half later and I didn't get the job as the Burnley Sports Development Officer because of the great job I was doing at Hyndburn, they weren't interested in that. What they were interested in was that I was running a Junior Football Club in Daneshouse with ethnic minority kids - something that had never been done before. What they were saying was this is something that we value and we want someone like this to come, as the targets they had with Asian communities, because of

102

the disturbances, meant there was also targeted funding in these areas. So they thought well, we've got someone who's doing it for free, let's bring him in and pay him, and let him do it. For six years I did that job and I was paid to do a job that I loved. It didn't feel like I was going in to work. One of the things that I will never do is, I will never give up the work that I do with the Daneshouse Football Club because that's what gave me a start. It started me off as a volunteer and I ended up doing the job that I love. I'm now working as a School Sport Partnership Manager and looking after the Spirit of Sport facility at Blessed Trinity College, and for me that's been a different stage. I mean I've moved on, but I've still carried on doing the volunteering.

Working in a Roman Catholic College has brought me closer to my own religion. It probably sounds daft me saying that but the way that's happened is, every morning when we used to go into work, with it being a Roman Catholic College, there's a briefing in the morning for staff and they say a prayer. All the pupils are doing it and all the staff pray as well. And being a Muslim, listening, sometimes you start realising that it doesn't matter which god you're praying to, and at the same time you're starting off with a good prayer. A good start to the day adds moral values and things like that and for me it's a case of right. I thought, that's a great way to start the day and to end the day and wishing well for the people that are around you, thanking God for everything that he's given you. There's no harm in that. All it's doing is it's making you a better person. So as a result of that, I started going to the mosque more and getting more involved in my own local mosque and, helped set up The Ghausia Centre, which was derelict at the time, but the football club and the Ghausia Centre and the voluntary side of it has just sort of snowballed and it's open every single day of the week. Ladies are using it, kids are using it. We've got over 300 kids who are members of the club; we've got 13 coaches who are volunteers and giving up their own time. For me, volunteering is the key and I think one emphasis that I would always push is the emphasis on volunteering.

It's nice to get the recognition of my peers for the work that I do. I think the local community and the people that I work with, and in particular the young people that we work with, I think they do value what we do. I think that's because of the hard work that we do put in. They see that. I think the biggest contribution or the biggest thing

that stands out is that in the Asian community we're not brilliant at saying thanks, and the odd occasion when you do get a child come up to you at the end of a session or after a game, and say thank you, I think – it's somebody putting a smile on someone's face. I had a parent ring me up a couple of years ago and she thanked me. She said, "I'd just like to say thank you for all the time that you put in with our kids." And I said, "Well, it's what we do. That's what we're there for as a club and, you know, that's what it's about," and she turned round and she said, "No," she said, "My kids have had it really tough and if it hadn't been for the football, God knows where they'd be today." The other thing that stands out for me is remembering when we first started playing football down at Towneley and we were getting beat 21-0 or something silly like that. This old man, with his flat cap on and walking stick, walked past. He was walking his dog and he said, "Do you know what, boys? You need to stick to playing cricket." That was ten years ago when we were starting off and I could have walked away and said, "You know what, let's stick to playing cricket, this isn't for us," but we

Above: Daneshouse FC under-16's, winners of the inter-Madrassah Annual Tournament 2012

Below: Daneshouse FC under-10's, League and Cup champions 2011-12

Above: Daneshouse FC under-8's taking part in a half-time match at Turf Moor in 2012

Below: Building Bridges Burnley organised a Women's Only trip to Jerusalem, Afrasiab accompanied them

persevered on freezing cold mornings, on Sunday mornings, going out there and getting on with it and doing it. But last week we had an under-16s game and we were 3-0 down at half-time and we managed to scrape back to 3-3; at the end of full-time it was 4-4 and we went into extra time at 5-5 but we lost on penalties.

Ten years ago when choosing a name for the club, the actual ward was called Daneshouse so we named the club after the ward. If you'd ever opened a paper and you'd read the word Daneshouse it was always associated with negative connotations about the disturbances, the riots, or to do with poverty and so on. But now all you need to do ten years on is go on Google, put in the word 'daneshouse' in the search engine and the football club pops up with pictures and images of the football club. I think that itself speaks of the work that we've done. So now whenever you mention Daneshouse to a wider population, especially the field I'm in, straightaway people turn around and say, "Oh yeah, football club." Or they say, "Yeah. We beat you" or "you're rubbish" or whatever – fair enough. At the same time, because we've invested in our young people, one of the things that we have found is that we're improving as a footballing side as well - I think 2008 was the first time we won a league and cup double. Last year we won the league and cup double with the under-10s and our current under-10s are top of the league and hopefully we'll do the double again this year. So we are improving as a side. But the most important thing is giving ownership to our local community, they've got something that belongs to them and hopefully will be around for years to come.

When I think of the significant influences in my life, it's my mum and dad. My dad always emphasised the value of education. I can see now their wisdom in sending us to schools where we would mix with people from different backgrounds; I can see that wisdom now. The analogy my dad always used with me was, he'd say, "You can go out and buy a posh car. You can go out and get lots and lots of money but something could go wrong and you could lose it. But, if you go and get yourself whatever's in there in your mind, nobody can ever take that away from you." He said he wanted something better for us than to be working in mills, you've got younger siblings, they'll look up to you and they want to do the same. Considering they weren't educated themselves I think that's very, very important. Your family, it makes you who you are in your community. I had an opportunity to stay and work in London but I'd seen the whole of it change and I knew I wanted to go back and make a contribution and make something happen in my own town, that's made me who I am. I want to be proud of Burnley. Faith has had the biggest influence because it's always been about doing the right thing, because the personal gain I've got from doing all of this has been that God's been looking down on me and he's been giving me opportunities to get other jobs and I've progressed professionally. I know that my intentions are good for the people that I work with and that's something that I pass on to the volunteers: do what you feel is a hundred per cent right. And if it does rub people up the wrong way - if you've upset people along the way, it means that you've stood up for something that you believe in.

Chapter 11 - Public sector

Transport

Ghulam Nabi Chowdhary

My name is Ghulam Nabi Chowdhary I was born in Karachi when it was still part of India. My father was in the British Royal Air Force so he was in service in Karachi where I was born. Then they transferred my father to various places and in Partition, in 1947, we moved from Delhi to mid-Pakistan, to Peshawar. I actually started my education in Peshawar. It was alright, those were nice days. I really enjoyed my childhood. It was very nice because my father was in the Air Force from

early on and our living standards were very good and our education was very good. I was in Peshawar for eight years then my father retired and we moved back to Jhelum, our original place. I finished the last two years of my schooling in Jhelum then started a job as an apprentice electrician. I had training for three years as an electrician and in 1961 I came to England. It was actually our families' decision that we should go abroad. At that time, many people were coming, especially from Kashmir. We were following

Above: Ghulam Nabi Chowdhary, first Pakistani heritage Bus Conductor, Driver and Instructor on Burnley, Colne and Nelson (BCN) Joint Transport

Below: Fauji Textile Mills, Jhelum Pakistan Electrical Department employees (Ghulam Nabi Chowdhary circled)

LEST WE FORGET
PHOTOGRAPH TAKEN ON THE FAREWEL PARTY GIVEN TO
Mr. MOHD MUKHTAR Astt: Foreman
By The Electrical Department Fauji Textile Mill Jhelum.
22-3-61

Ground (L to R)   Ghulam Mohd   Mian Nazar Hussain   Ehsan Ellahi

Chairs: (L to R)   M/s Mohd Ayub   Mohd Akram   Capt. Mohd Aslam (L. O.)   A. R. Mirza (A.E. & M.E.)   Mohd Mukhtar(Astt. Foreman)
A. Q. Awan (Chief Engineer)   M. A. Bhatti(Weaving Master)   Sh. Ikhlaq Ahmed (B.D.&F. Master)   Capt. Abdul Rahman (M.O.)

Standing L-R 1st Row   Zaka Naseem   Raja Mohammad Afzal Khan   Bashir Ahmed   Mirza Saleem Baig   S. Sarfraz Ali Shah   Mohd Afzal   Mohd Asharaf
Mohd Bakhash   Mir Afzal   Barkat Ali   Ghulam Nabi   Mushtaq Ahmed   Mohd Younus Khan (Guest)   Ashiq Hussain Shah
Ghulam Sarwar   Karam Elahi   Said Akbar   Sadiq Ali.

2nd Row   Mohd Sharif Sufi   Abdul Aziz   Fazal Mohd   Manazar Hussain   Bashir Ahmed   Karam Elahi   Adalat Khan   Pea   Walait Khan.

Right: Ghulam Nabi
Chowdhary working in the
Spinning Department of
Fauji Textiles Mills, Jhelum,
Pakistan

Below: Ghulam Nabi
Chowdhary with his double-
decker bus, at the Laneshaw
Bridge stand in Colne

them and it was actually for economic reasons.
When we came, everybody had the same ideas.
We came thinking, we will stay for only five
years, earn money and then go back and start our
business or something else. We used to joke about
it with our friends saying we came for five years
imprisonment with hard labour, now we've got
life imprisonment.

I settled in Burnley because of the job. I started
my first job at Smith and Nephew in the Spinning
Department. I had a little training in spinning in
Pakistan so I got the job easily. That time of year
in 1961-1962 was very bad. We were looking for
our own house because we were paying rent so
we decided to get our own house and the first
house we got was in Burnley. We bought it for
£200, it was nearer to Brierfield. It was a private
mortgage because we could not afford £200. I
can't remember the exact figure the mortgage
was but we paid by instalments. I think there was
no building society then; lending for housing,
so many people were getting a private mortgage
between one solicitor and lender. It was a three
bed-roomed house; no bath, and only one fire
which was in the living room. There was no
heating at all. We had a bath once a week on
Saturday at the public baths. It was a very hard
life. We couldn't get our food; there were no
Asian shops from Colne to Preston as far as
I know. As we couldn't eat meat unless it was

G.N.CHOWDHARY RING SPINNING

DOFING

halal, every Saturday we were going out to the
countryside to buy chicken; slaughter it there,
clean it, put it in a bag and bring it home. That's
the luxury – we had a good meal at the weekend,
the rest of the days we were eating imported
vegetables in tins like cauliflower, sprouts,
potatoes etc. It was a hard time but a pleasant
time, busy working. I was working five nights in
Smith and Nephew and the wage was around £12
a week and 8 hours a day doing 40 hours. It was
not bad, not that expensive or difficult as life is
now. We could survive with £12.
A bag of flour cost ten shillings
(50p) at that time.

There were not many of us
Asians but people were very
helpful to each other. One
example is; the first house
we lived in, our landlord did
not collect money from the
unemployed and the people who
were employed in that household
were offering three meals and
everything to unemployed
people so that they didn't have
any problems. When I was
looking for a job I didn't know
any place in Burnley, I didn't
know the buses timetable either,
I just looked for the chimney of
the nearest factory; walked there,
asked for a job and obviously
they would say, sorry. Then I
went looking for the next nearest
chimney, went there, asked the

B.C.N BUS AT LANSHAWBRDGE (COLNE) STAND

DCW 357C. Year 1965. Fleet 257. D/Decker
Leyland PD 2A/27. Body N.Counties.H37/27FD

same question and got the same answer. I went on doing that so many times up to Nelson, Colne and Accrington. It was a difficult time to get a job but later on it wasn't too bad. The first time I applied for benefits was after my retirement in 1998. Back then, for six months, I was unemployed. I went to Blackburn – no jobs. I didn't know how to apply for unemployment benefits. I could get £4.50 and nobody knew. So for six months I didn't get any income. The first job I got, I had my insurance card and I gave it to them. They asked me "Where have you been because there are no records?" I said, "I was here." They said, "You should have returned this to the employment office and you could have got some money." I said I didn't know. That was too late anyway. So, the first time I applied for income support was after my retirement. I was married when I came here, so I thought I should have my family here and decided to bring my wife here. My parents were against it. Nobody advised me to do so because nobody expected our women to come here; nobody thought they would be here for long or permanently. Some people married here but it did not last. So my wife was the first Pakistani lady to come to Burnley, I had no children then and she was the first lady from our district. My first son was born in 1966 and we moved to Canning Street, the first house we had. I worked for about ten years in the textile industry.

Around 1966, 1967, a lot of people bought houses and moved to Burnley. We thought we should have an organisation to help each other. So with Mr Malik and some of our other friends we decided to make an association or something for the needy people. We worked a long time for that, as at those times there were no facilities at all, especially, people who were coming over here had no knowledge of English. Some people died here and they wished to be buried back in Pakistan. They needed some money so we would organise donations to help arrange for funeral costs and we all worked very well together. We had good friends working with us even though some have passed away but we will still remember them; they were very helpful.

In 1967, I saw advertisements at the bus station, jobs for conductors. I thought I should give it a try as I had worked for a long time in the mills. I went for a test and my application was not successful but they didn't give any reason. I went to the Citizens' Advice Bureau and there was Dr Hajela, working voluntarily. I mentioned to him that my application was not successful and they didn't give any reason. He rang the manager who made excuses such as they think Asian people may not be able to do such jobs. Dr Hajela said to him that he himself was Asian and a doctor, and a conductor's job was not as complicated as

B.C.N BUS AT COLNE (HEIFERLANE) BUS DEPOT

HHG 75F. Year 1968. Fleet 75. Panther Leyland PSUR 1/1R. Body N.Counties B50ST19FD

a doctor's. The manager had no answer. Actually there were union bans. It was the General Transport Union. They had decided not to employ any coloured people. We briefly had meetings with the councillor who came to our door from the Labour Party because it was election time, and we put questions to them, told them we had rights to get jobs and this is semi-government transport, it isn't privately owned. There was no Race Relations Act then. They promised everyone that they would look into it. This issue also came into the media, with headlines saying, 'Race Discrimination on Transport.' That was difficult for the transport union. They had a meeting between unions and workers. It was a big issue then. The union said they will have to start letting some coloured people apply, only 6%. So my

Right: Ghulam Nabi
Chowdhary's first Driving
Instructor Certificate issued
on 28 June 1976

friend and I applied again and another Asian person from Colne applied as well and we were taken on. The three of us started there but they were not co-operating, the staff and workers. They were also threatening those people who were willing to train us and they were sending un-named letters to the press stating that anyone who co-operates with the Asian people, we will send them to Coventry. We carried on through this and got the training. When I started my own job, I had to go with the driver. The first day, the driver refused to work with me. So they had to change the driver. This was at the beginning but many years later, they found out that Asians were very hard working, good time-keepers and everything and they added some more. The union couldn't stop it.

I started as the first Asian conductor, first Asian driver and first Asian staff instructor in Burnley and Pendle. It was actually Burnley, Colne and Nelson Joint Transport when I started but they changed the name later. The first staff instructors were unqualified but a law came out saying that they had to be trained. The reason I applied was because I had some qualifications for driving. It was my hobby to drive. I read books and then I was given a test for advanced driving and I passed it. Then, I was given a test for the Lancashire Constabulary driving course. These were my entire certificates, I showed them to the management and they selected me and two English people to go for training. Three of us went, and one failed and the two of us passed. We were certified by the Manchester Commissioner for Transport who was taking the examinations for driving. They allowed us to take the examination and we were qualified for that and given the licence. Our

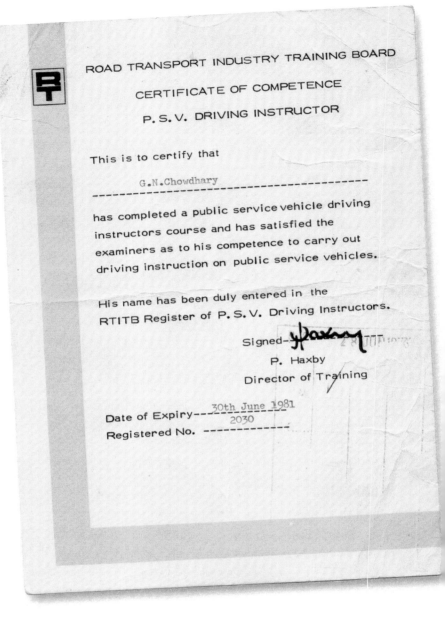

job selection was more than the inspectors bit; we had to train the conductors, drivers and the inspectors and maintain standards. Those were our jobs standards but our pay scales were about the same as the inspectors. I was very happy and the management was happy too. Then, having been the first, after so much opposition from staff, we had 70 Pakistanis working in transport. We decided we wouldn't run away. It was our right and we succeeded. From our relationships with the staff, later, more staff changed their minds. In my own opinion, they had the wrong idea about us. They didn't know us; they had no experiences with the Asian people. When they worked with us, they found it very different from what they thought. Only a few racist people didn't accept us but later they left the job. Otherwise, after that, there were no problems. They may have thought that they ruled the whole world by taking us as their slaves and so on. Also, they didn't know our behaviour, our religion and everything. So they had some wrong ideas. After the experience with us they became very good friends with us.

I would say our behaviour changed their attitude. If our behaviour was good with a person it made them think twice. After that, I had many experiences attending places like high schools with girls and boys from grammar schools as well. They wanted to know about Islam and they would invite me to meetings in a house on Sunday. It was different houses at different times to answer some questions. I would go there at night. They wanted me to explain about our culture and religion. Some questioned why women walked behind the men. I told them it was a custom not religion. One of them once asked me why Asian women go to the greengrocers' shop and pick up and taste food to see if they like it. I explained to them that back in Pakistan, shopkeepers allowed them to taste products. In time our women will learn the custom here. They were learning from me and I was learning from them as well. It was a religious group. They were Christians and every Sunday they were meeting and having prayers with questions and answers on their religion and sometimes they would invite me. Also, some girls from high school were coming to Asian ladies to teach them English at home. My wife

was learning as well, and some others. They were teaching them voluntarily.

I am not a racist myself; I think all human beings are the same. So, if somebody else is wrong and I do the same thing there is no difference between him and me. So the best thing is if I change his opinion. I learned this from studying after I left school, as reading was a hobby. I used to read a lot of books on different subjects, everything really. I kept what I was reading in my mind, picking up good things and changing myself, not staying at the same level. I was educating myself. With the workers, staff, colleagues at the transport service and before that in the factory, I thought, if my behaviour is good, I can change other people's behaviour. You should have patience and with time they will change. The problem was both communities were staying apart. If they stay together, they learn from each other and they change each other.

My English was not very good, I was doing a lot of reading of books for the job and giving other instructors help with questions they had. I was organising everything, even our manager left everything to me. I was reading books and writing questions for our trainees and they used them in the classroom. There was no classroom before, trainees would just go on the road but I started the classroom training as well. So

there was driving theory as well instead of just practical driving. I was making a lot of copies at the office for this and somebody complained to the manager that I do hundreds of copies. So the manager asked me to bring what I was photocopying. I took those things to the manager and explained what I did with them. He was impressed with that but the questions had a lot of spelling mistakes. I told him, my trainees understand it and that's what is important and if I had proper English I would have been in your place. He laughed. They were very helpful. I was very happy.

I retired from there in 1977 then started my own business. I had the business for twenty years; providing the service for electronic goods on Brougham Street in the Stoneyholme area of Burnley. I wanted to do something and I was looking to see what business I could do. There were no electronic goods or business in Asian shops. For a few years it was very good but later on the recession came and there wasn't much profit from it, but at the same time, the video came on the market so we changed for an experiment and we found it much better than just fancy and electronic goods. We changed to fancy goods, electronics and video; now these days, videos are gone as well. Videos were very expensive in those days and it was hard to get Asian films. I was travelling to Manchester every second Thursday to get the films. Later on we got the deliveries but in the beginning it was very hard. It was very popular in the Asian community because they had no other entertainment, especially for families to enjoy together. Business-wise it was very good; it was a successful business but it also made me close to the community. I would visit most houses delivering videos and we had some connections with them and relations with other communities like the Bengali community, the Pathan and Punjabis in the community. I was visiting most homes and I tried to be helpful to them because I delivered videos and colour TVs, as there weren't many coloured TVs then, and I would deliver night or day. Two o'clock in the morning, I would get a phone call that their video was not working and I would go there and help them. I didn't tell them to wait until tomorrow because I knew they had a programme to watch, I didn't want to spoil it – I wanted them to enjoy the experience. I don't live in Burnley now, I live in Blackburn. My work was more than 20 years ago but I still remember those young boys and girls wherever they meet me now. I don't recognise them but they do

recognise me and they respect me and mention the old days. I am very happy, very pleased that they still remember me and they didn't forget me. Many of the boys and girls are married now and have families but whenever they see me they respect me. I was very lucky.

I was very close to my religion. I always respected it and tried to practise it as much as possible. I and my friends; Mr Malik and some others – five, six people – we decided, as we had no mosque in Burnley, to collect donations from the community for a mosque. We bought a house on Rectory Road and converted it into a mosque near our Islamic centre and about six people were working on it. We had close contact through the mosque. One of our friends I always remember was Mr Yaqub, and he had a very good knowledge of the religion. We were working very hard even though there was some opposition from the community but we didn't bother about it. We succeeded and now I think we have about six mosques over here. But that was the first religious place we started before 1978.

Lancashire is my home. As I mentioned before, we came here hoping to stay for five years. After I brought my wife here and the children were born, I was thinking this is our country not Pakistan. A lot of people have close contact with Pakistan so they think their children will go back. I have no property, not a single thing in Pakistan. I stayed in Pakistan for 8 years after my retirement for my daughter's education, especially to learn about the culture. She knows both sides of east and west culture now but I stayed in a rented house, not my own. I don't believe I should have any property there because I understand that we can't go back and I think it's a stupid idea that our children should go back. I think we are better off here. My children are settled and now I have fourteen grandchildren.

Chapter 12 - Private sector

Catering

Abdul Majeed

My name is Abdul Majeed I was born in Pakistan. At that time, my dad came to live in England; I was mainly brought up by my mum. The first time my dad came to this country was in 1962; I did come to join my dad a couple of times in England; while I was here, I attended school and college but I didn't stay long. In the beginning I didn't think much of this country; I was missing home because my mum, my sisters were all in Pakistan. When I came, I wanted to go back. Obviously, I was born and brought up in Pakistan – I went to school and college there. My mum, sisters, friends and all the rest of the family were there, so that's more than enough to miss for a youngster. Then I came here in 1979 and that's when I got practically involved in the restaurant trade with my uncle and it's what I've done for the last thirty-three years. I got involved straight away in restaurants, when the first Pakistani restaurant 'Koh-i-noor' was opened by my uncle on Manchester Road in Burnley. The involvement with restaurants never came to an end; I'm still doing it and enjoying it.

Coming from another country and starting in a new trade was tough; it wasn't easy. First of all, I didn't have any prior experience; new country, new people, new trade, new business, it was difficult but I never gave up. I did work hard and I still remember I took my first day and night off six months after I started. That shows my determination. I did work hard to learn everything; still it took me a little time to learn all the patience and the tolerance that this kind of business needs. The attitude of English people of that generation towards Indian/Pakistani restaurants was a little more abusive, whereas now they appreciate me. It was tough but I stood firm and got through all the tough times.

The abusiveness was happening on a regular basis, sometimes I would feel very uncomfortable, sometimes during the night (I used to live upstairs in the same building), I used to go crying to my room and say, what am I doing here, why am I doing this? But the day after, when you re-open, you feel a little fresh and then people walking in were family people. They were so nice, very supportive, very helpful, they would talk to you and you'd feel very comfortable; that's what helped keep me going. We had mainly English families coming

Above: Abdul Majeed is the longest serving restaurateur in Asian cuisine at 'Aroma' restaurant, Church Street, Burnley

Below: Abdul Majeed happily showing his 'Recipe 4 Health' Award

— 10 — *Masala*

Prize-winning restaurant raises standards

An Asian restaurant in Burnley, Lancashire, has won the county's highest health award.

Lancashire County Council's Recipe 4 Health certificate has been awarded to the town's Aroma Restaurant, owned by Abdul Majeed, after strict inspection of menus and environmental standards by both Burnley Borough Council and county council.

Aroma Restaurant owner Abdul Majeed of Aroma with the Recipe 4 Health certificate.

The award recognises achievements of caterers who help their customers make healthy choices and aid the environment through their business practices.

Aroma is claimed to be one of Burnley's most stylish restaurants with a contemporary interior and mezzanine floor overlooking a central island bar. The outstanding layout complements what can only be described as a tantalising menu featuring many classic-style curries and a host of signature dishes.

It is the first Asian restaurant in Burnley, and one of the first in Lancashire, to attain the Recipe 4 Health award.

Owner Majeed expressed his pleasure at winning, adding: "It is a great delight to know that our good practices are helping raise the standards of catering and customer satisfaction.

"The award is a tribute to our investment and the hard work of our staff."

aroma

in with their children, and then gradually I got to know them and they were so nice and then I used to say to myself, look at these nice people, so that's the positive side of English people and I'm not going to get put off by a few idiots. That's what supported me and helped to keep going, there was great support. There were many, many nice people who became regulars, people we saw every week, every fortnight, and some people we even saw them a few times a week. So we got to know them and gradually they became more than customers, you know, more friends than customers and it is great support that has helped.

I did get a lot of support from our own Pakistani community, the local community and people from Burnley, Nelson. There were some organisations that used to organise certain functions and some were political, some were social events and it was always a pleasure and great fun in catering for them. They used to and still do, it's been happening on a regular basis. Then I was catering for both communities and I was getting support, you know a lot of love came from both communities. They probably liked what I did for them, what I had to offer. At that time there weren't many restaurants around here. If I look at the type of restaurants we have now, my restaurant, the first restaurant, it wasn't very modern or out of this world but still, having said that it was very nice and very well-known. When people talked about a local Burnley restaurant, the first name and the first thing that would come in their mind was the 'Koh-i-noor' – that was the proper local restaurant. Then when I moved

to new premises I renamed it 'Shalimar'. The Shalimar became more like a local restaurant, when either Asian or English people talked about the local Asian restaurant, they talked about my restaurant. That's why I was always involved in person, so it was a bit of personal touch and it was always appreciated and I always enjoyed that.

In my working life, I feel proud that every time I made a move (from Manchester Road I came to Church Street). I had something much better to offer every time I made any changes. It was something different, always something different, something better and people always acknowledged that, people always appreciated that and it has provided me with a lot of satisfaction, a lot of strength and that's what helped me keep going. It's almost thirty-three years now and that makes me the senior restaurateur or caterer in this region. Not just locally, in Burnley, but this whole region and I feel very proud of that.

I have an older son who is twenty-two years old and at Manchester University. He's into music, so he's not interested in the restaurant trade and I don't want to force him. Once he's graduated, if he does feel he should come into it, then he knows everything because he has been coming in and out of the restaurant since he was a little boy. I was shocked when he said "Oh, I want to do music", but I said fine, do well, whatever you want to do, as long as you do well, I am happy. So he's doing well, I'm quite happy and content but at a certain stage, at one stage if he wants to get into that, I wouldn't mind, I would only support him.

I would say the tough early days probably happen to everybody who goes in to a new trade or starts their practical life; but with experience, you know, you feel more relaxed, feel more comfortable and then you're cruising. It's quite nice and easy so that's what happened to me. Now everything is smooth, very much in order after that, it was just tough in the early days. To tell the truth, when I first got involved I wasn't very keen. I wouldn't say that was because of the business but the kind of

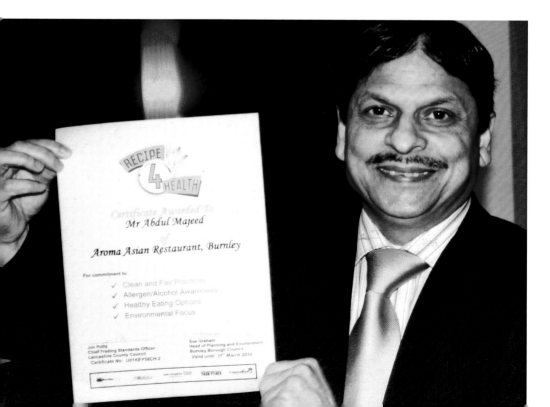

attitude to this business running at that time, I'm talking about the late 70s and early 80s and the negative attitude people normally had towards the curry houses. In the beginning, I wasn't that impressed but then gradually you know I got more and more impressed because I got more and more involved in it, then I said to myself I should get a little bit more serious and when I had that feeling I did work hard, I was completely devoted, I did work hard, very hard; and that hard work never came to an end, even today.

I'm still enjoying it, I keep making some changes to my system or the staff, even 'Shalimar' when it was opened in 1987, it was the finest and the biggest Burnley ever had then. In 2006, because I wanted to create a little bit of excitement we closed it down, we completely redesigned it and rebuilt it, gave it a modern and very contemporary look, a new look; I even gave it a new name 'Aroma,' and rebranded it. I proved to people that an Asian restaurant can look like that. The menu was completely reorganised, a lot of research and study went behind that giving it a modern touch, with very contemporary and high-class tableware and glassware as well as everything else. It gave me a lot of strength and excitement as it gave people a lot to appreciate – that Burnley could deliver a restaurant you would only find in big cities like Manchester and London, the design and the kind of layout. It's gone well.

Risk is a basic part of every business that you

start, even in 1987 when I took these premises and converted them to a restaurant, even at that time it was a very big risk, it was a huge property, a very big restaurant in 1987. Even though it was huge, I was always confident because by that time I had built a very, very strong relationship with the public of Burnley and I was more than sure that I would receive a lot of support to carry on with the business and to appreciate the business which did happen.

Time is a wonderful thing because I've personally experienced that with time, people's minds, their attitudes, their conception of curry houses, it changed big time. When I started this career, the majority of people, especially the youngsters, the concept was let's get drunk and then think of curry or a curry house, let's go have a curry and give a lot of abuse. But with time, it all changed, they've realised that curry is not something that they can only enjoy when they have had about 10 - 12 pints; it's something to enjoy, the flavour, the cuisine, the taste, it's something to enjoy when you're sober. You will only enjoy or appreciate it more when sober. As soon as they started realising that, their ideas, their mindsets, their thoughts about curry completely changed and it's so lovely to see that. I mean if I considered my times, opening times compared to what it was in the early days of my career, it's a completely different story - that says it all. Now I can close at 11 o'clock in the evening and go home and by half past eleven I'm at home. At one time, I couldn't imagine being able to do that. I can

still remember the first restaurant's times were 6pm till 3am weekdays and we were open until 4am on weekends.

I think we reshaped English culture and their attitude to part of our culture through the curry house. It took time but it has happened and it's so nice to see; especially for me because I've gone through all that and I've witnessed all the changes and I thank God the changes have only been positive, good ones, so I really feel very pleased about the changes

With the new design and new layout because it's very modern, we not only carried on welcoming our regular customers, the people who have been coming to me for years and years, it also attracted a good number of youngsters. It's modern, it goes with their expectations, it goes well with the time. We get a lot of youngsters and believe me; their attitude is completely different to what it was thirty years ago. And this new generation, there's another reason why they're so well-behaved with me, so good to me - I know their parents, I know their grandparents, they've known me since they were babies, they were probably brought up on my curries! So they will never be disrespectful to me, they respect me for all the services I provided and the changes I provided and what I'm doing now, even now with their generation they appreciate that, they acknowledge that.

But my relationship has been equally good with all parts of the communities. I've no reason to believe that Burnley is generally racist or anything, there could be some examples but they occasionally mean nothing. I've never faced any serious problems or anything; my relationship is still very strong and equally good with the Asian and English communities. But there have been big changes and all positive, I'm glad to say

all positive; they're closer to each other than ever, I mean especially the new generation. They mix with each other so they have white friends as well as friends from their own community. They go out and have fun and laugh, they play together. It's good to see them living together in good harmony and being good human beings. That's what I've seen.

For me, Burnley is my town, Burnley belongs to me and I belong to Burnley, this is my home, I'm not going anywhere; even when I retire I would still belong to Burnley, this is my home. Whatever I have done, I'm very happy and very proud of that. I provided, I mean I think I provided an excellent service to the public of Burnley which does make me feel very proud. I'm still enjoying it, and I'm going to carry on for as long as my health allows me to do so. And my message to everybody is work hard, never give up; you will have tough times, hurdles - all kinds of problems but don't give up, carry on. I've not forgotten my roots, I'm still very proud I was born and brought up in Pakistan. I still go back on a very regular basis but this is where I belong now. I think religion is very much a personal matter and I've never mixed my religion with my business. Your faith is for you to follow and it should be respected in every way and that's what I believe. However, the basic teaching of any religion is to be honest and I have been honest and very sincere to my business, to the people involved in the business; the staff, people you deal with, the customers and the clients.

Chapter 13 - Private sector

Law

Waseem Chowdhary

My name is Waseem Ahmed Choudhary. I was born in Burnley, Lancashire on 26th of October 1979. When my father came to the UK he was employed as a spinner, at Smith & Nephew in Burnley where they used to make healthcare products for the hospitals. That was his main work. My mother was a housewife, bringing up the family at home. That was in the early 1970s when my father and mother came over. The number one reason for migrating from Pakistan to the United Kingdom was employment. Also, all my father's family were settled in the United Kingdom so it was one after the other, which meant they followed.

When I was a boy I attended Heasandford Primary School in Burnley. It is still down my street which I see first thing in the morning whenever I'm on my way to work. I was there till 1992. Then I went to Gawthorpe High School, the secondary school in Padiham and left it in 1996. When I left school, I went to Burnley College and studied for the General National Vocational Qualification in business. I also did some IT courses sponsored by various companies for which certificates were awarded. A year later, I followed that up with my A-Levels and also progressing on further to do another National Vocational course. I was at college until 1999 when I moved on to university. I initially started at Manchester Metropolitan University to do an LLB Honours degree and it was only a year later, due to some medical difficulties, I had to transfer over to Preston University, now called the University of Central Lancashire. I completed my three-year degree course there and qualified in 2003 as an LLB Honours degree holder. Then my career moved on, while staying with the University of Central Lancashire, doing the legal practice course as I wanted to become a solicitor

Above: Waseem Chowdhary the first university graduate and solicitor in his extended family

Below left: Waseem Chowdhary as a child

Below: Waseem Chowdhary holding his LLB (Hons)

UNIVERSITY OF CENTRAL LANCASHIRE

practising in England and Wales. I started that in 2004 and finished in 2006. Luckily, before completion of that course I was enquiring and searching around to see whether there were any training contracts available. My good luck was that as I was pursuing my legal practice course with the University of Central Lancashire, I had obtained part-time work in the legal profession working for a local solicitors' firm in Nelson - Bukhari & Co. I found that to be very interesting as it was my first step in the career which built me up, more than anything, because I was employed as a paralegal. In 2006, while still at Bukhari & Co, I went on to do my training contract with a firm in Darwen called Darwen Law Chambers, which was being run through Bukhari & Co. That completed in 2008 in accordance with the Law Society Guidelines as a two-year contract that you have to complete. On completion of that, I qualified as a solicitor in the Supreme Court of England and Wales and started my first role as a solicitor in 2008. Since then I have been practising as a solicitor in immigration law and criminal law, although I have experience in other fields of law as well.

Above: Waseem Chowdhary receiving his Legal Practice Certificate (LPC) from the University of Central Lancashire (UCLan)

While I was studying at Burnley College, I did a part-time weekend job at the local Asda store and then on 8th of March 2008, went on to work with them permanently. I worked with Asda for ten years until I qualified and I've got to say that when I was a trainee solicitor, I was still working with Asda Superstores in Burnley. I worked through the various departments and I gained vast experience and knowledge. But more than anything, my reason for working at Asda, or having any sort of part-time employment, was to support my funding for my courses and other commitments which I had around the home. As you find nowadays, funding is very important especially when you're going on to universities, but for me I think it was a challenge; that is why I am where I am today. I'm now a duty solicitor, a criminal litigation accredited member of the Law Society and approved, which shows employers the real effort made to get to this stage. It has been a very challenging journey, especially when my mother and father migrated to the UK as they were illiterate, they found it very difficult speaking in English, understanding the system, approaching other individuals for help. However, being the oldest child, more responsibilities had fallen on me and I was pushed to get here. I'm delighted with their efforts because today I'm a recognised member of society. More than anything I'm proud as the eldest child of the family. I've also brought up the name for the rest of the members of my family as I am the only family member who has actually gone on to university, got a degree and been recognised in society.

A lot of times, what I've learned about myself is when I see other individuals hurt and other individuals needing help, I want to approach them and I want to give them as much help as I can. I am actually still doing that voluntary role now. I find myself working the hours of 9.00am 'til 5.00pm, sometimes I get called out in the middle of the night because it's my job. They say it's not nice defending criminals but unfortunately it is part of the job. I also find a lot of the time, individuals, members of the public, ring me out of hours for certain services that they need; for example, urgent passport documents need signing, some important advice that's required. As a prominent member of society, I've always found that it's more to do with community involvement as well rather than just being the professional working 9.00am 'til 5.00pm. When you go back to looking at the ways of thinking and what it is that led me to go into this, overall this is what it is. It's like a circle, you've found problems, you tackle those problems if you've been a victim, and you want to strive and move on. When I was working up towards my college days, I also felt like a victim during an incident when I was wrongfully given in to the hands of the police. The hardest part, more than anything, was that I wasn't listened to and from that experience I realised the only way you can actually make somebody understand is when you get to a proper level of professional standard. What I was unable to articulate to the police when wrongfully arrested, I have been able to achieve through the study and qualifications I have gained subsequently. In the legal profession, the most rewarding aspect for me is where a member of the public is considered to be a client for us when they approach us, when they are lost and have no hope, thinking about where they will land, what position they are in and what steps they need to take further. Being a solicitor, you can always advise your client by giving them options, not making the decisions for them. It's a matter for them to make their own decisions but professional standards always have to be borne in mind, along with integrity.

It's like, for example, I'm actually going back to 1998 and I was aged 18. I've got to say I went through a lot of stress, emotional, physical, all sorts. More than anything, it was for me to approach the right people, get them involved, ask them for help, it was more of a plea than anything and the support and the offers were always there. Today, I'm in a position where I believe that I can return the support and assistance to those same people when they require it, I feel the need to give that to them. When I see another individual who has been through the same process, same stage as me, it gives me a flashback and I think this person is where I was - at that stage, at that time and this person needs help. I give them my full support. I think, sometimes, it's not who you are it's what your level of understanding and knowledge of the system is.

That network of support was the local councillors in the community who obviously volunteered to come forward. One of the support services we had, I mean it's not a legal body but certain individuals voluntarily assist here, and that organisation is where I am sitting today, Jinnah Community Development Services. They can always put you in the right direction in terms of the right individual, firm, or organisation to support and assist you. So that level of support, I find, was always there and is still there from these people. I would also say that education is something which can never be stolen from an individual but it's a long-term commitment which can always go with you from the beginning to the end, and your knowledge just continues to extend and make you a recognisable figure in society. If it wasn't for my parents I probably wouldn't be

here today. Other figures, for example, who have always treated me like a nephew, are Mr Malik himself, also Mr Mohammed Najib. They've always been proud of me and they've always helped me in my days when it was difficult for me to move on. They have always given me good advice. Whenever there's been an issue, I feel sometimes I've found they were closer to me than my parents, but that was more to do with, not just with household things but also educational things, which they helped me along with even though my mother and father were there. The understanding or the knowledge could only be obtained from them because they had experience that they passed on to me. I remember when I was a paralegal, they say you always learn from your teachers, from your elders. I remember when I used to work at Bukhari & Co and I had my first case; I didn't know how to prepare, I didn't how to conduct the advocacy hearing and my main senior supervisor was ill in hospital undergoing an operation. I had attended Bradford Court with the preparation I had done and I won a victory for my client. I believe that the strength and the teachings that you get given from your seniors can always be very useful. The voluntary work I've done in the past for the St John's Ambulance, working at the local library and also working with some insurance organisations and more than anything, with charity groups; the NSPCC, fund raising with Barnardo's, I have found rewarding. I may not have the time now, but the only thing I can probably offer now is obviously money for charity.

I live in Burnley, I was born and bred in Burnley; it's home. Not just the fact that, obviously, I've lived here all my life, but I believe that this is where my roots lie now. I think if I was to go and settle in Pakistan it would be extremely difficult, we cannot adapt in that society. Here, you should always get on with one another irrespective of differing cultural origins. It's an effort, that's all I've got to say. I have gone through that and I'm proud of myself. Burnley is still my home.

Above: Waseem Chowdhary with his parents holding LLB (Hons) Degree during his graduation ceremony

Chapter 14 - Private sector

Manufacturing/Retail

Riaz Ahmed

Above: Riaz Ahmed is a hardworking businessman who employs over 250 workers at Sweet Dreams on Colne Road, Burnley

My name is Riaz Ahmed. I was born in Pakistan in 1949. My parents worked in the farming industry. I came here to join my older family; the initial reason would have been financial, they thought they'd be better off here with more opportunities for work and other things. It's just how things happen, it was a coincidence really. I started my business in Nelson. I came to do some colour photocopying here in Burnley, I think that was at Livingstone Mill. When I passed by, I saw the Queensworks stone building for sale. I always liked that type of building and I thought, okay, I'll make some enquiries, and I managed to buy that, and that's how I came to Burnley really, for business.

I was working for a bed manufacturer in Barnoldswick; that was my job, at Silent Night, and I was there for a total of 17 years. I worked hard as much as I could and management appreciated it. After one or two years I became a training instructor to teach new employees how to do various jobs. My Asian background did help me to learn most of the departments because some of the people starting there couldn't speak English, so I trained them properly in various departments. Then after a few years, Silent Night decided to set up a factory in the Middle East, UAE, in '78, and they offered me a job there as a works manager. I went there and started that factory from scratch, along with the managing director from Barnoldswick. I was stationed there 'til 1984. When I came back to the UK, they couldn't find me a similar level job here so it gave me an opportunity to start my own business. I started my business basically on my own. I used to make headboards during the day, load them in the evening, set off early in the morning to deliver somewhere in Yorkshire and then come back.

When I went to UAE it gave me a knowledge of business because it was a small operation. Rather than just being works' manager looking after the production side of it, over there, if there was no sales manager, because of my English background they sent me down to see the customer. I learnt what the business was and I found it quite interesting. I trained all the people over there; I recruited them from Pakistan around my village and that area, so I basically started it from scratch. I knew how to make things, how to handle things and I think that was the reason I started my own business.

The first few months were very hard because I didn't know how to do business in the UK, although I had a bit of experience of the Middle East, it was really hard because I was doing everything. I was making it, I was selling it, I was delivering it, and I didn't have the finances to have a few people or small team from day one. It was a very basic start, which again helps you later on but the thing is, either you make a start there or you don't. Like my children, they're starting halfway, but I didn't have any option. I can still remember I used to see where I could find a customer, I'd get the Yellow Pages and go to the library and get different Yellow Pages for different areas, find the furniture retailer then when I went to Manchester it might take me four hours to find that customer. Lots of one-way streets, because I wasn't used to that area! So it really took some time.

As I started from scratch, I was talking to people and asking "Where do I find furniture retailers?" You know, at that time there was no internet. Naturally, Yellow Pages from this area will have furniture retailers from this area only, then I thought, I want to supply to Manchester, new customers. As I expanded, I went into the local library to find certain addresses. When I started, I was supplying very small, local retailers like those in Nelson, Burnley and Clitheroe and then when I knew a few, then I was thinking, how I can expand? I think some of these things just happen, I mean one day I was making headboards and a gentleman came in and said hello, and introduced himself, he was a sales agent. He'd been trying to comb one-off retailers and he was looking for the agency and someone told him, "There's a lad in Burnley who's very keen, go and see him, he might be able to give you something." So he came down and we had a talk. Up to that point

Above: Riaz Ahmed with his sons, Adnan and Majid, at Sweet Dreams warehouse

I didn't know you could have a sales agent, I was thinking you can only employ people to sell and my business wasn't big enough to take anybody on. When he came, he explained and said he has other agencies and he's looking for a headboard agency. He was a nice gentleman, hardworking, and I found it interesting. I said, "Yeah, that's fine," because at that time, if you're a sales agent there's no commitment. Now even sales agencies have gone, as sales employers have come on. So I took him on and I think that was another big step forward because I gave him the agency and, whereas before I was getting small orders, now within two, three days he posted me ten orders. He knew all the retailers around that area and around Lancashire – he was covering the whole of Lancashire. It's business, you have the van or you don't, everybody's different. I'm a very basic person, very basic, and I make it work. Some people could be very educated, intelligent; each individual will have different abilities. I mean politics, I knew from the start it wasn't my field, I don't even try but doing the business, I can talk about the subject of business all day.

If you do your job well you will progress, and you need to be honest and straight and I think all the people who know me, or work with me, know I keep it very simple. If a person were to come to my business - my desk now, mostly I aim every day to keep it tidy. Alright, some days you have a few papers there but you keep it clean, tidy, straight, and people should know who you are. I mean that's the beauty of business, a personality,

they should be able to read you easily, whatever you are. Don't try to be what you are not. If you try to be what you are, and honest and straight, I think things come your way.

I think it's the way you're brought up early on; you see your parents, they talk at home, if they're honest they talk straight, at the time you can't see it but register it in your mind and when you grow later on, then you naturally act that way. Maybe it's in your genes and maybe you learn from people around you. I think what I experience, you must have faith, because without any faith you are a lost person. Faith does play a big role, you have a direction and faith again - to be frank, live with everybody, respect each other, and respect other faiths. If you're true to that, I think it will help you for the future and you feel good about it because you're doing it right. I'm a very ethical sort of guy; I'm not a businessman in that sense when you look at clever businesses. I can give you a small example. When I was in Dubai, we had an accountant from Karachi who'd been working in bigger organisations. When he came down and joined us, I was there as a manager on the factory side and lads from the village, they were working, and whenever they went they would borrow money from me sometimes. I was too friendly with them and the accountant used to laugh and say, "Riaz, you'll never be a businessman." But I wish I could speak to him now, he's moved to the States and I haven't got his phone number, but I would really like to tell him that you don't need to be extra clever to be a successful businessman. And that's why I'm saying, he saw all this that I was doing, normally people use others, and yes, they were using me in a way, but there was a friendly sort of attitude, they were borrowing something, it's only a small thing, but they'll always return it. I was in a position to help them, nothing wrong with that. I used to sit with them on the stairs or wherever, if you have the personality to shine, or if you haven't got the personality just to show, people will know, it's as simple as that. Some people see you in the street and they want to talk to you, not because of your wealth, but because they know that you won't say anything which will hurt them, you won't act in a clever way, and that is the reality of life. Like I said earlier on, when I used to start in the morning and then deliver headboards, come back, and the neighbours used to say, "Hey Riaz, you were early this morning," I would say, "How do you know I set off at five o'clock?" They would say, "The whole street knows because this old diesel van makes a big noise!" But you know, I'm proud of that, and that van was my family car as well because I couldn't afford a car, so I was taking family out in that.

I think anybody's strength is their character. If you are straight and honest I think you are alright because you've got 90 per cent of strength before you start. At that time, I thought about how I could bring the awareness in my children and I thought, okay, do something different. I mean, if I put them into private school they'd maybe think, Dad is sending us to an important school, there is a reason for it. At the same time I was thinking I had the three children at the school then, I couldn't easily afford all three but I thought if I'm going to send one, send all three or don't send any. The next two, three years, my total income was their school fees, which was my investment, rather than building or buying land in Pakistan at that time. My generation are like that because you always want to get something which you don't have early on. But I thought I'll go another way and I put them in a school and gradually, after a year, two, three years, I could easily afford it. Out of three children, one – he was 11 – he said, "Oh Dad, I want to be a footballer" I thought, yeah, everybody dreams, alright, good luck, but I didn't discourage him, I encouraged him really. Our generation at that time wanted their children to be doctors and engineers, but thank God he's given me the thought which meant I grew myself out of that way of thinking. I thought, yeah, fine, playing football is good, try your luck, and I think he was 12 when he managed to get

Left: Riaz Ahmed the owner of Sweet Dreams in his office

into Bury Football Club Academy. So from 12 to 14, he played at Bury, then at the age of 14, Manchester United approached him and he was at their United Schoolboys, from 14 to 16, and then he got a scholarship at Huddersfield Town. He made his debut in 2003, played for the first team and he achieved it, which was good. Early on, when he was at school, I never pushed him for grades, I never put pressure on him, because his profession was different. I could see what he wanted to do so I never really said, "What grades did you get?" You know, these are little things but you need to help them and I used to take him to Bury myself, and even United, most of the time because he used to do two days training, Tuesday and Thursday, and then Saturday was the game, and I can't remember ever missing his game. Even at that level they play all over the UK. I watched nearly every game early on wherever he played from 12 to 16; these are little things which can help and thank God he made it in his profession, so he plays at Huddersfield Town, Tranmere Rovers and in Hungary, Ferencvárosi, their Premiership club. Last year he was in Iran, masha'Allah and he played 20-odd games for Pakistan. He scored four goals against India. He recently played in New Delhi, the SAFF Cup. His achievement was a lot harder than mine. Okay, we work hard and in business, if there is a little bit of a tough time we can get together, have a coffee. In football you have yourself, you have to prove everything and everybody's watching you. If the ball slips, or the pass is not right, it's a lot of pressure and he did it alright, and he toured all over the world really, with the Pakistan team; China, The Maldives and Bangladesh, and I've seen most of them because I went to watch them, so it's good.

I've been very basic and I'm always working. I'm practical, sensible, and I'm not a silly worker.

Below: Riaz Ahmed and Tim Webber, Barnfield Construction, at the ground breaking ceremony for a large extension to Sweet Dreams Head Office on Colne Road, Burnley

Also, I never say if you work 18 hours you're very hardworking; this is fine, but over time you change. I mean I've given a lot of time to my kids and many times they'll ask me, "Go on, get out, have you nothing else to do?" You can find that if you work, quality work, eight hours is enough. I have really given them the time they wanted, as they went into universities. I never went myself, but I can remember reading the university guides all night to learn which was the best university, what was there. I was very close to them and I wanted them to have the best facilities possible. If you want to do something you will learn, that is the beauty of it. Same as business; I find it good. I come in the morning, look forward to coming to work, not thinking of, oh another eight hours. Your business, again, is your team and you must have the ability to pick a good team. If you can't do that you can't progress. You, yourself, can only do so much. Like I said, I mean I'm a very basic sort of guy on the educational front, but we have a first class facility at work; our accounts are up to date, we do management, monthly management

accounts, and we have people. We've got all the IT up to date and it's working fine.

I think in business we are proud, really, of what we achieved. It's not the business growth - we're not the biggest and we'll never be, because I don't want 20 factories, because I like to do what I can handle and do it well. Without overstating it, I think the business model we have we're proud of, it is a special business model and it is showing in the trade. We have a team, people who come, stay. Like if somebody's looking for a job in our sales department they have to wait till somebody retires, which is really good. I mean, a guy in London retired, and recently we recruited somebody in Lancashire because the other gentleman retired. So that is a good achievement and other people working in the office, my national sales manager Jacquie, she's been with us 20 years, grown with the business, and other staff also. I think the beauty of it is to have a good atmosphere, you come to work, are treated like a family, like home, and it always pays back.

I think Burnley is a very nice town and I found it very helpful. I work with Burnley Council; we work very closely with them and all of the departments and they're very helpful so there's no reason to change. I don't change things very often anyway, that's my nature. My accountants started with me 30 years ago, but it works so there's no need to change. My solicitor and my bank are the same. Burnley is a nice town and the people are very good and the facilities are there, so why change? It is no good changing for the sake of changing. If there is a reason, you always look for opportunity but there are a lot of opportunities here. The way I see it personally, there are too many opportunities and I have to be selective. I don't want to take all and like I said, I pull myself back to look after my family and other matters, I don't get carried away with the business. But opportunity-wise we are growing, even in this climate. I never believe in recessions, although these last few years it has been hard, but thank God we are not feeling it, we're pushing on. We just managed to get the site next door to us, a two and a half acre site, an old builders' centre. Last week I gave the go-ahead to a local company to build a 50,000 square-foot extension. So even on that side, there are a lot of opportunities business-wise, a lot of employment and going against the trend. The way I'm thinking, my next two, three projects are all manufacturing in Burnley, not just trading, so those are moving on. One project, upholstery, is making sofas in-house. I started

that about two years ago, rather than bringing them in from China and the Far East, to compete with them. You can compete; I think if you focus and look deeply, don't be scared of going to the bottom of it, you can compete.

In reality, you learn all your life and then when you learn something new you think, why didn't you learn it before? It's been good, but things have been hard also. I mean it is life and never expect it to be rosy all the time. But as I said before, if you're honest and straight you have the right foundation. Nothing will ever be perfect; it is not possible, so you need to be ready for challenges. Even in my business career that I started in '85, up to 2005, each year we've grown, continuously, some years 5%, some 4%, some 50%, some 70% up to 2005. I never thought it could go wrong as well, just kept pushing on. In 2005, I set up my own factory in the Middle East, Dubai. I had a sofa company in Burnley other than my bed company and everything was going great. Tragedy happened in 2005; one of my factories caught fire and I lost roughly two million pounds overnight, it was full of stock, and the whole thing burned down. Normally, we keep everything very up to date and the last thing I was worrying about was something would not be right. My credit insurance was taken away, I was thrown into specialised lending in Manchester and on top of that, my biggest customer went into administration. We'd been dealing with him for the last 15 years. Those four, five months were the toughest time of my life because all the kids were used to an easy lifestyle. I'm very easy-going, and I mean people are different but I don't mind giving the kids responsibility, I don't control them. But they have to behave, and they have to look after themselves, they don't need to be controlled. They were all living a good life and we were right at the edge. So those three, or four months were very tough.

There were no other assets because I was putting every penny back in to the business. That was not a clever business strategy because you should safeguard yourself when things are good. I'm not saying it was a good thing I did! But I did it. I'd rather have a very small business and a good business, than a big business and an unethical business. Immediately the following year, we made our best ever profit and we learnt a lot from that. What I didn't learn in 20, 25 years I learnt more in one year because after that, we safeguarded ourselves also, and we controlled the business better. That's when the recession came –

we already had tidied things up, and we didn't feel anything.

It was tough, a good thing Pendle Hill was here! I was walking on weekends quite a lot, getting a bit of fresh air, just keeping myself going really. The sort of guy I am, a bit too ethical or too reserved, I wouldn't discuss business in those four months not even with friends like Mr Malik. I just kept it normal; talking to them, going out, and having a meal. But I did discuss it afterwards because I didn't want anybody else to feel worried, also because I was going through a rough patch, and I knew it was me who had to handle it in the end, along with the team. With hard work, we had to make some very tough decisions. We had to close the UAE operation immediately and I had to close the sofa company to safeguard Sweet Dreams, but because you're straight with people, it will always pay back. Our suppliers, they supplied us on normal terms because they believed if Riaz says he'll pay, he will pay. That is the belief they had although business ethics would suggest they were wrong to trust us on good faith alone, because there was no credit insurance whatsoever. But we paid them every penny and we came out dead clean and that's really what I'm proud of, going through all that. I don't owe anybody a single penny, paid everybody dead-on and came out nice and clean, and that's how you build your reputation. Banks; 99%, they thought we wouldn't pull it off!

I think the children learnt a lot, I mean I would say more than me because, I'm very close to family, and we were talking. They knew my movements and even if you are father and children; if you have a good relationship there is a different feeling than just a father and daughter, father and son. I can see sometimes when I talk to them they have learnt about being a little bit careful and responsible. Anything I do now I think twice. Before, I would buy machines anywhere and even tell the accountant afterwards because I thought he might stop me! Now things have changed, now I consult him and we ask, does it stack up? It gives you more confidence. We didn't make any excuses like "Oh we are in trouble, and can you please knock 20% off?" No, why? They supplied in good faith, they need to get paid in good faith, and I think that does help. Even our suppliers in the Far East we used to import stuff, they approached me and they said, "Riaz, we heard the bad news and if you need any help we are here to help you," which was a very good thing because they're abroad and they

Below: Riaz Ahmed with his management team, holding the award they won at the Burnley Annual Business Awards

can't chase the money here anyway. But this is the beauty and enjoyment of the business; having a nice relationship, people trusting you and you respecting them, and that is wonderful. I can still remember, because at that time everybody goes after their own money. They're thinking, oh, they are in trouble anyway, they're going to go anytime, so what about us? But they believed what we told them and the business model was good, even then, Sweet Dreams itself was good, we were just running out of cash. I learnt how the cash flow in business works! Before, I never believed it. If you think business is going well, how can it go wrong? But it can go wrong, so I learned from it. Now if somebody wants very big orders we watch it, what percentage of our production is going to that particular customer? If it is too high we think about it, because it's a risk.

I spent most of my life here, the children were born here, grew up here, so we treat this as a main home. We have two real homes, you know, Pakistan and here, but we have very much a feeling for Burnley and the people here because we've lived with them so long. Again, people, in any community are very nice people; I mean we see Pakistani, English, they're all the same to me because we're so close with both communities and there are some very nice people. All I have achieved, without local support or without my staff, we couldn't have done it. I'm the one who's explaining now, but the reason for this success is the team. Without a team you cannot do anything, you have to have the ability to delegate, and delegate to the right

people. That is a skill and that is the ability I can say I have. I'm good at selecting people or talking to people. Production, innovation, introducing new things. I can work all day long and like it but in some areas, I don't have any skill, but I can find a person who can do the work better than me and that is the reason for my success. Even now, we have the biggest retailer from the UK in the office. My sales manager Jacquie's dealing with them and she can make a decision, she doesn't need me, she will negotiate with them and that is the beauty of running a business or leadership; to trust people and choose the right people. That is what is good because when people work for you, they depend on you. They're not there for money, they're there for you and you need to really make them feel good so they can talk to you; and give them respect – that is the key more than giving them another few hundred pounds. It goes a long way. I think that is the key anyway because people are your business. Your biggest asset is your team. Other things – machinery, money - anybody can have that. So, if somebody's rich he can buy all those things ten times better than you, but if you have a better team he won't compete with you, you will be the winner, because winning is the team.

I think, basically, my advice to anybody is to always keep things simple; do what you like, do it honestly, straightforwardly, and there is no limit to what you can achieve. Like I said, I'm a very basic person and people who are higher up or lower down, they're all people. If they are good with you, you get up, shake hands with them, and respect them. If an elder person comes from my family, I still act as a junior towards them. I'll get up, I'll give them tea, and that is the beauty of a good life. The same as when I was in Dubai; I can still remember sitting with workers on the stairs and, because over there the culture is different, there were some saying, "Oh look, he's the mill owner, he's sitting there," – it makes no difference. What I'm saying is, keep things straight and simple and people should read you, and read you hopefully as a good, straightforward-thinking person not as anything else. And there is room for everybody; I mean you don't need to be a specialist in any field. I think if you do things right, opportunities come your way.

Manufacturing/Retail

Basri Chowdhary

My husband, Mr Ghulam Nabi Chowdhary, migrated to the UK in 1961. He sponsored me to join him as a spouse in 1963.

I was the first Pakistani female who came to Burnley. It was good; there was no crime or theft like we see today. Nobody was involved in drugs. Elders used to drink alcohol but young people, both English and Asian, weren't involved in anything like that. Now a lot of our young generation especially, even the white youths, are involved in drugs. They are going to ruin their lives.

I worked at Lucas. I also did sewing. I worked for about 17-18 years. I have four children whom I also looked after. When my sister arrived in 1966, I gave birth to my first child, Iftekhar (probably the first Pakistani child born in Burnley) and then a year later my second son was born. So while my sister was here in the UK another son Zulfiqar was born. She used to look after my kids then. That is how I managed to continue to work. It was extremely difficult. I used to start work at 7am and finish around 4:30pm; come home, clean up the house and prepare the food, which was normal as an Asian lady. It was hard and a few years later another Pakistani lady came to Brierfield. I started to visit her at the weekend when my husband was home.

I think when Nisar was about to be born and Iftekhar was about 8 months old, I first met Mrs Malik in the clinic. She had a baby boy Zahid and I had Iftekhar. So this is where I met her and then we started to see each other on a regular basis. It wasn't seen as bad if you went out to the park, unlike today. We don't go to the park any more, we used to finish all our work and take the children to the park with us. It was very safe and we sometimes left our doors unlocked. Nobody used to bother you or steal your stuff. You didn't feel worried that there wasn't another Asian around. What people describe as 'bored' it wasn't the case at all. People were so caring and loving then, which isn't the case now.

I personally feel as society has progressed and been educated, we have lost other values and traditions. This is my own opinion. You see people who are extremely educated but they don't get on with each other. I feel there's no more love and feelings for each other, it's all fake nowadays. When I develop or form a relationship I do it for life. I made friends with Mrs Malik and Mrs Bukhari and I don't make too many friends, it is not my nature.

Above: Basri Chowdhary was the first Pakistani lady to work at Lucas Electrical Compay, Eastern Avenue

Above: Basri Chowdhary's first born son, Iftekhar, in 1966

There weren't any baths in the houses. We didn't have gas, we used coal to keep our houses warm, and we had coals to burn. Yes, after some time when we bought another house we then installed a new bath in the house. We didn't have any carpet only lino where we mopped the floor.

But today, you have many luxuries and a lot more disease as well. I am so grateful to the Almighty,

considering my age I'm so fit and well.

Islam has played a positive role in my life, but it is all about application. If you apply your faith to your life you will reap the benefit. My son, Zulfiqar has passed away and left his widow and kids behind but I am still grateful to Allah the Almighty for everything he gave me. I live on my own since all my children are settled in their own houses. Make sure that you are sincere and honest and leave the rest to Allah. I am very happy with my life. I see my daughters-in-law as my daughters and I'm happy to see them.

Nowadays, our young generation is giving a bad name to the whole community from their actions, especially Muslim kids who are doing harm to the image of Islam and we have to defend our religion in front of non-Muslims. If I have an English neighbour, regardless of her faith whether she is Hindu or Christian, I will try my best to support and help her.

My neighbour works in a care home, she has shift work but whenever I see her and whatever food I have cooked, I offer her. I try my best to lead my life as a good human being. I treat everyone fairly and hope this may encourage them to retain or accept Islam. If I treat them badly then it will make them think about what kind of Muslim I am. This is my point of view.

When I came from Pakistan, although we lacked facilities it didn't bother me. We had grocers who used to visit Burnley on a weekly basis and collect our orders and deliver groceries. We didn't have any Asian grocers in Burnley at that time. I didn't have to go to the shop. The shopkeeper used to deliver everything to our homes each week. People used to come round and sell Asian clothes as well. Certainly it was really hard, when comparing it with today, when everything is available at the door-step, by the grace of Allah. I

am grateful to the Almighty for everything. I have suffered a lot in life so I hardly remember good times.

My kids have now grown up. I have many granddaughters and grandsons and by the grace of Allah, Aisha is just turned 21 now. I am not worthy of all this but Allah is kind.

If we look at our actions then we are zero and deserve nothing. Just look at ourselves, how many of us offer prayers and remember Him but he still gives us happiness. I am always so grateful to the Almighty that my sons are practising Muslims and offer daily prayers. Alhamdulillah, I don't deserve anything that he has bestowed upon me and my kids. My daughters-in-law are all so wonderful too. They respect me like a mother and I wonder what more I need.

I made clear to myself I'm not going to repeat with my daughters-in-law what I suffered from. I always seek Allah's blessing to guide me to the right path and I am looking for this, I require nothing but His pleasure.

I make this du'a (supplication) for everyone. I brought up my children and worked as well and maintained this balance. Only by the grace of Allah, it was purely through his blessing that I have lead a very active life, I never felt tiredness in doing things and it's only his blessing and kindness that enabled me to do; what I had to do I brought up my children and I am fond of cleaning.

I was very young when I came to Burnley (UK), my home, by the grace of Allah, who has made Burnley my home and granted me everything I needed. Why shouldn't I be so grateful and consider Burnley my home? May the Almighty help this country succeed and prosper. I always make du'a to grant prosperity, peace and harmony for the UK. Whether it's Pakistan or the UK, both were made by the same Creator. Although it is at the back of our minds that the UK isn't our homeland, but it is the place where we live. So I consider from the core of my heart that England is my homeland and Burnley is my home.

Manufacturing/Retail

Iftekhar Chowdhary

My name is Iftekhar Chowdhary. I was born in Burnley on the 1st of May 1966. I was born on Canning Street, opposite a parish building of some sort, which is now 'Hubie Street Plumbers'. At the time, there was my brother a year younger than me and there were a couple of other families. I believe I was the first Pakistani heritage baby born in Burnley. I don't remember anybody besides a couple of others, but they were younger than me. I think I was the first, second-generation Pakistani born in Burnley.

My father worked in the mills, cotton mills, when he first came over. Then he started working in Burnley at that time. He started driving, then he became an instructor for the buses, he was an inspector as well at one point and he retired in about 1979. My father came in '61 and my mother came in '63. They were amongst the first families to come over. I think the job opportunities more than anything else made them settle in Burnley. There were a lot of mills around the Burnley area. When my uncle came over in late '66 he started work in the area, in Bradford I think. The industry, it was lacking in people or the manpower and obviously our people looked at opportunity there and that's where they started.

I went to Stoneyholme Primary School, literally across the road from where I lived. The nursery I went to was on Elm Street but the infants and the primary school was Stoneyholme, which isn't there anymore; the building has been knocked down, demolished. When I left high school I went to Burnley College. Prior to Burnley College I went to the Information Technology Centre for a year, did computing and electronics. In college I went down the route of electronics; electronic servicing in particular, that's repairing video and TV. I did that for three to four years. The fourth year was in Blackburn, they didn't do it in Burnley. I started working in Blackburn with a private company doing repair, the video side of things. We also had a video shop, a rental library on Brougham Street at that time and I was doing

some repairs via the shop there as well. That was my father's business. I think I was influenced in my career by my dad. I think it has, because my younger brothers didn't go into the business until later and that was in the mid-to-late '80s. Because I was there from when we opened, I took an interest in it. So that part stuck with me. I didn't think of it at that time but obviously, you find out later on in time that that's what it was. Mum was hard-working, she's still like that now. I think their work ethic has rubbed off on me. I work for Comet now. I have been for the last 17 years. I'm a sales manager, that's my current position. I was at Blackburn, now I'm at Burnley. I do enjoy my work hence I'm still here after so long.

Above: Iftekhar Chowdhary, the first Pakistani child born in Burnley, Bank Hall Hospital in 1966

Below: Iftekhar Chowdhary standing on the footpath near Blackpool Tower

I remember when I was about three; early memories, living on Canning Street, playing around the area with my tricycle at that time. I remember my father's car, I think it was an Austin. In terms of being Pakistani, I didn't really feel any different to anyone else, I think I fitted in because I spoke the language. There were some Pakistanis who came over and they were probably settled here but their English wasn't that good, and some were in secondary school, in particular Barden, where I went. There

Right: Iftekhar Chowdhary sitting on the floor of Stoneyholme Infants School Hall, (left) with his classmates

Below: Iftekhar Chowdhary's Award certificate for outstanding performance at COMET

were remedial classes for a lot of Pakistanis who came over. Mr Malik was one of the teachers for English as a second language and the late Mr Yaqub was at Barden as well, he was teaching the mainstream classes. There was a bit of tension, racial tension in the '70s but I didn't really come across it as much. You always find that the fellow students or the pupils basically said "No, he's one of us" even though I wasn't really one of them as such, because of the colour difference more than anything. There was an issue with the National

Front at that time. There were certain cases at Barden School which I'd come across, obviously they were at the height of it all but after that it quietened down really and the '80s wasn't that much of a problem as such. I didn't come across it anyway, personally.

Growing up, I remember the family business actually because I enjoyed that. I think it was in 1979 when we started the business on Brougham Street and I was still at school. I'd started taking an interest in the business and at the weekends in particular, started helping out because we did fancy goods as well, like radios and cassette players. The rental library came as a secondary business but that took off. Maybe that's the reason I've gone into the same field today. My dad was a role model because he knew a lot about it in those days, the video side of it. In my work I find it rewarding where you get customers appreciating you, you can tell by the smile, praising, thank you, etc. You feel that you've achieved something by doing that. Because at the end of the day, if a customer's happy, they'll return and that's the reward I think, and the company obviously wants that as well; they want positive rather than negative feedback. I think in this day and age this is a really important

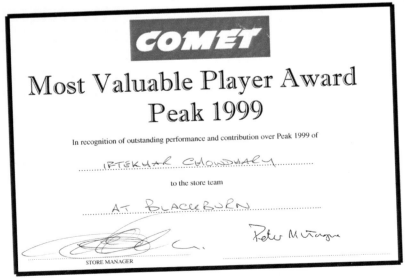

Respect to all colleagues

COMET

Most Valuable Player Award
Peak 1999

In recognition of outstanding performance and contribution over Peak 1999 of

IFTEKHAR CHOWDHARY

to the store team

AT BLACKBURN

STORE MANAGER

Dedicated to customers

Deliver the best

Working together, through mutual respect and support, in an enjoyable environment

128

part of what you need to look at in a business.

I won't say I feel proud but I think over the years because technology's changing all the time and you pick it up, especially in the vision side which is the TV, DVD, etc, that's my speciality. Even in this day and age where you find people aren't too comfortable with the setting up of it, so they come in sometimes and I even go out and set it up for them. I don't charge them for it, it's just as a courtesy, really, more than anything else. And from that, it's another way of looking at it as you've achieved something and helped someone. And they in turn obviously feel that the company has provided that service and they feel valued so they come back again. It's another way of looking at it. In terms of faith, the way I see it, if my actions come across in a positive way and non-Muslims know I am a Muslim then they probably see that, yes, they're not all the same. There is a different side to it which they're not aware of. I do pray five times a day. I do believe in the values of Islam. In all faiths, obviously, you will get your

negative side and unfortunately that's what's perceived as normal for us Muslims, but it isn't.

Living on Canning Street there was, I don't remember the bathroom, having an inside bathroom, there was an outside toilet. I was only about four years old, when we were there. On Brougham Street, when we moved there, there was an upstairs toilet and bath so we did have hot running water which we didn't have in our first house. My parents were some of the earliest Pakistanis to settle in Burnley and my memories as a little boy, and thinking about my own experience now as a grown up and a parent myself, I notice a lot of differences, facilities more than anything else. Everything was done manually, like for washing. No washing machines, dishwashers. People used laundrettes; there were quite a lot of them around. But my mother in particular did everything herself; she did all that even though she was working as well. I remember from an early age she was working at Lucas Electrical which was in Elm Street in Daneshouse initially but then it moved to Widowhill Road; they made car parts. Mum was working on the production line at whatever section she was working on, but it was on the production line making car parts. She was doing that and bringing us up. It was probably about 1970-71 so I would have been about four or five years old then. My younger brother at the time, my late brother, was three years younger than me so he was obviously the youngest at that time.

Left: Iftekhar Chowdhary between his two brothers, Nisar and Zulfiqar, with his aunt and cousin

Below: Iftekhar Chowdhary between his mother and grandmother, three generations together

She used to get us ready in the morning, that was 7am she was getting us ready. She bathed us at that time, got us ready, everything; hair combed, clothes on, ready and then she used to walk to work. She did her part. I mean, that shows us up today and obviously we appreciate what she did for us. Today when we look at my own personal experience of it, it's a bit different in the sense that facilities like your washing machine, like your dishwasher, conveniences like hot running water, ease of use, you've got your own vehicle so it's a lot more convenient than anything else. Other facilities too, even having a television I suppose is your pastime, like your evening time; it's all a lot easier. But there is a bit of a difference where I remember, as in those days when we were young, probably in the late '70s, there were a lot of family gatherings. Everyone used to have them. On a weekend we used to have all the family like my uncles, aunties, so we used to have like family gatherings Saturday and Sundays. Watch a movie together on a video or go to the pictures. That was a regular thing. There is a lot less of that now. Everyone's busy in their lifestyle.

I think our religion is progressing more now than it was back then because of knowledge due to education more than anything else. In those days, especially people from Pakistan, they didn't have the information. Like I said, when I was little, telephones weren't really widely available. One person had one maybe, or could get to a phone maybe in next town. There was the radio; it was the only form of media that they had. There's more television now so again there is an element of education there. Not many people could read so what they learnt was from their families. But obviously technology has moved on and thinking positively, I think it's one of the things about technology, people do have access including via the internet so you can gain further knowledge through that.

My roots are in Pakistan but I would call Burnley home. I think myself, although I am heritage-wise obviously Pakistani, I think of myself as British even though the negative side to that is other people. The native people, if you would put it like that, don't think of me as British because of my colour or for my faith. But I do think of myself, as I know my brothers do think of themselves, as British. Last time I went to Pakistan was about six years ago, when my younger brother got married. You do feel that the native people there can tell you're not from there. I don't know whether it's from, not just from the conversation obviously, but it's from your appearance. Even when you wear the local clothing, obviously the traditional Pakistani Shalwar Kameez, they can still tell you're not from there. So you always stand out like a sore thumb. I don't, personally, feel that Pakistan is my home. It might be a different opinion from others who are from here but not me, this is my home. I always think of Burnley as home.

Chapter 15 - Private sector

Sport

Adnan Ahmed

My name is Adnan Ahmed. I was born in Burnley on the 7th of June 1984. I think my father had family members that were already here in the area due to the mill business at that time. I think they settled in Burnley because of the dynamics of their time really, because family members were already here. There was no choice really in that sense! To start off with, my dad was working for somebody when I was born and that was for a bed manufacturer called Silentnight. Eventually they got up the ladder really and they ended up setting up their own business and that was about 20 years ago now. So since that, obviously, they've been self-employed.

I went to Moorlands School in Clitheroe. I think our school upbringing was different to many of my cousins if you like because they were in the local school but we used to go to private school, which is about 20, 30 minutes from our house. The good thing with that was the mixture of people there. So we had a wide community there which was good for us, for our upbringing, because we got to deal with different types of people. I think from a young age we were always multicultural, which in a sense helped us as we got older. When I left school I was fortunate that I got an apprenticeship as a footballer; I went straight into that.

I started playing when I was about 10 or 11 years old. At that time, my father didn't know much about football to be honest but my elder brother Majid used to take us down to the local park and we used to just play, have a kick about. Then my brother realised that me and my younger brother (who used to train with us as well) we had a talent, so he started training us up. He had a coaching booklet so he used to go through it and we used to do different drills from the age of 11 onwards. From that age we just started, it was a hobby really. Then we signed for a local team aged about 11½. Again, they spotted our talent as well and they encouraged us. From there I ended up signing for a professional team called Bury, which is not far away. Two years,

I did really well, again they spotted my talent. From there I got spotted by Manchester United so I ended up there at 14 years old. I had two years over there, so I played with the likes of Dan Fletcher, Kieran Richardson. Unfortunately, I didn't get the apprenticeship there so I ended up going to Huddersfield, who were top of their championship by that time, which was the Second Division. The manager there, Steve Bruce, he spotted me because I was at Manchester United; I played with his son there. Basically that was the best move for me at that time. I went there, got the apprenticeship. Unfortunately I got injured, had a bad spell of injury. I'm used to training two, three times a week and then you go to full time and it's twice a day, so your body obviously is getting used to that and unfortunately mine didn't get used to it! So I ended up having a year out, injured. Luckily, Alhamdulillah, I managed to make it as a professional and then debut at 19. Since then, till now, I've been professional.

Above: Adnan Ahmed first Pakistani professional footballer from the North West of England

Below: Adnan Ahmed standing inside the family home

Above: Adnan with his father, Riaz Ahmed, (at the Sweet Dreams warehouse) and brother, Majid

Below: Adnan Ahmed playing for Droylsden Football Club, Manchester

If my mum and dad were that way inclined, to push me into the doctor/lawyer type profession, then I wouldn't be playing now - it's quite simple, to be honest. One of the blessings that I've had, is that my dad's been very supportive, specially because once I signed for a professional team and when at a young age (at 12) I signed for Bury, I think my dad realised that obviously I've got some kind of talent there. I think as a parent you should encourage that and not discourage. I think that's the key thing. Every child has a talent and if you were to suppress it and channel it into one area that you want them to do and they don't enjoy that, basically you're going to spoil their life in a sense. So I was fortunate that I was never pushed. I think my dad is proud of me, of what I've achieved and obviously my family is a big reason for my success really. I think that ethos has definitely come from my mum and dad. Again I have been fortunate.

There's one person really that helped me a lot called Walter Joyce, who's passed away now. He used to play for Burnley and I think he managed Burnley for a short spell as well, he's actually a legend in Burnley, and he was at Bury at the time. He moved to Manchester United and he's the one who took me there. But he really saw the talent in me and he said to me, basically encouraged me, and to my father and my brother "Look get him trained up, keep him strong, keep him focused

and he can make it." He was the one person I would say who really gave me a lot of hope in a sense. Because being Asian, you sometimes feel like the odd one out. You go into training and stuff and because people don't understand really, your culture and certain things. So I think, like, you need some backing and he was one that really backed me. Then when I got to Huddersfield it was the academy directors, in particular Jerry Murphy, who again has given me so much support. Through my injuries he could've easily said right, you're always injured, I'm not going to give you a contract, that kind of stuff. But he actually stuck by me and said, "Look I know you've been injured but I have confidence in you, you can do it." That's really why I pushed on. So those two are the main people I would say that really gave me a big help. But there've been so many others along the way.

I think I could've signed for Burnley really. Looking back it would've been better because it's local. But obviously football for me is always part of my life so I'm always following Burnley, seeing how they're getting on. Obviously as a local boy I try and follow it as much as I can and I try and play as much as I can. Football is always with me. In the past, I've had so many Asian people getting in touch to ask for advice, young boys, and that's something that I love to do because I know the difficulties I faced. If I can just help them in any little form or way, then it basically gives me satisfaction and hopefully they can progress further than I did. I was really close to getting to the Premier League and unfortunately, I got injured once I got playing and it didn't happen for me. But if I could help somebody who could get there, then I'm always willing to help.

I mean, every club that I've played for, I made history as the first Asian player to play there. So obviously, that gives me great pride to say that really and especially to be Pakistani, I'm the first ever Pakistani to do that. In the leagues I played in, I think I will be one of the first Pakistanis to ever play there in the league as well. So stuff like that gives me great pride. In the Hungarian Premier League, I went there and I was the first Pakistani to ever play there, so again that's history really, I created history in a sense. Stuff like that, you can't really buy stuff like that, It's just something you're lucky to either get it or not and there's no real value to that, it's just your personal pride. To be honest, I look at football as something that's developed me as a person.

Challenges I faced included racism, and I mean players have said it and especially in some of the games I've played, you're playing in front of big crowds. Stupid people really in a sense, they don't have any direction, they've got no fear, they've got no manners in a sense, no respect, so they'll say anything. To them it doesn't matter what they call you. Unfortunately I've had that. Luckily I've been strong enough to deal with that. I could've gone the other way where you end up trying to fight them. Looking back I should've reported some of the stuff and got it dealt with by the Football Association at the time, but as a youngster you don't really think about it too much, you just get on with it. So those were big hurdles. As a young lad when you hear that, it is quite daunting, you're like, well what's that about? So that's the sad thing really about that. But again you have to be strong to deal with that

and don't let them win. Still, I think there has been a big improvement in football. We can't say there hasn't been. But, I think for Asian players because there aren't many in there, it's a new thing, so it's a different type of racism, say, to what the black players had. I think that has improved tremendously with the black players. When the first black players came through, they had bananas thrown at them. So from those days, of course it's improved. Now I think with the Asian players, the British Pakistani players coming through, I think it's going to be a different type of racism. It's going to religious, Islamophobia is going to come through, which I've felt and seen. To be honest I'm quite strong with my faith so if I was weak minded then I'd go in a shell, but I challenge them and say, well what you're hearing is wrong.

The reward is that you can influence many thousands of people here and in Pakistan as well because obviously I play for the national team there. So I have a big following from over there as well. Of course you get a feeling of satisfaction really when you know that people are looking up to you. Unfortunately with football, when you become a footballer, you're a role model whether you like it or not. And whether you choose to be a good one or a bad one, I mean that's down to the person. I just try to be a good person and hope that people who I do come into contact with, basically they see a good example. I mean the first time, it was quite daunting really. It was in 2007, it seems a long time ago. But it was the World Cup qualifier against Iraq and it just came out of the blue really. It was me and Zeeshan; we were the only professional players. So before that they never really had been in touch. I don't think they really knew about foreign Pakistani players until there was a group of lads from the UK who had started to help the Pakistani Football Federation. They then obviously got in touch and said, okay come down, and obviously we went there. And since then, I've never looked back. I've enjoyed every time we go back home, in a sense, to see, obviously the country that your parents are from, I think it's important people don't lose touch. People say, well you're born here, you should play for England, but I say, obviously, to play for England is very difficult. as my parents were born in Pakistan. So, for an English person who was born in Dubai, this is the question I always ask; if you were born in Dubai would you class yourself as an Arab? And they wouldn't, people class themself as English. I'm saying here that my parents are both from

Pakistan and I class myself as a British Pakistani really.

Normally, we'll do the training and then we'll go to different countries where the tournament is. Luckily, I think I've been to about ten countries at least, through Pakistan, and so there have been some fantastic trips there. That's another perk of being international. I've been to the Maldives, India, and Syria to name a few. You wouldn't really get to go to these types of countries. So for that reason, again it's been a blessing to visit these countries. Whilst we're in Pakistan, we normally stay in Lahore because of security reasons. They always keep us there. Attendance has been good. Obviously we haven't had many home matches to be honest, we've only had about, I would say, two or three in the six years I've been there. The crowds have been good but not brilliant like the cricket, obviously cricket's number one. So hopefully that will change in time. I would say we get a crowd of 10,000 max at the moment. It depends where you are. I believe in Karachi they can get up to 40,000, 50,000, it's quite a footballing place, Karachi is. But for security reasons, we're not allowed to really play there. So in Lahore, normally, we're looking at about 10,000 approximately. As I've played here, I've played with a lot bigger crowds, 40,000 and more. Crowds obviously can make you nervous if it's your first game, it can be quite petrifying to be

honest. But once you're used to it, I mean every footballer will say the same thing. You get on the pitch and you forget what's around you in a sense. That's the same thing with myself. Once you're on the pitch you kind of forget that the crowds are there until after the game. I suppose once you play you kind of blank it out.

I think my plan's always been different. I've never been that dictated to by football. Never been like that. I've always had a plan to go into business, help my father out and that's always been a big ambition for me really, as well as the football. So whilst I was playing in the summertime obviously, we used to get a good month off and I always used to go into the factory, learn things. My plan was always around the age of 27, 28 to go into business. For some reason, I don't know why that was the case, but I've always had that since a young age. I believe football is all well and good but family comes first and I think the business side of things, it's a greater thing really for your family and for looking after your family. Now I'm at the stage where really I'm looking into that side now. I'm very ambitious as well in that I enjoy doing that. I think working for yourself or obviously for your father, your family business, there's no greater feeling to be honest because you're managing your own time, so if you're coming in early or you're finishing late, it's your own time, you're working for yourself. Whereas

sometimes, if it's football, you're working for somebody else and sometimes, I don't like the ethos of certain things and you can't really say anything, you have to do what you're told. I've always had that thing, I like to be my own person, I like to do what I want to do in a sense. I think that's where now, the business side of things, I'm looking forward to doing that and doing my own thing and developing the business side as much as I can. In the long run, what I want to do is set up academies, football academies, not for British Asian players only, but to give them a fairer chance really to come there and play and to see that there is an opportunity to move forward. I think now, it is very limited, to be honest, for British Asian players; they don't know where to go. You speak to many of them they're saying "Well how can I make it, I'm a good player, I'm 16" or they say "Oh so and so's a good player." I ask them the question, where are they playing? Nowhere. That's a common theme.

Why is that? Basically, it's education. They kind of fear, so they don't step out of - it's like a comfort zone. They're in their comfort zone and to step out of that takes a lot of courage. I think a lot of British Asians tend to stay in that comfort zone. It's not just for boys, many tend to stay with their families, tend to stay within their group of friends, and until you come out of that bubble, if you like, you're not going to achieve great things in life. It's a fact. In whatever you do, whether you want to become a doctor or whatever, you have to come out of that environment, you have to push yourself and do that. I think that's what's lacking at the moment; there are not enough British Asian players playing football and British Pakistani players in particular. Unless you've got exceptional talent you're going to find it difficult. I think that's one thing I want to promote, to start playing at a young age, at 10 or 11. Football's that kind of sport that the coaching at that age is exceptional, so if you're missing out on that then you're going to miss out in the long run. That's the reason that eventually I want to set up my own academies. That's where the business side comes in, insha'Allah, that's the ambition I've got, really, for the future.

I got to, I think, about 20 or 21, when people were asking me questions about my religion because of the bad things that happened with September 11th. I didn't know the answers to be honest. I was embarrassed because sometimes when asked, what is the belief? And I didn't really know. Obviously my mother and father tried to instil

in us at a young age but, at school and stuff, the environment you get into, it's quite easy to get out of it. Once I was reading about the Prophet Mohammad's life, that's when you realise the beauty of the message. Everything that I was reading was beautiful. There was nothing that was negative, there was nothing about bombings, and there was nothing about what you hear on the news. When you read that and, that's what I told many of my team mates and stuff, that's what I said to them, I'd give them books to read which were simple books, it's not a case of always forcing anything on anyone. It's just basic knowledge, once you get that, you go yourself and you find certain things. That's when you find out what the truth is. Until you do that, you can't rely on media and stuff like that because I think a lot of the media is negative, let's be honest, you don't hear about the good things in Pakistan. Like, when I was there, I saw there was this athletics day and, obviously, girls were segregated in a sense, but they were doing the running, the boys were doing the running and they were cheering and stuff like that. You won't hear about that, and the unity that I saw that day. Stuff like that obviously, going back, I was really happy to see that in Pakistan. I was looking and I was thinking, you never see anything like this in the news, these kids smiling and stuff like that. But going back to the faith again, when you find out things for yourself you see the beauty of it. When you really believe in something and you find it out yourself, not just because your parents have told you to do it; and that's one thing I am, I don't do it because somebody's told me to do it, it's like literally, it's like a new finding for me in a sense. Most of the British born Muslims, we are born Muslims, it doesn't mean that we really know what it means to be a Muslim. We're all born and we all say we're Muslim. That's when you have to go out and find what it means to be a Muslim. Then when you find, like the book I read is a book called, I remember it clearly, it's called Tell Me About Mohammad and that book was for kids, but I read it and it was beautiful so I recommend that to many people who don't really know about Islam or, basically, when they're like myself where they're looking to come into the religion or want to learn about it. That book is brilliant; it is basically about the life of the Prophet and at the time of the Prophet in Medinah, how it was in Makkah, the beauty of the people around and the message. It was so simple, something so simple that it really hit me then. I felt it was beautiful, and everything that I was thinking about it was wrong. And that's the thing. Once you see that, then it's like a jigsaw really, pieces coming together. Then I remember at that time I used to listen to Yusuf Islam who was Cat Stevens, I got a CD as well because, obviously, I was into my music as well and another way of going is like listening Nasheeds. Some of Yusuf Islam's songs really appealed to me because I like philosophy and it's how I look at life. When you see things that you relate to you think, hang on, right, that's for me. I think from that moment, I really took to it. It's a gradual step and no Muslim's ever perfect, you never really will be to be honest. But you gradually try to be the best person you can be, you try and pray on time, obviously it's not easy at times but you try and do the basics that you can do. I remember once I started to pray, I actually got into the first team which was literally three months later. Straight away I saw the results. The benefit that I get from that is that basically you don't react to things in a negative sense, you don't think, oh why me, oh why has that happened to me? You always think that it's happened for a reason, it's a blessing why it's happened. That's important. I think many people don't see that. They'll say well God hasn't given me this, or I'm not happy, I'm not going to pray, why should I pray?

To be honest, what I see in this country is something special. Law and order, what's here, is by far the most transparent country and a country with great law. Whatever happens, you're accountable for and the justice system is fantastic. I was born and bred here, I see it as home. Definitely, without a doubt, I would say it is home. I'm proud to say that because of the country itself, what they actually provide as a nation to all their communities, not just to Pakistanis to everyone, is justice. In many countries that I've been to, the infrastructure, justice, you can see that it's not there. People are getting away with things and bribery and stuff like that is rife in other countries and you can feel that when you go to many countries really. Whereas the UK, you don't feel that, you feel, there are a lot of beautiful things in this country so we should be proud of that and feel lucky and be grateful for what we've got.

Chapter 16 - Private sector

Transport

Nazia Khan

Above: Nazia Khan a Law graduate and first Pakistani Pathan commercial pilot in Burnley

Below left: Nazia Khan with her dad, Younis Khan

My name is Nazia. I was actually born here in Burnley. My father used to be in business, and he used to own a café but he's since retired. My mother was a housewife all the time. They came in the 1970s. I went to school at Walshaw High School; it's called Sir John Thursby Community College now. I went to college, then I went to university and I studied law. I graduated obviously, in law, and then carried on practising law. After I did 'A' Levels I wanted to go into journalism but I didn't think I'd have the confidence. Then I got interested in law. I got quite high grades in law which persuaded me to get into that field but then I left because I wanted to pursue being a pilot.

I've always wanted to do something regarding piloting, but I thought it was something that wouldn't be easy to get into for a normal person like myself. But I was determined to get into it, perhaps I should have gone into piloting from day one but it had just been a childhood dream. I'd always wanted to, when I was little, but I thought it's something that you dream about - it's like saying I want to win the lottery, something that's never really going to happen. Then suddenly I started investigating, I started looking into it and I realised it was for normal people, you can do it if you're more determined, and I was obviously. You need determination and money, and fortunately I had both. I did my training in Greece, not here, because of the weather here. We fly in small aircraft; the weather does matter, and obviously in England the weather's always depressing, it's raining. It's not suitable for flying, not for learning to fly. I thought, I've been to Greece quite a number of times, and I love it there, so I found a school there and that's when I just went for it. The other option was to go to America, which is a lot cheaper but because it was really far away, I couldn't come home whenever I wanted to and because I've never been abroad alone, I've always had someone with me. When I did get there, on the first day I thought, oh my God, why did I do this, but like I said I was really determined to become a pilot, and I did it. It wasn't something I expected because I thought it would all be about flying, and wasn't prepared for the Crown exams. There are ten exams for the CPL, Commercial Pilot Licence.

It took me about a year, now actually I'm trying to progress further and get the ultimate licence which is ATPL, Airline Transport Pilot's Licence and I'm finding that really, really challenging. But I'm enjoying it as well. That means that I will be qualified to pilot the Boeings 747s and I'll have more options, it'll open more doors for me. I've always wanted to get the ultimate licence, or, say it's a degree or whatever it is, I have to go for the main one. That's what I'm doing at the moment. It is quite hard, like I said, the Crown exam it's not just about flying. I always say, what you need to become a doctor, meteorologist etc, you need to be good at physics, maths, everything. It's really hard because I'm not good at maths or physics, I find it extremely dull. But you have to know it, you can't just learn it, you have to know it and understand it.

Above: Nazia Khan's dream comes true. She is in the cockpit learning the skills to be a pilot

Right: Nazia Khan's father on his return from Hajj (pilgrimage) enjoying a warm welcome from friends and family

I love the practical side of flying. The first time I was taking the aircraft, I was all over the place because I was trying to control it like a car. Obviously it's not a car and it's totally different, but I got the hang of it and then after about 17 hours in the aircraft I went solo, which means you don't have the instructor with you. There's nobody with you and you have to do a touch and go landing, everything alone. It's really scary, but I just pretended to myself there was someone sitting with me. Because I'm quite religious as well, have faith in God, I said I'm not dying here, because you have to be calm, you can't be panicky. It's all about yourself basically, even if the engine fails, you can control it if you don't have that fear. It's not going to be easy not having any fear, if you're in that situation. The hardest part is the actual solo navigation. Oh my God, it's hard!

We fly under VFR which means visually you have to see the ground as well. So you see everything, but everything's quite small. You have to base it on charts and maps so you have to be a good navigator to fly. You see everything but you're obviously looking from up in the air. I love it. There's a saying, 'Once you fly; you will walk with your eyes skyward.' So yes, it's fun. I was always thinking I'm not going to be happy not having

lived my dream, and most people are still chasing their dreams, I wanted to be one of those people who leaves this world having lived their life properly. And I say properly, in terms of living their dream.

The family wasn't too thrilled about the safety element but because of all the negatives, I was more determined. My father didn't know. I wanted to keep it a secret. I wanted to surprise him. My mother knew, she said she wasn't happy but she wouldn't stand in my way because it was something I wanted to do, the rest of my brothers and sisters knew about it as well. After I finished my skill test, when I'd completed everything, I phoned my family but no one picked up the phone. Finally, I got through to my sister-in-law and I said, you can break the news to everyone now, I'm actually a pilot. That's when she told my father, and he's like, no, how did that happen? I thought she was doing something to do with the law. I'm not proud of myself but I did lie, I said I'm doing something to do with law. But I wouldn't really talk about it because, obviously, it was nothing to do with law, and he fell for it. I know, he was shocked, but he's happy. He's really proud; it's really rare to make him proud. But he is really proud, you can see it. Amazingly they are so happy for me, I'm getting everyone congratulating me. I didn't realise the reaction would be this big, you feel like a celebrity without really being one, feels quite good.

Quite a few young people have approached me saying that it's something they would like to get into as well, and asked me what they should be looking at. I said, the first thing is family life, safety, and of course determination to succeed, as well as money. You spend thousands. Pathans, those from the North West Frontier of Pakistan, are very strict and they focus more on the men, well they used to, and for a girl having achieved something like I have - I think it's woken them up a bit. The Pathan part of the Pakistani community in Burnley responded well too. I didn't expect them to be this happy for me, but I think it's woken them up a bit as well having a woman, a Pathan woman, achieve something like this. I was saying this to my mother the other day, because the focus is always on the men, whether we like it or not. I think most of them are helping their own daughters now, into whatever they want to do, not piloting of course, but I think they're more open-minded.

But now they're looking at me and they're saying, if she can go and do something like this, so can others. Parents are encouraging, and it's quite good. I believe in studying further, I don't think you should stop, I believe in a good education. I'm glad that it helps others. A mother actually told my mother that she was having big problems

Above: Nazia Khan ready to fly

with her daughter wanting to go away to study further, but she wasn't too happy about that. And my mum said, well, look at my daughter, I am so glad that she has done what she's done. My mother wasn't really happy at the time because of concerns for my safety in the air. Since then, the daughter has gone to university and the mother did say to us that it was because of me; she had thought why not? I think it's good that other people are learning from this and using this as an example to go further.

I'm a Muslim obviously, and I try to be a good Muslim, which means I try to pray and give a lot to charity; I'm part of quite a number of charities in fact. I paused halfway into my piloting, because I always fear for my life to be honest with you. A lot of people say there are more accidents on the roads. But when you are in the air, you're always scared that you might not make it to your destination and I thought, I don't know what's going to happen to me. So I left everything; I came back to England and I persuaded my father to do Hajj with me, the pilgrimage a Muslim

Below: Nazia Khan clad in Ihram (Hajj dress) in the Khaana Ka'aba (House of Allah) in Makkah

has to perform at least once in his or her life. I thought I might as well do it whilst I'm young and I did.

My father and mother both went last year. Wonderful, I'd like to go there again. It was like, this year I wish I could go but because I'm studying further it's not possible. I'm so glad I went there; it's amazing, because I'm young and more active than most people, who go when they're quite old. The only thing I would like to say is if anyone wants to pursue their dream, it is possible. They should go and do it because whether it's piloting, law, anything, I think it's all down to you. And nothing is impossible, I actually believe that.

Chapter 16 - Public sector

Utilities

Mohammad Younas

My name is Mohammad Younas. I was born in Kashmir in 1953. I came from Pakistan, initially, at the age of 12 and I was actually reading in seventh class in Pakistan when I came over here. I started schooling

over here and continued for about 14 months before I left school and started a career. I went to a school in Derbyshire called Arlington Secondary School and when I completed school I left with a basic secondary education.

It wasn't my intention to come and settle in Burnley, I qualified as a civil engineer and throughout my career I worked in various places starting with Bury Council, Preston Council, South Liverpool Council and, of course, ended up with Burnley Council so I decided to move to Burnley as well to be near work. At the moment I am a network engineer for United Utilities for the North of England. Basically, we supply water and take water away and treat it before we take it back to the river. The things that go on in-between, we look after them.

My memories as a child in this country were enjoyable. When I came here, it was more of an adventure. I didn't know what I would face. When I started school here, I didn't know any English at all. For the first few months, I was sitting in the classroom trying to pick up the language and basically developed from there. One thing I remember when I came to this country there were a few of our people in the area and they lived together. People came from all sorts of backgrounds but when they came here they were like brothers. They understood each other's needs,

Above: Mohammad Younas secretary and project director of purpose built Ghausia Mosque, on Abel Street Burnley

Left: Mohammad Younas at Arlington Secondary School, Derby

Below: Mohammad Younas in uniform as a cadet (back row, third from the right)

LEADING the parade — the band of No. 126 Squadron A.T.C.

Above: Member of the No.126 Squadron Band (in the middle of second row)

Below: Mohammad Younas in a new suit, on his 21st birthday

playground playing football and hockey and it was very enjoyable.

I was quite lucky, when I left school I had to try different jobs. I ended up getting an apprenticeship with Rolls Royce. So, I think I was one of the very first Asian people lucky enough to train with Rolls Royce. At that time it was hard to get an apprenticeship with Rolls Royce. I had an opportunity to train in all aspects of engineering. Rolls Royce was one of the best training employers in the country; it was a privilege to be a Rolls Royce apprentice. The language was actually a barrier as you can't pick language up overnight, you learn throughout life and I am still learning now.

they helped each other along the way; they put people up when they had no room because of course they were countrymen, they were bound to help each other out.

At that time, in the school that I went to there were only two Asians boys, myself and one other boy and we were treated with curiosity as the young children had not seen many coloured people at that time, or anyone from Pakistan before. Even though we couldn't speak the language, through activities we could actually communicate with other children in the

Part of my success in getting these opportunities was because I think I have always been a very keen and enthusiastic person right from my early beginnings. I went for the test at Rolls Royce and when I did the interview, the interviewer was quite impressed that I could speak two languages because of the fact I had been in the country for a very short period of time and could speak the language - they thought it was very good English. So, I got taken on. I think a positive approach does actually help, being enthusiastic and being forthcoming helps and I think a smile also helps. I think it's something that comes naturally.

There have been some people in my life that I got very close to and who influenced me. They have been very encouraging. One of the people I came across at an early age was a student who came from India; he was over here to do a PhD. One day he asked me "What are you going to do with your life?" So I told him what I was doing and he said, "Later on in your life, do you not want to do something that you could be proud of and say yes, I accomplished this?" It was something in the back of my mind, driving me all the time. I think the aim is to do the best you can, don't just end up in a job and say this is it. You need to push yourself. I think it's a personal drive. You know, we came here to achieve something in this 'other' country where you can achieve your dreams. Education is free, training is free. In fact you get paid for going to college which is not possible in Asian countries. It's basically a gift and you must make the most of it.

Left: Mohammad Younas overseeing construction work for United Utilities

Below: At the opening of the purpose built Ghausia Mosque on Abel Street, with the Mosque Committee Members, third from the left

out why you are getting the flooding and so forth and one of the jobs that I did 25 years ago was on a particular road. There was a fire station and a playground that occasionally flooded and when I joined Burnley Council, my duty was to find the problem and sort it. We did an investigation and ended up laying quite large pipes to deal with the flooding issues. Now that whole complex has been rebuilt. The school has been built where there used to be green fields. We actually created the ideal facilities for them to be able to deal with the problem, by our actions 25 years ago. Now they have come along and made use of the services that I provided at that time. We have this land, it's going to be developed, I said. Now I see there is a school and the fire station has been rebuilt and there is a big housing estate that was built four or five years ago. So it's good to see something that you started and, obviously, other people have come along and they have made use of that. Looking back at that and other jobs, I feel I have achieved something.

Recently, I have become a member of the Ghausia Mosque. I am on the committee as well and we used to occupy a small Masjid on Colne Road. Everybody started talking about building the new mosque 10 years ago and being on the committee, it was my responsibility to see it through and that's another accomplishment which I am proud of. It probably started about six years ago, a time when we were lucky to acquire a former working men's club which actually had a car park attached to it, and we were looking for various possibilities as to what we could do. We decided to use the existing car park to build the new mosque and keep the old building for other uses. We are a very small community, the membership of our Masjid is around 200 people and when we actually started the project, initially I told people it was going to cost us £740,000 to build the mosque, the estimated figure. We ended up using about a

Life itself is a challenge and every day we find different challenges. When I left school I had no recognised qualifications. In those days people used to do GCSEs, CSEs. In secondary school, I didn't actually have an opportunity to gain recognised qualifications such as GCSEs. I left school at the age of 15. My present place in engineering is as an associate member in civil engineering. My job is quite important. I am an engineer and we cover most of the North West. It's challenging all the way really. It's something you go through on a daily basis and you take things as they come.

To young people, I would say, be true to yourself and drive yourself. The world has opportunities and you have to go and find them. I think the driving force behind it was that I always wanted to do something all my life through. That is the main thing really. You've got to be ambitious and you need to drive yourself and follow it. I have seen this myself it's the way things have developed and accepting the challenges of life to make progress regardless. When I came to Burnley, I was behind the completion of several engineering schemes throughout the borough. Basically, you are taking away all the problems. If you get flooding in this area, you go and find

Above: Mohammad Younas (in white cap) with some friends from Burnley, observing the devastation caused by the earthquake in Kashmir, Pakistan in 2007

£1,000,000 and everyone who sees the mosque seems to admire it. It was actually an achievement for the community itself. We did have to go to cities to raise funds, but the Burnley community did 95% of the funding.

Unfortunately, the economic situation is a challenge for the youngsters these days. They are finding it quite difficult, not only our Asian youths, but the white locals as well. Things are not as good economically as they used to be. We try to encourage young people to be part of the masjid. If they become part of it, at least you are trying to help hundreds of them, something we should all be doing. So, for example, they could be on a street corner, smoking, and we are trying to discourage them from doing this. We have an existing community centre which provides facilities that encourage them to come and mix with others. There is of course, a football club as well at our masjid centre. We are encouraging youngsters to take part in the wider community as well. A masjid is at the heart of our society and is a place of meeting for the whole of the community. It's fascinating to hear the importance of the masjid to people so clearly and it's good to hear it from different voices. We don't have social clubs, and we don't go to

pubs. It keeps us close and brings us together so it plays an important role in society. I have been putting more time in to it, basically all my spare time. I don't play games, I don't watch TV, I just go to the masjid and play my part. I believe in doing something good for somebody else. To be honest, that comes from our faith. It teaches us to do things for other people. Don't just think of yourself. I would like to see my son following in my footsteps but that may take some time because he is busy with his own life. He is going to university soon. He has started his career. So I am hoping one day he will follow in our footsteps.

You guide your children when you have an opportunity because you don't have them for long, when they become 16, you lose them. So you've got to make the most of it and so I made sure I made the most of it when he was young. I took him to masjid, in the evening in Ramadhan, in Jum'ah and so on and so forth. I set a path for him to follow. When a father and son spend time together and when you go to mosque together, you go home together then you can discuss at home together how you liked certain things, like a particular lecture by the Imam and so on.

When I was younger one of my uncles had a

big impact on me and his words are still at the back of my mind. He said "If you had a donkey you release it in the morning, it will go all day, feed itself and it will come back full. And if you are going to do the same thing, just look after yourself, you are no better than the donkey. Even if the donkey has a full stomach it can't think of others." I thought that was a very powerful statement and that's why I always made sure that my extended family was taken care of.

I have seen Islam as very important in life. It teaches us things that maybe we tend to forget. It brings us closer to our Allah and of course, at the end of the day, what brings us closer to our Allah is our masjid, our community. One rewards the other. Our community depends on Islam and Islam depends on our community. Both things go hand-in-hand. The way I look at it, I was in Pakistan for 12 years and now I have been here nearly 40 years, Burnley is my home now. My useful life, I have spent it in this country. So I see myself as a British Pakistani even though I was born in Pakistan, all my youth has actually been spent here and my family is here.

Left: Mohammad Younas in the garden at home with his first child

Below: Mohammad Younas with his wife, children and grandchildren

Chapter 17 - Third sector

Voluntary, Community, Faith and Youth

Maulana Abuzar Afzal

Above: Maulana Abuzar Afzal is the first homegrown English speaking Imam at Abu Bakr Mosque, Brougham Street, Burnley

My name is Abuzar Afzal. I was actually born in Copenhagen, Denmark in January 1985. I moved here quite young, so I can't really remember too much. My father was mainly in the property development business, where he basically bought and sold properties over the years. My father came here in the early '70s. There was actually quite a lot of work, a lot of mills at that time. We had relatives here as well, so when they came over and people said that there's a lot of work in this area, gradually, we settled down in Burnley.

I attended Barden Junior School. I went to nursery school, primary and junior school in Burnley. I grew up here, lived here and now I'm working here. The school's been demolished now but I used to go back every now and then; I had a rapport with the teachers, I would talk to them. I kind of reflect and look back at things, in order to positively contribute towards the community. I do go back to my roots and I remember the school times and playing areas and dinner breaks and things. I actually went to a boarding school in Bolton. It was called the Jamia Islamia. It was a private college where I did further studies in Islamic theology and Arabic syntax. So I studied for six years there in Bolton and then graduated with a scholarship in Islam. Everything I do is more or less around faith. Islam basically, is everything to me.

What I find motivates me is I like to help people. People come to me at difficult times because of my position in the community, an Imam in the mosque. A lot of vulnerable people, a lot of elderly people, mixed people, young, old, come to me so I try and adapt to everyone and help everyone. One of the most important factors of being a Muslim is that you help people, you realise the values of other people, you learn to treat other people with respect and kindness and this is what the teachings of Islam are based

on. The Prophet, peace be upon him, came to this world. This was one of the leading factors – that he was known as trustworthy, he was known as kind, he was known as truthful, before he was actually granted Prophethood. People will recognise him with these titles - that he is truthful, he is helpful, he is the most kind, and he is the most generous. Obviously as a Muslim I would like to follow in the footsteps of our Prophet, peace be upon him, and living in this day and age I find it is very seldom that people want to actually help others or to be of any use to other people. I feel that it's my responsibility as a community leader and member of the community so I try and play my role in helping the society and helping the community. That is very important to me because obviously I feel that if I am spending my life in a good way and I'm helping other people, then my life is of value, and I'm not wasting my life. I feel that I'm spending my time wisely and I'm valuing my own life which Allah has given to me.

To actually lead a congregation in prayer, to reciting the Qur'an in prayer with a congregation of 500-plus people behind you is a great honour and I feel that it's a great responsibility as well. It's just the actual position that I'm in, that I've been put into. It matures you; you seem to feel situations more deeply. You have to deal with different people, with different temperaments and moods and it's all a part of a learning experience of life really. This is the mission of my life more or less. I take it as part of my life and a part of my life I wanted to do and part of my ambitions and my objectives. This is what I wanted to do from day one, and I have a good life - all praise be to Allah that I am in this field and I am doing what I wanted to do. I feel that it's a duty of every person to help and value others, and obviously ourselves as Imams and community leaders, we are examples to the people, and the people then follow in the footsteps of the leaders, so we try and live and do everything according to what Islam has said. To understand Islam truly, we can't just always go back to the media or what the media is saying, but truly to understand Islam you need to look at the life of the Prophet, peace be upon him, and then the life of his followers; how they lived, and even in this day and age we have people who are truly Muslims, and those true Muslims are those who are generous, kind and helpful. We need to actually look at Islam, not through the eyes of the media, but through the eyes of Islam itself.

It's very easy for us to relate to our youngsters when we come from a religious point of view. I've seen this with our youth, especially in Burnley, they are motivated. There are numerous examples as I meet a lot of the youngsters. Sometimes in the subway at the bottom here, outside the Jinnah Centre, and sometimes they're actually on the canal, consuming alcohol, drugs etc and all the bad habits. Obviously I do talk to them from a religious point of view and I do say to them that, as Muslims, we are not even allowed to consume one drop of alcohol because it contaminates the mind and it contaminates the body, and a person loses control of his body and then certain accidents happen, or certain things are said, which are not done or said when a person is in his total senses. That's why our Prophet, peace be upon him, said that as Muslims we are not allowed to drink or consume even a drop of alcohol and thereafter drugs as well, anything that intoxicates you is forbidden for a Muslim because as Muslims we have to keep our senses clear.

Below: Maulana Abuzar Afzal sitting with book in hand talking to a fellow delegate at a meeting of the faith leaders

With the youngsters, I feel that when we come from this point of view and we tell them about the teachings of the Prophet, and we tell them about the teaching of the Qur'an - it really does help because they start coming to the mosque and they start praying and worshipping, and slowly, slowly, we see that they leave these habits behind. There are numerous examples where youngsters have actually turned away from evil and sin. They've changed their lives for the better and then they help other people. They counsel others, they mentor others, become mentors themselves.

This is a positive point about religion, where through religion we can work on these youngsters and get them out of these habits and these drugs that they're stuck into and show them there's more to life, there's a future for them. Rather than not doing anything, you can actually become something or become someone who then can be an example for others for many, many years to come. I say to them that, for example, the Prophet, peace be upon him, came over 1400 years ago and still he is an example for every person today, like myself. I would look back at the life of the Prophet and he came at a time when there were no rights for women, people in that culture were burying their own daughters alive. But when the Prophet came, he taught them the values of life. He told them that your women are a part of you, you must treat them with kindness, you must provide for them. You must feed them, you must clothe them. Your children are part of your life. Girls and boys all come from God, so the values of life were taught to them and that's when they became followers of the Prophet and then slowly, slowly, from generation to generation, this passed over until this same religion came to us and the Qur'an itself; it's been over 1400 years. Not a letter of the Qur'an has been changed in any way or been diluted in any way. It's been preserved, and just like it was recited in those days, the Qur'an is still recited in this day and age. Just like it motivated and moved people in those days, when the Qur'an is recited today it still motivates and moves people emotionally and this is the biggest thing that we hold onto. This is where we derive our spiritual guidance, spiritual nourishment as they say, by reciting the Qur'an and we see that in the youngsters. At first they struggle; it's very hard, or more or less close to impossible, to actually recite or want to recite something or repeat something which you don't understand. The Qur'an is such a book, it's in Arabic and Arabic is not our mother tongue. Yet we see over and over again that youngsters will keep reciting repeatedly and they'll feel a kind of pleasure in reciting, yet they don't understand what they're reading. But still they'll want to read it all, over and over again. What we do then is try, we have the Qur'an translation and youngsters read the translation as well and try to understand what the Qur'an is trying to say to them. The Qur'an is full of guidance, models, etiquettes and slowly, slowly, it seeps into their hearts and before you know it, a youngster has changed his ways. Now he becomes a valuable person whereas before nobody looked at him; now he's become an example, a role model for his friends, for his family, for his community and he's referred to for that reason. I feel Islam is used in a positive way and when I've heard a youngster or person becomes more practising, then he realises the value of life, realises the value of a person, realises the value of being a human being. In a way, in the Qur'an, we are first told to become human beings. Then after, we are Muslims, but first we are human beings, where we have to value life and today we see that life is not valued, we're at each other's throats all the time and there are so many killings going on, and so many murders, because life is not valued. We don't take human beings as human beings, and life is not worth anything. But first, we have to build ourselves to a level where we can actually value life and value another human being, and this is where care and kindness come into it. Thereafter, we have Eman, we have faith in God, in the Qur'an, in the Prophet Mohammad, peace be upon him, and we are told to follow the ways of God, the ways of the Prophet Mohammad, peace be upon him. Then we have an objective in mind, we have life after death. So Islam teaches us many things and then, when we are living, we are actually living with an objective in mind, and we have got so much more. So with the youngsters, when they realise these things, then they change their bad ways, you know, and they come onto the correct way. And this is what we want for every person; that they leave the evil and they turn towards the good.

Obviously those who are Muslims but have deviated or gone away from the straight path, they read the Qur'an, translation of the Qur'an, and they come back onto the path. In Burnley itself, we've had many youth programmes when scholars come from out of town and talk to the congregation. We've even had events here in the

Jinnah Centre where we've called meetings, even with the local Council, for example, the police and local school teachers, where we actually open ourselves up to the rest of the community and people have positively contributed, and we've had positive feedback from the members of the community as well.

When I think of my roots, obviously my roots are in Pakistan. I have relatives in Pakistan. I have a great love for Pakistan. In Pakistan it's a different lifestyle, it's a different culture to here. So it's nice to sometimes come out of the routine that you live in and go back to a village lifestyle where you find chickens and hens and sheep and lambs running around. So it is quite interesting. It's quite different, and obviously, more sunshine! But Burnley is where I grew up. This is where I attended school and I know the people. Burnley is what I consider my home.

Above: A group photograph of Muslim and Christian faith leaders on a visit to Westminister with Kitty Usher MP. Maulana Abuzar Afzal standing far left

Voluntary, Community, Faith and Youth

Alamzeb Khan

Above: Alamzeb Khan is a community, youth and faith leader and secretary of Abu Bakr Mosque, Stoneyholme, Burnley

Below: Alamzeb Khan sitting (left) on the floor of Heasandford Primary School with his classmates

My name is Alamzeb Khan. I was born in 1975 in Pakistan, in a small village called Waisa, which is in Attock, near Islamabad. My parents, my father came to this country a long while ago. Probably one of the first Pakistani people that arrived in Burnley, he used to work in the steel foundry. First he went to Sheffield; he used to work in the steel mills in Sheffield. His friends were in Burnley and they invited him here, so when he arrived here there was a lot of work here as well, there were a lot of mills in Burnley. So he used to say that he would go to the mills and, for example, you were working in one job that day, you could go to another employer and there would be work there, there would always be work, so Burnley was a thriving place for work at the time. His friends were here so he felt comfortable. Then a lot of his relatives also came here; Burnley became a place where a lot of my family came to and they have been here since the 1960s.

I went to Stoneyholme Nursery, and then I went to Stoneyholme Primary School for 3 years. We moved houses and we lived up at Harle Syke. Then I went to Thursby Road School. I remember there were only two Asians in the whole school, me and another guy called Zahid. That was an experience because I came from a school where it was like 90% Asians, Stoneyholme, and then I went to Heasandford; it was a bit of a shock but I could handle it, it was no issue. I lived in an area that was predominantly white, as well as moving from Stoneyholme where it was all Asian to an area where all of my friends then were English lads and I used to associate with them without any problems, but it was a bit different, it was a learning curve actually.

When I left school, I went to college, Burnley College and I did a BTEC in business and finance, I got a merit in it actually. Then I applied to go to university and that was in 1995 I think, so I got my place at Preston UCLan and I was going to do business management. But I was only there 4-5 weeks and then unfortunately my father passed

away. That was in 1995, I was only about 21years old. We had a business as well a shop my brother used to run and he needed help, so I couldn't carry on with my studies because I had to help him. In a way, I kind of sacrificed my studies for the family business but looking back, reflecting, it was a good thing I was with my elder brother. He had a lot more responsibilities after my father passed away, so I was kind of helping. I was very young, very naive, it was a good thing because it made me mature at a young age. I had a lot more responsibilities; my family, my mother, my sisters. Before, I never used to even think, everything was normal; my dad was alive everything was good but when something like that happens, the responsibility it comes on you and you realise – you think I have to step up, so Alhamdulillah I did, and it was good. I worked in the shop and my brother was the boss for a few years. After about 5 years I took over the business, I ran it for 6-7 years, I made good money, I used to have a good life style, so I have no regrets but I didn't go back to study.

One day what happened was, Mr Malik saw me. He's a good family friend and he says to me, what are you doing with yourself? I said, oh I'm happy, content; I am providing for my family with my little business. He said you could do more, come to Jinnah and work part-time for just a few hours, so I did. That was in 2006 so I've been here 5-6 years now at Jinnah. When I started I was very raw. I was used to the community dealing because I've had a shop and in a shop, to be honest, you're like an agony aunt. People come in with their problems, so I used to know everything that was happening in the community because people used to come and tell me; a little corner shop – it's amazing. When I came to Jinnah I realised that most of these same people, because it was in the community, are the same people. Slowly, it took me a bit of time to get used to things but with the guidance of my peers, Mr Malik and others, I got it, it became so natural and now it's absolutely really easy and I'm really comfortable with it.

When I think about the influences in my life, I think in my family we've always kind of been business men, my father had a café on Standish Street in the '70s and my mum used to say he used to earn so much money that he used to hide it under the carpet. That was in the 1970s. His brothers helped him, and then we had a shop on Burn Street in the '80s. My dad ran that for about 10 years and then, obviously, there are the shops that I run. So I think in the whole family we've always had the business-minded approach. I

know when I was growing up my father used to say to me, these shops, I'm not worried about the money, I realise I want to know where you guys are, so in a way it was to keep us safe. I used to go to work, my brother used to be at work, so when we were not at home we'd be at the shop. He felt very comfortable because it is dangerous for kids to grow up in such surroundings. Some get side-tracked, peer group pressure and all the rest, especially the alcohol. Alhamdulillah, I survived all of that because I was at work and my father, I remember him saying you know, when we used to have a quiet day for example, "The sales were down this month" my mum would ask my dad, he'd say "Ooh the business, oh I'm not bothered about the business, do you know where your sons are?" She'd say "Yes", he'd say "That's all I care about." So thinking about that, I realise the idea was to keep us busy and occupied and I've got that mind-set now. When I'm not at Jinnah I'll keep myself busy, I'm not in the limelight, I'm doing my own thing and that in a way keeps you out of trouble. I've got kids now Alhamdulillah, I want to teach them, same kind of philosophy. My parents were very, very strict, I'm Pathan in origin and generally our families are a bit stricter. Back then when we were growing up, it was like 25-30 years ago, so I think their mind-set was of the Pakistani ideas but now, obviously, I've been brought up here. I was one year old when I came to England and I've been to Pakistan a few times but it's for no longer than a couple of months, my home is here. When I go to Pakistan and I'm sitting on a plane, I can't wait to get there but after a few weeks, after about a month, I want to get back home. Home is Burnley and obviously my parents are here, my mum's here, my sisters are here – immediate family – so it feels like home. Every weekend my sisters will come to my house on a Saturday and Sunday. It's like a youth club, masha'Allah we've got about 20 kids roaming the house and my mum, I can see her, she's so happy. I think their happiness comes at that age from the kids, it kind of gives them an extension of life and it gives them that motivation, so Alhamdulillah they're happy and content.

In terms of faith, I wasn't really a practising Muslim before, what I mean by practising was I never used to read my namaaz regularly, I used to read one Jum'ah on a Friday. I used to try and make myself go to Jum'ah every Friday because I felt I had to. I didn't really have interest in the religion but in 2010, when Mr Malik went to Hajj that year I went as well. It was just a coincidence, we didn't plan it like that but in March 2010, I went to Umrah, so Umrah is not Hajj, it's not compulsory. So when I went to Umrah, I saw Allah's house for the first time, in March, and I was amazed, it did something to me that nothing has ever done before. When we pray in front of the Kabbah, it's just when you see that in front of your eyes, the black cloth around it, the smell coming off it, it's amazing. When I saw that the first time, before I went they'd say to me, whatever you do, whatever you wish for, when you see the black stone it comes true, so I said to myself oh Allah bring me back here frequently and bring me back this year for Hajj. Allah works in mysterious ways. I thought to myself, my religion is true because one thing I firmly believe is that Islam, it tells you to question it, because it has all the answers; if it doesn't have the answers then it's not your religion.
So all this was an experience for me and I believe, on a very serious note, that our purpose in life is not to earn money because everybody earns money, it's about finding God in your own way.

I'd like to think my dad would be very happy with me if he was here today. He was a very simple guy but sincere. Today he'd be very happy because to be honest he was also a people person, he used to help people. I realised that, growing up in my family, the front room of our house used to always be occupied and my mum used to be cooking for ever. I used to think who is here now; people from Sheffield, people from London and this was frequent, every weekend and in the evenings. Then when we had the shop, my dad used to sit upstairs and he had made a nice little area for himself and every single day, people used to come in from all over, relatives, friends. Then I realised that these people have been here since the '60's and '70's. They've been friends, they've lent each other money, money's a valuable thing, nobody gives it to you. My mum was telling me that where we live on Clive Street, we didn't have much money so dad's friends paid for the house. I was thinking I wouldn't pay for a friend's house now - I wouldn't get it back! So they had so much trust and everything between themselves, it was amazing. If my dad was alive today, he'd be happy because he was a religious guy. I remember growing up, and going to the mosque with him at the age of six or seven, so it was normal. Our routine was kind of a religious routine in our homes, so he'd be proud, he'd definitely be proud. Obviously I've got kids and everything's moved on, so it would be a good thing if he was here but some things are not meant to be.

When I came to Jinnah Development Trust, I had no idea. I used to be a shopkeeper and my motivation in a way was money, and I used to earn money and I was happy. When I came to Jinnah, in the beginning it took me time to learn everything to be computer literate. I went to college and it had been 10 years since I used a computer, just basic things. So it was funny, because when I started, even typing used to take me forever and Mr Malik used to say, didn't you go to college? I said, yes, but it was 10 years ago, bring me a till, I know all about a till now, but I forgot how to use a computer. When I started at Jinnah, I remember doing basic courses. I used to go on a Saturday to Burnley College; they've got an adult centre downtown. I remember going at 10 o'clock and the people that were there were absolutely illiterate. I said, I've done a GNVQ to the woman there, as she taught the basics and it came back to me straight away and after

Above: Alamzeb Khan's late father as a young man, in the 50s

Below: Alamzeb Khan's late father with his late brother, Wasil Khan

a few sessions I was back to normal. I first met all of these council executives types; all of these in my mind, big people. I used to think they were. They all used to come in for a meeting. Mr Malik used to say to me, "Can you take the minutes?" I used to be petrified. I used to think, oh no, what if they ask me a question? They all used to come in their suits, it was a big thing. I realise today, now when I sit in these meetings, sometimes for a second I just reflect and I remember, and I think about when I started I was a nervous wreck then I look to where I've got to today and like anything, I think any trade, any business, anything, you have to give it time and with experience it becomes absolutely normal.

Now I've become a lot more confident. I want to help the community, masha'Allah I'm doing a lot of work with the mosque, we've done a lot of work with the mosque through Jinnah. The organisation called the Burnley Council of Mosques was organised by Jinnah. I actually registered it as its own charity; all of this stuff I never did before, all of these are learning curves. So we registered it as a charity, we made a constitution for it. We changed the management committee of the mosque, of Abu Bakr Mosque. It's been there for 15-16years, the management were all the old school, they never had a public meeting, and they never had any finance income statements or expenditure statements displayed in the mosque. Don't get me wrong, it ran beautifully like it did. So, what happened was, after 15-16 years, Mr Malik he was like mainly in charge of it, he said we needed a change, so anyway we've introduced a 12-member management committee, who are younger, 30 plus, 35 plus and the work that we've done in the two years since the management committee has changed is amazing. We've got a new front end, the front part of the mosque which we did exclusively for the ladies so they can use it as a community hub as well. They can come in, do what they have to do. They teach them the basics of Islam on a Saturday and Sunday now, from A to Z, because we realise that life is busy, and what you've learnt in childhood doesn't necessarily mean that you

remember it now, so let's go back to basics. There's no need to be shy, lets learn the basic stuff from the beginning again; so we're doing that for the ladies. The mosque is acting as a community centre as well, that's what we want; I think that's the idea behind a mosque. We've just built new classrooms upstairs, four brand new classrooms, new rooms, new carpets, everything's getting refurbished. All of the Maulanas are young, all the teachers are young, and they've all been CRB cleared. They realise they're all complying with the new laws, we brief them about them; obviously stuff like you can't hit a kid, no, they all know about that and other issues. We've never had a problem; they've all been fire-marshall trained. It's a big thing, the mosque runs very efficiently, even the heating system, everything, on a timing system where it wasn't before. It is a very, very big mosque, so all of the costs and everything, this new committee are putting everything into place and it's making sense. I think, so far so good, we have achieved a lot and Insha'Allah hopefully will carry on.

As I said before in terms of home, when I go back to Pakistan, I feel a sense of attachment because our families are there, our roots are there. My father, when he passed away, we've actually buried him in Pakistan because that was one of his wishes. He wanted us to do that for him. So, we did that and when we go there, the first thing we do is go to his grave. So it's a sense of yes, I need to go there anyway because I've got something there and secondly, my uncles are there, we've got family houses there, so I think even if somebody doesn't want to be part of that culture, they are. When I go back, I feel very happy when people talk about my father so I feel a sense of belonging. But like I said, after about 6 - 7 weeks, my heart is saying to me, get back to Burnley, get back home. When I'm on that plane and it touches down in Manchester, I feel yes, I feel that I'm home. I feel comfortable.

Voluntary, Community, Faith and Youth

Nasreen Malik

My name is Nasreen Malik. I was born in Lahore. I went to school there and when I left school I got married. I came to Britain in December 1965. My brother and a few friends were here so my husband and I decided to stay with them.

Mainly, my life has been all about working as a volunteer. My husband was working in all these volunteer roles so I was involved in it too and helping him. And then we formed an association, the Pakistan Women's Association, in 1977 because we thought we needed to have a forum where we could all be together and get out of our houses and have a bit of freedom from the children! And also, to get together and feel less isolated. In the '60s, we were amongst the first Pakistanis to come to Burnley; we were only two, three families at that time. I was elected as the chairperson. We've been working since then. We've been working for charities as well, all the fundraising we did from different functions like the Eid Party or Pakistan Day, we gave to different charities and especially to the Mayor's charity fund.

For over 30 years we've always helped the people, all people, because my husband was a councillor and all English, all Asian community came to get help from him. So it's like helping your own town, isn't it? So it's Burnley, and whoever makes up Burnley, we wanted to help them all and that's why the Mayoral charity was a key way to make a contribution. I was already working to help the ladies; when somebody had to go to hospital and needed an interpreter for schools or social services, anything. So I did interpretation for other ladies that had come from Pakistan.

I learnt English in Pakistan but when I came here it took nearly three months before I could speak English. It's the first necessity. I didn't go to any college or get tutoring, but I learnt it from

television. All of a sudden I realised I could understand them. Over time, I was involved in nearly everything; that included schools, I was also Labour Party executive member in Burnley, I was on the Racial Equality Council's Executive and I was a JP as well. I think I wanted to know the system, how it worked. Also I wanted to be involved a bit more in my adopted country's justice system, and to know what goes on with the people who commit crimes. I think it was a wonderful experience. There was one other Pakistani woman doing this back then. I think it was making me feel more at home by involving myself more in this country and in this area. It was like a sort of community work because it's done voluntarily. I thought I must do as much as I can to be involved. I'm sure that people felt

Above: Nasreen Malik was the first Pakistani 'First Lady' as Mayoress of Burnley, 2000-01, and Chair of Pakistan Women's Association (PWA) since the mid '70s

Below: Nasreen Malik presenting, a cheque for the Mayor's Charity to the Mayor, Irene Cooney and her Mayoress on behalf of Pakistan Women's Association, Burnley

comfortable when they saw me in court. Maybe some of them were ashamed, as well. Oh my God, now Mrs Malik knows! It wasn't nice because they respected me; some of them, they were like my children. I've recognised people in there, which really upset me, but I think it upset them as well that I had found out. I also think it may have helped them to resist from committing illegal activities in the future. You can sit there and you can hand out justice. And you're sure that you're applying justice there, because sometimes when you're not involved in this sort of field you don't know what's going on in the court. That really impressed me a lot about the justice system of this country - that they apply justice quickly and impartially.

Being the Mayoress was a wonderful experience as well. I think it was amazing because I met all the communities this way and I worked a lot for the charity as well. We did a lot of fundraising and we still do through the Association and it's a voluntary organisation. But we do try to help charities. Through that, I went to every corner of Burnley. I must say there were parts I didn't even know that people are living in, I mean I had been living in Burnley for over 35 years, I thought I knew Burnley, but I didn't until I became Mayoress. I was pleased that I was Mayoress for everybody; I think it brought both communities together, closer. Also I enjoyed going to different places and meeting different people.

There are so many memories to tell you the truth, every day we had amazing experiences. But especially when I went to London, to Buckingham Palace; it wasn't the first time, I had been a few times before as well but this was even more wonderful - when we were passing in the Mayor's car, people just looked at the car and said, "Oh, there are Asian people sitting in the car. Who are they?" Oh my God, it was a wonderful experience. Incredible. I think maybe people were surprised, but they must also have been thinking, there is equality in this country. The inaugural day, when I became Mayoress, was the happiest day of my life - after marrying Mr Malik, of course! I used to go to functions, because he was the Mayor and I used to go to the Mayor's parties before that because he was a councillor. I also went to the Mayor's Ball and the Mayor-making ceremony, but I never felt it was so wonderful until my own turn came. Then I realised, oh my God, it's so, so amazing. It was another especially beautiful day when they asked me to make a speech to the Mayoress's Committee. There were around 200 women there, and they were all English ladies. I had to make a speech there in front of them. So I

Left: Nasreen Malik standing between the Mayor and Peter Pike MP, on Remembrance Day in the Peace Garden in 2000

Below: Nasreen Malik selling poppies in the town centre together with the Mayor and an officer of the British Legion

the town centre. I felt a real part of it; that we were doing our share.

I started working first as a factory worker because at that time, you know, there were no jobs in bilingual support. It was a very different experience and hard work and I realised how hard people had to work to earn money. You have to use your hands all the time and I had four children at that time as well. Then I worked as an assistant teacher, a bilingual teacher, in Barden Infant School. That was another wonderful experience. I mainly used to teach Pakistani children because when they start from Reception class, some of them didn't know any English at all and they couldn't even say that they wanted to go to the toilet, they couldn't even ask that. So I was there and I gave them comfort as if they had come out of their house from one mother, and then were looked after by another mother in a different place. Also it was about building their confidence. It was not only them; sometimes English children came to me as well. In Assembly, at the Eid Day party or Christmas parties they used to ask me if I wanted them to read something and I used to ask them to read rhymes or poems in Urdu. I was most amazed that English children were joining in as well. The whole class would do it, even the class teacher would sing with us as well. What made me very, very happy a few times was when I went out of school, after we finished the practise, children would be leaving with their mother, English children, singing all the Urdu rhymes and poems I'd been teaching. I remember them, I remember one little boy doing this and his mum was surprised and puzzled. But he and I knew what he was singing. So he said, "That's Mrs Malik, she's been teaching us all these rhymes."

think the chief executive was next to me and somebody else, important, from Burnley Council. They all had their speeches with them to read, I had nothing in my hand. I thought well, I shall see when the time comes. So when I started speaking, I don't know how I carried on. I carried on and on and on. They cracked up laughing with enjoyment. I didn't know my speech was so funny, but they thoroughly enjoyed it. Then as soon as it was finished, I think I had to give them some prizes as well for the good work that they had done and everybody was saying, "Oh the Mayoress made a beautiful speech," and they told the Mayor, "Oh, the Mayoress – we all had our papers that we were looking at and the Mayoress had nothing in her hands and she made people laugh and they enjoyed it so much." It's just I didn't know I was capable of doing that. It was nice, very nice.

Remembrance Sunday was a very nice experience. I had never been involved like this before. It's generally only the males, who go to where you can put the flowers, in remembrance. But it made me think about how wonderful people had been, and how they gave their lives for their country and that it is important to remember them, every year, on Remembrance Day. To tell you the truth, we had all these wars together. At that time Pakistan and India were together, we had these wars together, England and the other countries. I read all about it in history at school, about India, and I was amazed, all the memories came back with what I read, and we were practically there. I was really blessed that we do remember those days and that time, which is many years ago now, we still remember that these people had done so much for others, to save them, and then they've lost their lives. And we very much appreciate and admire them for their sacrifice. I sold poppies, myself, as well as the Mayor, walking through the town selling poppies to aid the servicemen. That was a lovely experience with people and children coming around us to buy poppies, especially when children were running to say that the Mayor and Mayoress were selling the poppies in

Right: Princess Anne enjoying a joke with Nasreen Malik and Rafique Malik at the Annual Dinner of the Standing Conference of the Pakistani Organisations (SCOPO) in the UK

Right: Princess Anne enjoying a joke with Nasreen Malik and Rafique Malik at the Annual Dinner of the Standing Conference of the Pakistani Organisations (SCOPO) in the UK

Below: Before attending the Queen's Garden Party in July 1977, Rafique and Nasreen Malik visiting Trafalgar Square with their children

One day a long time later, a few girls came to my door and they started singing for Christmas. When I opened the door and gave them some money, they said, "Mrs Malik, do you recognise us?" I said, "No." Then they sang one of the old rhymes I had taught them and said, "Do you remember, you used to teach us all these rhymes."

But what was so stunning about that was because we're talking about something that had happened over 10 years ago, and it was one of my greatest

memories of real integration there. I think it was everybody. It was English children and Asian children. It was really breaking down barriers in a way that even today we struggle to do, lots of organisations struggle to do, and I just thought it was a really powerful memory. I felt that they should understand their mother tongue and their heritage as well as that sense of being British.

My husband and I were invited to the Queen's Garden Party a few times. The first time we went to the Queen's Garden Party, or we were going to meet the Queen, I can't remember exactly, but the local newspapers were waiting for us at Euston railway station. It was a big event, we were going by train and we were a bit late. I think it's maybe the first time in the history of this country that the train had to wait like that. The train had to wait for five minutes! When we reached Euston, the newspapers were taking our photographs and they asked me, "Mrs Malik, what if you'd missed the train, what would you have done?" I said, "Well, we would have got a taxi!" At Euston, there were newspaper journalists, photographers, and TV cameras there as well. They were making a

film of us all the way from Euston to Buckingham Palace. They asked us to go to Trafalgar Square and for our children to get out and feed the pigeons there and they all did. Well, I mean at that time people were looking and they were staring and wondering what was going on. That was actually an amazing experience. At the gates of Buckingham Palace, we had to say goodbye to them. We went inside. In there was the Queen, but then I had dinner with Princess Anne in the Hilton Hotel and honestly that was a wonderful experience. I mean, to talk to her and to be in front of her and have dinner with her - she was Princess. She was so polite, she was so nice and it was amazing. And then I was hoping that I would have a photograph taken with her but my photograph was taken with the Archbishop of Canterbury. It went on the front page of our local English newspapers. Okay, that was nice, I think! All the Ministers and politicians were there; William Whitelaw, Merlyn Rees and David Steele and lots of famous people were there and we all had a meal together. And of course, the Archbishop of Canterbury's wife was there, and it was wonderful.

Actually when I think back, I got married when I was in the last year of school. It was just in matriculation, a few days before I finished. Then I passed the exam. That was so embarrassing; I remember thinking what if I failed it. What would my in-laws say, but it went very well. I passed in the first division and it was wonderful. Then, I came here. I had one friend here; she used to run the post office. That was the only one we had at that time. When she came to our house I didn't understand a word she was saying – her name was Mrs Green, Florence Green. I thought, what is she saying? I couldn't understand. I couldn't even understand 'yes' because she was saying 'yeah' rather than 'yes'. We learned English as a subject in school but I couldn't understand her.

I remember she took me out once and she said something about, oh yeah, in the car. I said car? What is car? Car? I kept thinking. And then she touched her car and she said, car. I said car? You mean car? She didn't pronounce the 'r' because of her northern accent so I couldn't understand. I mean there was so much difference at that time. One day she came and brought me a cake, she made a cake for me, and when she was going I said, "Thanks for coming and thanks for the cake." That was the first full sentence I said in English. I thought, I'll never be able to learn it because I can't understand it but I used to watch

a lot of television. Then suddenly I realised, yes, I can understand what they're saying. And that's how I came to speak this language. I didn't find it difficult at all.

Back then it was a busy time, I think, I had a lot of energy and strength despite bringing up seven children in all, working and volunteering. It was

Below: Rafique and Nasreen Malik at the gates of Buckingham Palace, ready to attend the Queen's Garden Party in 1977

like a fire in me, I had to do something, I had to do something. Especially because my husband was involved in these things and then suddenly, we were both more or less the same, you know, we had exactly the same interests, same hobbies; he was a strong influence on me. It was a very, very hard time. People didn't have phones at that time. If anybody, English or Pakistani had to use one, at that time there were mostly English people around us and nobody had a phone, if they wanted to use the phone they'd knock on our door. People used the phone or asked us to help them about anything. I mean my husband was a councillor and even if somebody lost their cat at night, they'd come and knock on our door, "Mr Malik, I can't find my cat!" People were knocking on the door, people were ringing on the phone - it became a way of life. I didn't find it hard afterwards. It became normal.

Islam is my religion and it's with me all the time. I didn't find it difficult here because nobody has stopped me from practising it. Actually when we came here, there was no mosque, there was nothing. So we started by buying a building and getting the permission to use it as a mosque and say prayers there, and my children attended regularly as well. The first mosque was on Rectory Road. We bought two houses, converted them into a mosque and the children read their Qur'an there. I think I even became closer to Islam. When I came here, I felt I was in a foreign country and I had a sort of fear in my mind - maybe I would go away from my religion or from my culture. But nothing like that happened. In the beginning, we had a few difficulties but then we settled down and it's like home now and we don't have any problems or anything.

The more my children are growing, the more strongly they feel about wanting to understand every religion and culture - I do believe in this as well. We respect all religions and hold the faith. I am pleased, whether they read the Qur'an every day or they don't, but they are close to their religion and they understand it as well. I am proud of that. My children have done a lot through education. I didn't want them to be involved only in religion and neglecting to focus on their education. So I am really pleased they have acquired religious and secular education.

I call Burnley home but I can't live without Pakistan. I go there every year, and I stay there for about four to eight weeks, maybe a bit more, maybe a bit less, but then I come back home.

This is my home, my second home. Pakistan was my first home but because I was only a very, very young teenage girl when I came here and I've lived all my life here. I lived here longer than I lived in Lahore. You love your country, a native land where you were born; you were brought up, where your roots are. But Britain is my country now and Burnley is my home.

Voluntary, Community, Faith and Youth

Maulana Mohammad Iqbal and Abdul Haq Mian

Above: Maulana Mohammad Iqbal believes in universal brotherhood and unity in diversity

My name is Mohammad Iqbal; I was born in a small village, Buddo, in Pakistan on 8th June 1973. My parents are very simple people. They made sacrifices for my sake and for my education. I didn't realise it then but now I understand what they sacrificed for me and their other children. I studied Islamic Education in Gujranwala near Lahore for 8 years, including my degree, and then I studied for one year in Lahore. I finished my studies in 1998 and I started my job as an Islamic Studies teacher in my area, Gujrat and stayed there for six years. I came here in 2004 when our organisation, 'UK Islamic Mission' sponsored me to come here to provide religious duties and services for local people here in Burnley. They have got an Islamic centre here, a mosque education system to teach the children and day-to-day services to the Muslims as well as the wider community. So they invited me and that's what I've been doing for the last 8 years.

My name is Abdul Haq Mian: I was born in Gujrat, Pakistan. My father was a farmer. I did 'O' Levels in my own village at Channan High School then I went to Jhelum, a nearby district, for four years. I did my degree in Islamic Studies and Arabic. After that, I was a school teacher for four years in the same village school where I was a student. In 1996, I came to this country.

Maulana Mohammad Iqbal: Abdul Haq is the founding member who started the Ibrahim Mosque in Elm Street. We did a lot for this community, the people and the Muslim community at that time. Originally, there was only one masjid for local Muslim people but as the Muslim population increased; they needed more institutions and mosques. They built other mosques. Our own masjid, the Ibrahim Mosque in Elm Street, was bought in 1996. It was a sewing factory before so they did a lot of work to shape it as a mosque so that we could hold our services there.

Abdul Haq Mian: Let me clarify something, I was not the founding member of the community that started the first mosque at Rectory Road because

Above: Abdul Haq Mian is a faith leader at Ibrahim Mosque and Vice President of the UK Islamic Mission

Left: Maulana Mohammad Iqbal and Rafique Malik presenting a cheque for Palestinian Aid, on behalf of Burnley Council of Mosques

Above: Primary School pupils listening to an Imam during a visit to Ibrahim Mosque

Right: MP and Minister, Phil Woolas (in red tie), visiting Building Bridges Burnley, at Ibrahim Mosque. Maulana Mohammad Iqbal fifth from the left

I only arrived in the UK in 1986. May Allah, the Almighty, grant the late Mr Yaqub a place in paradise; he had a massive stroke ten days prior to my arrival. He was admitted to the hospital. Mian Abdul Waheed, who is also my father-in-law and who played a key role in building the first mosque, was with him. So I arrived very late after that, only 1986, so I'm not the founding member of the committee.

When we started the Ibrahim Mosque, we had our focus on two things: one – to reduce differences amongst our own communities, Alhamdulillah we have developed really good relationships with all sections of the community. We invite them and they invite us; too attempt to bring together the whole community, right from the beginning. We introduced a fresh idea, Mosque Open Days. It had never occurred before in Burnley. The UK Islamic mission is a nationwide organisation so we advertised the event in the newspapers, organised meals and around 400-500 people attended the event. It was an extremely successful event and I would like to share a comment from one of the attendees: a visitor who came to see someone in Burnley, did get the opportunity to visit the mosque at the open day and he was so impressed with the gathering that it encouraged him to write an article in the Burnley Express and he urged other non-Muslims to visit the mosque if they could. It is an opportunity not to be missed. I have the cutting from the paper somewhere in the mosque. Having read his comments I was extremely satisfied with our efforts and realised it was worthwhile to put up such an event in the mosque. This gave us so much motivation that we have been doing this event almost every year now. Besides this, we started to supply food to a number of people on the day of Eid. By the grace

of God, the Building Bridges office is situated in our mosque. We are striving to eliminate the differences between communities and improve relationships and understanding. Even amongst the Muslim community we must rise above these differences and work together. We must try to educate our local community about our role. Sometimes people just pretend to understand but have prejudices about you. Oh, he might be like this or like that whilst sitting in their houses.

When we sit together, talk, and see each other, that reduces misunderstandings and misconceptions and leads to positive relationships. As the Vice President of the UK Islamic Mission, I am trying to build stronger relationships with other communities. So by the grace of God, we are trying our level best to do whatever we can in our capacity.

Maulana Mohammad Iqbal: The feast was organised in 2005, which Mian Abdul Haq referred to and it was first time in the history of Burnley.

For the mosque open day we had our focus on the local community and invited them. We got all the departments involved in this programme; the Fire Brigade, Police, NHS, the local Council Mayor, the Deputy Mayor, solicitors and doctors. We also extended our invitation to local schools and colleges and as a result the turnout was wonderful. It was unexpected to witness nearly 500 community members attending the programme. It was a huge success. People from the community were so happy and impressed that they decided to organise a similar programme in a local church the following year and invited all the Muslims. We went there. It was also a very special event and in this event we also shared food. We talked together. We tried our best to understand each other with conversation, question/answer sessions and some brief talks as well. This was the first time in the history of Burnley. It takes place each year and by the grace of God, it is very successful. We are the pioneers in developing relationships with local schools and organised visits by their pupils to learn about mosque culture. We have a long waiting list of schools that are going to visit us. The aim of the visit is to understand the mosque system. What's this Mehrab? What do you do at specific times of the day? What are prayer times? They also visit kids' classes to see what's happening in the mosque. We are also engaged with a number of local authority services such as the Fire Brigade and they have delivered several programmes on many occasions to make the local community aware of how to save themselves from a fire.

Especially when people are going on pilgrimage to Makkah, they demonstrate a number of safety measures that people can take to protect themselves. We are also working with the NHS. Doctors visit us to develop a greater awareness about Islam. We are running special courses for them. By the grace of God we have introduced an 'openness' policy in the mosque to show the world that the mosque belongs to everyone and it is their right to visit the local mosque. We must share our culture with the local community simply to convey the message, 'nothing to hide here,' so by the grace of God we have delivered this. In partnership with Building Bridges in Burnley we collect some of the addresses and share amongst our members on special occasions like the Eid festival. We made everyone supply food to those families and share Eid with them. So we visited those families, supplied the food, had a chat and spent some time with them. This goes on now every year. One of the highlight of our services/programme is that we have encouraged the women in our mosque.

We tend to organise big gatherings for the women, as big as 200-300, and especially on Friday prayers we have special facilities for women, a separate wudu (ablution) facility through a separate entrance. They come here on Friday, and especially during the holy month of Ramadan, we have two separate rooms which get filled up completely and such a facility was not available before to women in any other mosque. We were the first to start it and it has been going on successfully. In addition to that, we have also tried to promote unity within the community and have met scholars, Ulemas and academics. It is understandable that people are sceptical about other people coming from other mosques, not knowing what they'd say. So we invited all the Imams from the local mosques in Burnley and arranged for each Imam to come and deliver a lecture each month and we give them a topic. Sometimes we have had breaks for some reasons but the programme has been running successfully. They start visiting us and giving lectures, particularly during the month of Rabi-ul-Awwal when Seerah programmes (the life story of Prophet Mohammad, peace be upon him) are conducted across the country. We invite the Imams from all the Burnley mosques. One of the most important events I would like to

Above: Maulana Mohammad Iqbal welcoming visiting Methodist Priests at the Building Bridges offices.

Below: An inter-faith dinner hosted at St. Peters Church, Church Street, Burnley

Above: Mian Saad Waheed, Mian Abdul Waheed, Maulana Mohammad Iqbal and Abdul Haq Mian at a wedding

share with you is the real contribution we have been able to make in offering Eid prayers in the local park and now 2013 is going to be our third consecutive year of praying in the park. We have already organised two Eid events in Queens Park and this was also the first time in the history of Burnley. We started in 2012 and we organised Eid prayers outside on the open ground. It went really well and one of the most important aspects was we had separate arrangements for women so the women also attended. The number of people increased in the second year. We also invited local authorities that included police, paramedics, the fire brigade and local council and in addition to that, we also received sponsorships from them. We faced criticism from some local Muslims, especially getting women in the park to say Eid Prayers. There's nothing wrong with this from an Islamic perspective and it also gives an opportunity to the local community to observe how we Muslims celebrate our events. It is exceptional to get everyone in the park together; women, children and men.

More than 70% of the organisations we invited showed their commitment. They fulfilled their promise and they came. Obviously a few people had some reservations. Their committee members thinking, 'oh, this mosque belongs to this school of thought, and they preach this sort of Islam.' It takes some time to break the ice and we are sure over time this perception will change.

We try to guide people at Friday prayers and teach them that there are two different things 'difference of opinion and difference of principle'. Consequently, we sometimes make our opinion as principle and principle as opinion. For instance, if I have an opinion this is my right. I expect you to have your opinion. Opinion is different from principle. When we make our opinion a

principle and try to impose it on others, that leads to hatred. One of our main objectives was to show ordinary people that there aren't any differences amongst religious leadership, and we have no quarrel with one another and principally we are all the same. If you have a difference of opinion then you have the right to do so, just show unity within the community and show ordinary people that they are all your imams and all the mosques belong to the community. So in a nutshell we are all one; we have the same faith, we all believe in one book, one god (Allah) and the prophet Mohammad, peace and blessing be upon him. So we should be one, especially as we have many other tasks in this community. So if we waste our energy in dividing the community then we won't be able to play a positive role. The main objective was to promote unity and particularly bring the local community and the religious community, especially religious leadership, together

It all depends upon your upbringing and mind-set, how you have developed, and the types of teachers you have had. So the people who trained me and educated me, they belonged to this type of school of thought. All schools of thought are there only to help others to understand Islam. The principles are the same. So if we develop our identity on the basis of a certain school of thought, then it's wrong. We are all Muslims, so we should be one. This was my training. It is important we apply the lessons we learnt from our teachers. We have always learnt the lesson of unity and always apply the same lesson to bring people together. You are absolutely right – this work requires sacrifice. If you try to get your name well-known and gain fame, then it's wrong and it won't work. It requires big sacrifices. For community gain and benefit, we tend to think beyond personal gain and rise above all those differences. This is our 'openness' policy and we are proud of it and that Allah has blessed us with this thinking and this vision. Things which are too small to understand or differences of opinion, we must not focus on them. We must always think about the big picture and big objectives. I would like to extend this further. We also have the vision that Islam is not just for Muslims. We are all creatures of Allah and this message is for everyone in the local community. Anyone who recites Kalima (takes Shahada) will be Muslim irrespective of their colour and creed. The message of Islam is not restricted to Muslims only. Allah, the Almighty, has given us this opportunity. It is our duty. You asked before what motivates us; it's a sense of responsibility. We are all answerable to our Lord. He may ask us, you were landed there and my message was for everyone and our beloved prophet Mohammad, peace and blessings be upon him, was descended as a mercy upon mankind. Whilst you were there you received all the benefits, what benefits did you give them in return? So he will ask how did you fulfil your responsibility and spread the message. This religion doesn't just belong to Black or Pakistani and Bangladeshi. This faith belongs to everyone in the world. This responsibility makes us think and do something about it. We must convey this message to all.

We are all answerable and Allah will ask us about it. We will have to answer one day. It is not considered as a sacrifice but a duty. We feel we are blessed that Allah has chosen us to do this job. It's neither our courage nor our hard work. There are many people who are more educated and intelligent than us but they are busy with worldly affairs. We feel that this is a special blessing from Allah upon us and some are calling it a sacrifice, but it's a source of satisfaction for us and we are so pleased that Allah has chosen us to do His work for the benefit of His creation. If we hadn't been there, then just in the last month of Ramadan, 8-10 people would not have accepted (embraced) Islam. It also helped to improve understanding. And because of us, if people gain a better understanding and get a positive message, then it is a great source of satisfaction for us in the hereafter. We do not consider this a sacrifice at all, but a blessing from the Almighty. To promote unity, what people say is "Love for all and hatred for none." We love everyone, we do not hate anyone and Allah created all of us. So this is everyone's right. We must reach out and get Allah's message across. This depends on one's understanding.

This is our belief – that men and women are equal in conveying this message and fulfilling their duty. Allah, the Almighty, has divided life into two parts; External and Internal. As far as internal life is concerned, the woman is the head at home. She is in charge of everything. So if we ignore them completely, how are they going to fulfil their responsibilities? Women are allowed to do anything in this society. So they get the opportunity once a week, twice a month to understand their faith, and the message, because they are equally accountable to Allah, the Almighty. They are responsible for looking after the children. So where are they going to learn from? Where will they find the opportunity to learn? They have equal rights in the mosque.

Even in the time of the Prophet Mohammad, peace and blessings be upon him, they used to go to the mosque and offer prayers. They used to listen to what Prophet Mohammad, peace and blessing be upon him, used to say. So unless we work together with women, we can't be successful. We complain that our kids aren't good, simply because we can't educate them. Women, especially their mothers, can. Unless we train our women, we cannot be successful in our mission. So this is why we feel that the mosque is a nucleus in our society and we believe women must have equal access to the mosque. Fair enough, we must respect rules and regulations and boundaries identified in Islam. We always adhere to restrictions identified in Islam. The women have separate facilities and work independently. They have separate entrance and wudu facility in our mosque. Now Ramadan is in summer so when people offer taraweeh prayers they feel hot and so we installed air conditioners. We face many difficulties, difficulties in reading. So we now feel we have air conditioning for the men, so we must install the same facility in the women's section too. They are entitled to the same facilities. We find the best example in the life of the Prophet Mohammad, peace and blessing be upon him, where a woman played a central role in spreading his message. This is how the message of Islam spread. Women's sacrifices are not less than those of men. We can't progress further so it's our responsibility to facilitate them.

First of all; community cohesion, better understanding, friendship, getting together, closeness, are just to name a few as we are part of this community. The women are also part of this community. We must not have such barriers and we must have at least a little bit of understanding. It is entirely up to us how we celebrate our events. So we must have this understanding because this is their right and we must share with them how we celebrate our events, which are a source of real happiness. It does not provide us with happiness just because we feed ourselves well and wear the best clothes in our house. Happiness only increases by sharing, the way we visit our relatives and they visit us and vice versa, food is shared so that we make the local community feel and realise that they are also our relatives, our neighbours and friends. Muslims don't live in isolation. So this is our intention, to celebrate our events and share them with the local community. When we got the list from them we told them, and it was all agreed beforehand that this particular person/family will deliver food to your house. And

Above: Ibrahim Mosque Committee visiting Pendleside Hospice and presenting a cheque. R-L: Mian Abdul Waheed, Hospice Representative, Maulana Mohammad Iqbal, Abdul Karim, Sarwar Baig (Chair) presenting the cheque

Besides this, I just remembered another unique incident, that the UK Islamic Mission is the only registered charity in this country which has helped local charities to raise funds, for example, at the local mosque. We raise funds for our charities like Muslim Aid and we include the British Heart Foundation and Cancer Research Foundation, all these charities are on our list during Ramadan and we make an appeal for them. When Mr Mohammad Najib was the Mayor of Burnley in 2006, he set up his own charity and he decided to raise £35-40k to buy a scanner to diagnose cancer of the throat at the initial stages, so we made an appeal in our mosque. In addition to that, the mosque committee visited Pendle Hospice and attended one of their meetings, and they said; it is the first time they have received representatives from the mosque. We believe that they are part of us and so we urged them to write a letter to us during the month of Ramadan and we would make an appeal. It's not your work, it's our work, because it is a charity hospital and we are now part of their committee.

similarly, Muslim families were given the name and address of the family who would receive the food. They were also waiting for us and the time was agreed, obviously in advance, because people had other commitments so the time had already been agreed. Both sides had their contact details and it was a unique experience we went through which was an exchange of happiness, a unique thing. It produced good effects and then we invited both sides into the mosque, the hosts and the guests together to come and share with us their feelings about this experience. They all expressed great joy over this experience as they had never witnessed such an event before in the community. First we got the opportunity to taste English food and see what it's like. I was reading a story once of a new Muslim who was travelling, and stayed with a Muslim family. His host had cooked Pilao rice and it made him feel and think that if the food is so nice, what about the beliefs of these people, how great would they be? Then he started studying Islam and embraced Islam afterwards. So food can sometimes become a source of interacting and of understanding one another. So we must invite others and share our food with them. The type of response we received from some of the families and their feelings about this experiment made us cry and understand how thirsty we are. It is our obligation; we are not fulfilling our responsibilities otherwise. They are so welcoming they are waiting. Western media portrays negative image of Islam but when people get closer to us and spend some time with us, it changes their views. Such experiences make them very emotional and they perceive the true picture of Islam.

We live here and we are part of this society. We must look after our basic requirements. We even supported Christie's Hospital in Manchester. We are part of the community and not separate at all. We live here and are citizens of this country. We must play our role and we tend to do it. Whilst I am talking about this I would like to mention that on two occasions we encouraged people to organise their Eid-ul-Adha and make a sacrifice here in the UK rather than in Pakistan and invite the community. People made their sacrifices here and collected all the meat for the mosque and we organised a big feast within the mosque. We advertised it in the local paper and as a result of that nearly 500 people attended the feast. Everyone came along to enjoy the Eid party; the elderly, children and all the Muslim community. We did that for two years. We have always been searching for new ideas to bring communities closer. We all have limitations but we always tend to strive for community cohesion. By the grace of God, the result of our efforts is positive. I don't exactly remember when but a lady health visitor visited my home and she met my daughter and wife. She asked my wife how many children she had. She replied that she had two sons and two daughters. She smiled and said "Oh, you are very lucky." My wife wondered why she was lucky. She said because she only had one daughter and they both had no other relatives in the world. On Christmas day we spend time together, just ourselves, as we have no other relatives. My wife told her that she had extended family in Burnley and the UK and not just here but even more relatives still in Pakistan, which was a surprise to her. It would be extremely beneficial if we could share this aspect of our culture which demonstrates that we love people and we enjoy living together, so we wish to go out and see people and invite people to come and see us and we always strive not to miss any single opportunity to promote community cohesion. By the grace of God, it is having a positive impact.

To be honest, I'd like to make it clear that most mosques are built on the basis of certain schools of thought but the Ibrahim Mosque wasn't set up on this basis. It is open to everyone. We have no problems whatsoever within the Muslim community. We strongly believe that the Ibrahim Mosque is mainly the second choice for people who may have had a different mosque as their first choice due to their family, tribe or area's affiliation for example the Abu Bakr Mosque, Farooq-e-Azam Mosque. Whenever their worshippers needed to make a second choice they would come to the Ibrahim Mosque because they knew that we didn't ask people which mosque they normally went to. We encourage people to go to all the mosques in the community. People know the Ibrahim Mosque is open to all. So if they were affiliated to a particular mosque due to their family, tribe or neighbourhood, whenever they got the opportunity to make a second choice, Ibrahim Mosque was their ultimate choice. As far as local authorities are concerned, I remember four years ago when Prince Charles was due to visit Burnley and the council invited all the community members like Mr Mohammad Rafique Malik, Building Bridges, councillors etc, when it came to inviting a representative from the mosque, they invited me.

Ibrahim Mosque is known to Parliamentarians as well. If any Minister visits Burnley, he or she tends to visit the Ibrahim Mosque, or visit muslim religious places and we also have Building Bridges office in our mosque which is a contribution from us. Everything is accessible to them and they receive delegations, organise meetings and they have full support from us. They also receive high level delegations, ministers or heads of organisations for

meetings and they all are familiar with the name of Ibrahim Mosque. Once the Head of the Methodist Church was on a tour of Lancashire and he had scheduled one meeting in Burnley. His local tour organiser made a decision to show him a mosque and his committee made the decision to take him to Ibrahim Mosque for a visit. Coincidentally, it was Friday and we invited him to share his views during Friday Sermon. So we allocated him time at Friday Sermon and allowed him to address the public, which he did. It was the first time in his life that he had addressed a Muslim congregation on their special day and special occasion. Apparently it was a positive message which he carried away with him. Any organisation, whether at local, regional or national level which is looking for a platform to deliver a project, will contact Ibrahim Mosque. This is our achievement.

This is purely the blessing and mercy from Allah, the Almighty, that we are not just serving a single sect or school of thought but Islam. We are satisfied with our services, may Allah accept it. We are doing it for the wider benefit, not just for one sect or one school of thought. We don't believe in these things. Our identity is that we are all Muslims. Our religion is Islam. Islam is not based on sectarian, tribal or a linguistic basis.

It is about 12-13 years ago when I used to live at 66 Elm Street. I walked out of the house and spotted a lady five house away from me. "I have got some luggage upstairs which is slightly heavy, please help me to bring it downstairs." she said. I wasn't sure whether she knew me or not. I went up and told her my name and address so that she felt comfortable with me but she said "I know you." I went up and helped her. It wasn't a big job.

Below: President of the Methodist Conference of Great Britain (standing), speaking to the worshippers at Ibrahim Mosque. Maulana Mohammad Iqbal sitting to the left of him

Above: Maulana Mohammad Iqbal (third from the left) and other delegates on an inter-faith visit to the Methodist Central Hall, Westminister

I don't remember exactly what I did, whether it was a mattress or something else I brought downstairs. After that I went to the mosque and came back in the afternoon. My wife asked me, "What have you done for this old lady?" I asked her, why, what has happened? She replied that the lady had come to our house. She knew so much about us, that we have two sons and two daughters and she brought us a fruit basket. She said "Your husband helped me so I got this fruit basket for your family." I came to the conclusion that if good deeds made any difference 1400 years ago, they are still valid today. People are generally good. They were good before and they are good today. I strongly believe if you treat people nicely you will get the same in return although there are a few exceptions in every society. Generally people are good. They treat you nicely so good people are everywhere in every community. I felt so good even though it wasn't a great job. If any elderly person asked me to do such a thing I would do it. She made a special effort and brought a fruit basket for us. She said, "I don't normally ask anyone except the people I know. I see you around and know your family." I always share this story with my friends, so that people notice and are aware of people around them. So whenever I get the opportunity I share this incident with my family and friends. It's not true at all that people don't respond to positive actions in a positive way.

I would like to draw your attention to another unique story. As far as I am aware, no one has ever done it before in the history of Burnley. I am talking about Ghausia Mosque which was being built from the ground up, and they follow a particular school of thought. If any mosque, other than the same school of thought mosque, helped them to raise funds for the project it was the Ibrahim Mosque. So we helped them to build that mosque and they never approached another except Ibrahim Mosque. It is their perception that people won't do it and we won't ask them either. But because of our trust, relationship and friendship with people in the community, we made an appeal on their behalf and raised funds. Shah Jalal Mosque is being built in this area by the Bangladeshi community. We have made an open offer to them, whenever they want, whether it's Ramadan or Friday, we are prepared to make an appeal for them. We believe they are all our mosques and you won't find such examples as here in any other mosque. We are trying to promote the culture that you can have your own opinion and you have the right to do so but remember, we are all Muslims so we must be united.

I believe this Philosophy is transferred from one generation to another. When an Imam of another mosque used to go somewhere and noticed a member of another mosque walking on the same side, he used to switch sides to avoid interaction. But it isn't the case with me. I am free to go anywhere and people are happy to see me. People feel happy when they see me and I notice this difference. This is the reward I have received for the work we have done and the culture we have promoted. Consequently, I have never seen anyone changing his side whilst confronting me or the colour of his face changing. Even I enjoy meeting people from other mosques; young, old they all greet me with pleasure. Even though people feel the difference when they meet someone from other mosques, I don't. They tell us because of this, families can be divided. Normally what tends to happen, especially on Eid, people would be divided due to different Eid days. Some of them may have been offering prayers at the Ibrahim Mosque regularly throughout the year but then due to different Eid days and due to the majority of their family members who were supposed to read Eid prayers in a different mosque, we encouraged them to join them happily. We even congratulate other mosques on Eid and celebrate with them. We have never made such things an issue and we see the results as people show great respect to us. People from other mosques love us and we also love them.

We invite youth, from time-to-time, internationally. We make arrangements of this kind, of meetings for younger people to bring unity and cohesion amongst them. We are happy to call them because we are British by choice. It is our country voluntarily. Burnley has been our home for 26 years. Whenever I go outside to Europe or Canada – I visit many places – I miss the UK and as soon as I come back I feel I am home, especially Burnley. It is a small town, so we don't have the facilities as much as people in Manchester or in London have, but even when we are visiting Birmingham, London or Manchester, we don't feel that same kind of happiness as we feel here in this small town of Burnley. Burnley is our home.

Voluntary, Community, Faith and Youth

Father James Petty

Above: Father James Petty is a life long anarchist and Priest

Below left: Father James Petty's Independent Labour Party membership card from 1961

Below: Father James Petty in Lucas Social Club with two friends in 1970 (on the left)

My name is Father James Petty. I was born in Burnley in 1933. My mother was a weaver; my father was out of work at that time. I attended Stoneyholme Primary School. When I left school I went to work in the cotton mill and became an apprentice eventually. I stayed in the cotton mill for nine years. I didn't have a career; I was simply interested in politics. I could have gone to Oxford actually but I thought I wanted a revolution believe it or not, it's perfectly true and going to Oxford wouldn't further this. I've regretted it since.

I first joined the Labour party when I was 14. We'd had the war, Churchill came here and everybody shouted. My family had been Labour for years and Churchill really didn't matter to us, we thought the man was a scandal so I simply followed in my family's tradition but it faded. I was also an Anglican Christian; an Anglican Catholic and it seemed as an Anglican Catholic that to love God and thy neighbour as thyself didn't fit in with Conservatism, it fitted in with Labour, so I got involved in that. I joined the Labour League of Youth which was marvellous; you met girls there who were interested in politics so you couldn't go wrong. We used to have marvellous weekends rambling; then public meetings and it always seemed that the revolution was just over the top. We used to believe in education, that you educated people, so we produced leaflets and magazines. Not just Burnley people in particular but from Bacup, Accrington, all the way round; it was really exciting and there was a good fellowship, we met regularly, we went to camps, fell out and everything else. But you seemed to be working for something, achieving something, there was spirit there which I really

Right: Father James Petty's Membership card of the North-East Lancashire Card and Blowing Room Operations and Ring Spinners Association from 1954

don't think there is now and of course on the weekend, I went to church.

Though I didn't know it then, I was looking for anarchism where people ran their own society, decided the mechanics of their own life and weren't dependant on the state. I grew to dislike the Labour party and the counsellors. After a while I began to see that I didn't agree with the things they did. They were nice people there, but they didn't want what I wanted, which was people to control their own lives. We did marvellous things; we gave out leaflets in the countryside, and we ended up with a horse and cart across the road. We had no experience with it and we hired it from this rag and bone merchant. It had its own mind and the result was all the traffic was stopped right at the top of Colne road, and there were cars all over the place. There weren't that many cars then, but they all seemed to navigate there at that moment and everyone was panicking. But that's what we used to do, we used to have discussions, oh it was an exciting life.

Well we wrote to the anarchists first of all, and they sent us some newspapers and virtually said 'sod off, we're not interested', if you'll forgive the French. We persevered, and gradually people came in and there was one thing about it; you weren't constrained by leadership, other people's leadership, and you could blossom and try things. We kept on with selling newspapers; it was awful, every Sunday afternoon for 10 years, and on Saturday for 40 years, I sold newspapers in Burnley centre, anarchy newspapers. Other ideas came up about housing communes, and education, and we developed all of these things as far as we could without having a great deal of skill, but I think we had a great deal of success. In Burnley, we once set up about five or six residence associations, all of which were going at the same time, and they were a pain in the neck because they were all Conservatives whereas all the others were Labourised and they were always clashing; so that was it. When I look back, it was mostly education. We prioritised it as I say, meetings and pamphlets. We used to produce papers, we used to produce pamphlets; the hard work was selling them, but they all went eventually.

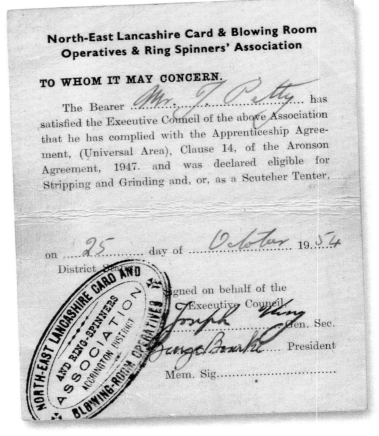

North-East Lancashire Card & Blowing Room Operatives & Ring Spinners' Association

TO WHOM IT MAY CONCERN.

The Bearer *Mr. J. Petty* has satisfied the Executive Council of the above Association that he has complied with the Apprenticeship Agreement, (Universal Area), Clause 14, of the Aronson Agreement, 1947. and was declared eligible for Stripping and Grinding and, or, as a Scutcher Tenter,

on 25 day of October 19 54

District ....

Signed on behalf of the Executive Council

Joseph ... Gen. Sec.

George Burke President

Mem. Sig. ....

The thing was, obviously, being an anarchist we believed one man was as good as another. I had a father, a step-father, who always thought you should never judge people and he said, if you mix with people, don't be put off by anybody else's opinion. He said treat them as you find them, which I always think is right.

I think it's like my father always taught me, and he was my step-father, and he said, judge a man on his character and how you find him, and I think he's right. I nearly married an Indian girl, but her dad thought I wasn't good enough. He was rigid, he'd been in the army, he had more medals than anybody I'd ever known and because I was an anarchist he had no sympathy. He showed it as well but that didn't bother me, he was entitled to his own opinions. Well it wasn't what I did but he moved to Leicester and it all fizzled out after that.

But with the influx of Asians I couldn't understand people... we'd just had a war where India had produced anywhere between 2 million and 3 million soldiers, everywhere the British army fought there were Indians there, Egypt, Asia, Malaya, and so on. I reckon they were as worthy to be reckoned as Englishmen as we were after all, with all these Scots, and Irish and Welsh, and what have you. To sort of single these people out for no good reason at all, which people did; I'll give you an instance. We had a man who bought a house on the street where I lived, he was a chemist. I came home from work one night and there was a mob of them. Things have changed, but women used to sort of run this area, and there was a mob of our neighbours and my mother amongst them, and so I said to me mother, "What's all this about?" She said, "He's Persian." So I said, "Ask him if he's got any carpets." So she thumped me – "Don't be cheeky with me." I knew what she was doing. I said, "Well, what are you complaining about?", she said, "We're not having it!" So I said, "Why aren't you having it?" I said,

"We have druggies further down the road and you're complaining about a chap because he's Persian." I said to her, "Does me dad know." So I went home and my dad said "I've tried to talk her out of it... oh well, he's different." So I said, "Why?" But when they got to know him, they wouldn't hear a word against him. I mean he had a lovely wife; I don't think she was Persian, I think she was Indian, she used to wear a sari.

In those days it was ignorance. They'd never met

an Asian or a black person, but on the whole they were very tolerant and kind people, but they had this fear. Well...chiefly it was fear, even then it was obvious, it was fear of people taking our jobs. They'd just come through this terrible war...my father died in the war, then he'd been a miner. He was in both world wars now they were frightened, mostly because of the jobs. Like everybody else, if they could have stayed away from Asian families, or Irish families for that matter – before it used to be Irish – if you could have stayed away from them, and isolated them, you could've hated them with complete abandonment. But once they met – I think they called him Ahmed, it's been so long now, who lived across the road, the Pakistani chap and his wife, they had this hate going. Oh it's ridiculous, they had this hate going against Ahmed and his wife; he was tall and she was very small. I came in one day and it was all silent, so I said, What's the matter? "What do you mean?" Well, I said, where's the hymn of hate? "Now there's no need for that." And I said, well it's been going on long enough. I said...well have they gone? "Well, no." Well, it turned out...oh simple souls... it turned out that this lady had brought some cake to me mother. Oh give over, I said, you're not going to be bought with a piece of cake. "Shut up, don't talk to me in that fashion," and that was about the level of it but they were frightened for their jobs.

When Asians and black people first came to Burnley, I mean, if you saw one in the street, even I turned round a few times when I was about 14 or 15. As soon as my step-dad met Ahmed and his wife and me mother it all crumbled, because I can remember saying to them, I said, oh come on, keep this up. They said, "What do you mean?" I said this hymn of hate; it's not the same coming in, without it. "Oh well, it's alright for you." I don't know if that was alright for me. It's typical of people round here you know, and basically they were frightened for the jobs. Most people are not as antagonistic as they were, there's not the same depth, I mean most people are like me mum and step-dad, I mean they were working-class people, they were frightened for their jobs really but what happens if unemployment comes again is a different matter. At times I've wondered that but I think there's no doubt that things have improved although there's still a big divide. It might not be amongst educated classes, but I remember there was an Indian girl who used to come to our meetings and we were going on a demonstration in Bradford. I met her at the bus station and I was walking to where the meeting was, and the hostility that we had got; now this wasn't from whites, or Europeans, or the local idiots, this was from the Asian community, and I don't know what they thought. I mean then, I was about 40 or 50 and she was only about 18; I don't know what they thought was happening, but there was a great deal of hostility.

I was born of a family who, 100 years ago, were socialists and there's always been a thread of that. I think things have changed, when you walked, about 20 or 30 years ago, people used to shout 'Paki Lover'. Then it was much deeper, within the English, the white English community, but then they used to dislike a lot of people in those days, they used to dislike the Irish as well. But the Pakistani community took over the hate and the dislike from the Irish, there was no good reason for it. I suppose it was economic; it was about jobs. It's shifted now because even now with the Conservative government it's comparatively easy. We have television and comfortable arm-chairs and so on, but I don't think it's gone away. I don't think its colour as such. The terrible thing is, if trouble comes, unemployment and poverty on the scale it used to be, this unpleasantness will arise again.

Back then we did things to build unity, like The European Friendship Society, which first started with European workers in the mill, and then it went on to Asian immigrants. The European workers were girls, which always attracted me, not that it did me any good because I was always tongue-tied and I used to think well, I'm in with a chance here but I always thought that they were very good. You met people, at first it was European workers; Germans, Poles, Ukrainians, who were victims of the war and they were brought over here to work in the mills. When I

worked in the mill, you met them there, men and women, and you mixed. You know, they were no different to us. Obviously no different from us. I began to wonder what the dislikes were. They'd taken our jobs, well, there were so many jobs then, and nobody in their right minds would go in a mill. It was dirty, dusty, and heavy. I mean the Asians who followed, same as the European workers, came because they needed jobs and money. By then, most of the work was with the Pakistani community. In the '60s it wasn't too bad, things were quiet, we held meetings but as anarchists. We developed a group with some Asian chaps, and one was called Shamshad. Along with Shamshad and a group of others, we used to go out every week leafleting. We used to go selling magazines, leafleting, holding meetings. We used to work with a lady who lived in Stoneyholme, Mrs Green, as well as Mr Malik and another chap Mr Yaqub. We had a society, the European Friendship Society, and I think it did very good work. People from both communities were active; leafleting, meetings, and doing all kinds of work. I think it did a very good job, but it was a voluntary thing, then later they had the community relations councils, and everything became more official. It showed that part of the community at least was united. The idea was that the Asian community didn't feel left out, or isolated; we used to leaflet meetings. Mr Malik used to put various events on, where people were invited, both communities. He was developing good relationships, getting people to know one another, and that was the sort of thing that went on, and we used to leaflet, and go on rallies, things like that.

They were funny times, things were changing, and looking back, in the '60s, when all the anti-National Front stuff was going on, it was practically a full-time job. You were out on weekends, you were at meetings, and we were leafleting, going to Blackpool. I went to party conferences at Blackpool, Manchester, getting in fights. It was all activity and it was all interesting, you met marvellous people. At first all the activity was sort of hit and miss, if you understand me, you had a leaflet and you would come across a group of fascists who were also there and then you sort of laughed and joked with them but in the '70s it changed.

I believe, obviously being a priest, if you believe in an Arab saviour, I would find it very hard to be discriminatory against an Asian or an Arab.

Voluntary, Community, Faith and Youth

Shahzad Ahmed Qadri

Above: Shahzad Ahmed Qadri is a young businessman turned TV anchor with Ummah Channel

Below: Shahzad Ahmed Qadri at a community gathering reporting for his TV channel from Birmingham

My name is Shahzad Ahmed Qadri. I was born here in Burnley, Lancashire, in 1976. My family comes from near Gujrat in Pakistan. My father came here back in the '60s. My grandfather came before everybody, before my father and his brothers and the rest of the family. My father was a mill worker, a factory worker, at a very popular factory called Smith and Nephew, which was based in Brierfield for about 20 years. After the Gulf War in 1991, the mill closed down because a lot of their cloth went to Iraq before the war. My father then opened his own shop, a grocery shop in Padiham on the outskirts of Burnley and worked there for the next 25 years; I worked there as well. I still remember the house on Claremont Street. It was the first house that my grandfather bought and was quite close to the factory, since then all the family have resided here in Burnley.

I went to Walter Street Primary School, even my own kids go there now. Then I went to Primet High School which is in Colne. At the time it was one of the best schools around and so I used to travel on the bus to Colne. Afterwards, I went to Burnley College; I did a BTEC National Diploma. I wasn't a person who enjoyed studying initially, I wanted to go out there into industry and work and earn money, but my father always used to say that education is important. I finished college

and I went to Derby University where I did a HND in Business and I was there for a couple of years. I then went to Staffordshire University and I studied there for three years. I did a BA Business Administration degree and then I came back to this area and it was just fortunate for me that I was in the right place at the right time when my uncle, Mushtaq Ahmed, asked me to go into business with him. We opened a double-glazing firm here in Padiham and for about eight years we ran that, it was a very successful business. I think, in the shortest period of time, it became one of the biggest double-glazing firms locally. I had the business for about eight years. Later, when the industry was not profitable any more - they say that when one door is closed Allah opens many more – and after that I didn't have to stop work and find other work but I moved into a TV career. That was also lucky for me but masha'Allah I went

into TV joined the Islam Channel team where I've been for the last three years now. I started by initially presenting small programmes and, as they say, the rest is history and today I'm Head of Production there and work hard. I believe

Allah always rewards you for the work that you have done, the hard work that you have put into something, he always gives you a reward for that.

Initially, I was there as a volunteer and I worked there for two years. I didn't know anything about media, I didn't know about presenting, I couldn't even speak Urdu; I've never learnt Urdu, how to speak it or read it or write it. Over the past three years sitting amongst people who all speak it, I did learn to speak Urdu which was very helpful in my Urdu television programmes; today they are the most successful programmes on the channel. During those three years, I never realised how popular I was until I started going out to Mehfils (religious meetings) around the country. It was only then that I realised I was popular. I went to Birmingham to a Milad Jalous (procession to celebrate the birth of the Holy Prophet, peace be upon Him). This is going back about a year and a half ago, and as soon as I got out of my car it took me a good forty minutes to actually reach that place because everybody was stopping me on the way, and it was only then that I realised that I was a public figure. I enjoyed it but at the same time I'd always learned from my father and from what I read that we must keep our feet firmly on the ground and Allah doesn't like arrogance. He doesn't like the people who even have an iota of arrogance within them and this is what we learn from the Holy Prophets of Allah as well, that arrogance is the first door towards the Shaitaan bringing you down. I maintain that belief and I've tried to be as humble as possible. But at the same time, I do say this to people, that you must work hard for your dreams and when Allah does give you success, he does give you the things that you want to achieve, he does give you that dream - that you make that dream into reality then preserve it. We must not get into this conflict within ourselves, the nafs (ego) conflict that we are something because at all times we must remember that Allah is everything and everybody else, they've always got room for improvement.

Going back to the year 2000, I made a New Year's Eve resolution and I can still remember I was amongst my friends and it was, I think, the second week of December of 2000. We were sitting down and just as mates do sometimes, said, right what's your New Year's Resolution, what are you going to do in the next year? We were just having this laugh and a joke that just like last year we're not going to do anything but at that point something I said became the focal and starting point of my success, of my journey towards what I am today. I said to them that from 1st January 2001, the New Year, I'm not going to miss any namaaz (prayers) and read all namaaz five times and I'm not going to leave any namaaz for the remainder of my life. At that time everybody took it as a joke and I think even myself probably, I probably only half- heartedly meant it but I didn't realise at that point those words were going to become reality and the turning point of my life. This isn't something I would like to see on camera, but if some youngster is watching this or reading the interview in a book, the reason why I will say this is that since 2001, Allah subhanu wa ta'ala accepted the little that I've been doing and the five times namaaz that I've been praying. I think these acts are the essence of my success because namaaz became my oxygen. If I didn't read it, I was like somebody who can't breathe, my day wasn't complete or something was missing and mentally, I wasn't right if I did miss namaaz. So my five times namaaz became my essence, the essence of purity that I used to keep myself clean; I used to enjoy reading namaaz. After six months it became hard. It wasn't easy; the journey wasn't going to be easy. I realised that, after six months, because my mind started going, back towards the previous years and I wanted to go back into the world I came from. I think for three months I really, really struggled. I didn't want to read namaaz, I wanted to go where my mates were going, I wanted to go back into that company but then I spoke to a Shaykh and I said to him, this is my problem; I'm becoming weak, what do I do? And he said that this is what the Shaitaan does to you, he tries to override you when you're at your weakest, when your heart's at your weakest and your mind's at your weakest, that's when he attacks. So you stick to your guns, you keep reading namaaz, keep yourself clean and in sha allah you will overcome this period. I still remember that it was in 2001, I started reading namaaz. It was only after that period of hardship that I went through, as regards my mental state and my head was saying something else, it was only after that that I kept a beard and because somebody said to me that if you do keep the beard, then automatically in your own mind you will not want to keep that kind of company, because you'll feel ashamed of yourself for having a beard. So I kept the beard and, Alhamdulillah that was right and it helped me stay connected with the religious side of life.

In 2001, I got married and I've got three beautiful children. So it's been a beautiful journey for

Above: Shahzad Ahmed Qadri's father, Mohammad Ramzan (middle), his grandfather, Haji Ali Ahmed (left), and his grandmother Raj Bhari (right)

the last ten years and I think everything was set in place. The only downside in the last ten years was the death of my father, Mohammad Ramzan, who was a councillor in Brierfield. He was a mayor of Brierfield as well; a very popular person and he helped the community. I know that the local people will know this because the local people knew him. He was so popular, initially, because when people used to want to get immigration forms filled in for their spouses or for visa purposes, my father used to go with Mr Malik to get it done. Mr Malik himself is one of the most beautiful personalities; my father used to say Malik saab is gold. I can remember we were sitting in a restaurant in Wilmslow Road, my father had taken me with him, it was some sort of party I think for winning the elections and he made a speech, and my father said that Malik saab for us is gold and it's that kind of gold that increases the value of him and the value of him becomes much more as the months and years go by and since my father passed away, Mr Malik has helped me. He has always looked after me and he's always advised me whenever I've needed it.

When I first joined Ummah Channel I used to do a programme called YQA, Your Questions Answered. There, I learnt my presenting skills; it took me about a year and a half to actually achieve that because I didn't have any presenting skills, initially. I was shy of the camera but I think as time passed, and due to experience and everything, I became confident and it was only then I realised, I've got a big opportunity here so I decided to take this opportunity to promote the love for the Holy Prophets of Allah subhanu wa ta'ala and the importance of loving him. The

Below: Shahzad Ahmed Qadri's father, Mohammad Ramzan, with his Mayoral Chains on (right)

Prophet, peace be upon him, said we should love Allah subhanahu wa' ta'ala more than our own parents, our own children, our own wealth and everything that we have got in life. I took this into my head and I thought I'm going to take this opportunity to promote this belief and to get the young generation in particular, on the right path. The Prophet, peace be upon him, because he was an example himself, only then was he able to get other people to implement and adopt his characteristics so until I can become an example for others, I will not be able to achieve this, that's why I said that this is a very tough path. You've got to watch what you say, you've got to watch what you do and you can't wash your dirty laundry in the outside world and you've got to be mindful of that. If I'm saying to others you've got to be good with your wife or your children then I've got to start it in my home. Be good with your family, your mother, your brother, and sisters, your immediate family and then your relatives and your friends, you've got to balance life out. So I have tried doing that. It's very, very tough but I think doing one of my favourite programmes, one that I set up myself, and this was for anybody who starts reciting Durood-e-Paak. I thought, if I get everybody to start reciting Durood-e-Paak that's going to get people motivated and that is

going to be my starting point for people. Today I've done 'Durood Bank' and 'Aqa Ka Milaad Aya', two of the most successful programmes over the past two years on any Islamic television, not just on Ummah Channel. Youngsters, children of 4, 5, 6, 7 years they're having competitions in school break times, they're reading through the Durood-e-Paak who can read the most. So you can just imagine the people that I've reached. And the elders who never used to read Durood-e-Paak, they started reading Durood-e-Paak and then Milaad Mehfils at home, people started conducting Milaad Mehfils. So I think I've gone a long way towards achieving what I want to achieve in terms of the importance of love for the Holy Prophets of Allah. The media is huge in this day and age, it's what everybody looks at and people tend to read books less compared to watching TV. There are many Islamic television channels, but what Ummah Channel has done, what it has achieved, is phenomenal and thanks to Allah, I always say to my team there that I only do one programme a week, it's brought me many blessings, it's brought me so much in my personal life and so many du'as (supplication in prayer) from people. The other greatest memory that I have is when my father got an invitation from the Queen. He got invited to the Buckingham Palace garden party, and I travelled with my father, my mother, and my sister Sadia.

MAYOR MAKING: Former Mayor of Brierfield Coun. Margaret Parker hands over the chain of office to Coun. Mohammed Ramzan. (LTN9133)

The first citizen
New Mayor's future hopes

THE new Mayor of Brierfield, Coun. Mohammed Ramzan, has set out his aims for the next 12 months.

In his first speech as Mayor, at the annual general meeting of Brierfield Town Council on Monday, Coun. Ramzan said he would carry on with many of the battles the town council has been fighting since its inception in 1991.

He said: "I want to try and achieve a litter free town, more security for Brierfield

that area being provided with an adequate playground.

"I shall continue the work of my predecessor in pushing for CCTV cameras for the town centre and I hope to be able to approach the teenagers in Brierfield and achieve and understanding with them."

Coun. Margaret Parker, in her last

when they disagreed over management of the town hall.

And she added that £7,884 had been given to finance projects such as cleaning back streets, traffic calming on Veevers Street, and the provision of play equipment on Chatburn Park Drive.

Mrs Parker has now taken the role as Mayoress of Brierfield

It was the proudest day in my father's life because at that point, he said, so many people have done so much hard work, more than I have, but they never got invited to the garden party, and I have. I think that was his proudest moment. I saw his smile, and I can still remember that the Queen was just a couple of feet away from him and he was like a little boy. Some people might not think like that in front of the Queen but it is a proud moment because all these things reflect on the fact that you've achieved something. I'm proud that he was a very successful person. Sometimes you only realise how intelligent a person is after he has passed away. I remember when my father kissed me on my cheek when I got my degree. That was a moment that I've preserved in photos. I look back at those photos and I feel that was my proudest moment, because my father was there and my father was also proud. Since then, although I enjoy my mother's smile, to be honest I live life as a traveller; I live life because we've got to live the life. I live life because you've got to live it for your children. On a personal note, I don't want anything; I'm telling you the truth here. I have no big dreams any more. I enjoy going to Makkah, I enjoy going to Madinah, and I enjoy my little life that I've got with my family. I have no desire for the worldly things, and I think people who know me would also tell you that about me.

At the age of 35 now, Allah has given me so much that a person at the age of 60 has to go through the whole of his life to achieve what I have achieved in 35 years. I just want to live a relaxed life, a normal life. But I want to do so much, I want to do so much for my religion, and the only reason for that is so that I have some good deed to take with me and on the day of Judgement I'm not ashamed in front of the Holy Prophets.

I've spent all my life in Burnley. I can never think of ever leaving Burnley because this is where my heart is. Whatever I've had, I've invested in Burnley. People know me here, I've got respect. Through the media you can go anywhere and I always say this to my fellow colleagues that the most important place is where you live. If you don't have the respect there – people in London, Scotland, Germany or other places, they only know me from the TV, but the people who I'm going to be interacting with every day, they are the people who are important to me. That they've got good words to say about me, they've got respect for me, that is what I want to maintain. The difference from Brierfield to Padiham is five miles, and my father hated living in Padiham; he always came back here because this is where his heart was. And it's the same with me, Burnley, Brierfield, Nelson, are the shores for me and I will never, ever leave this home for anything or anyone.

Above: Shahzad Ahmed Qadri hosting a programme of Mehfil-e-Milaad in Victoria Mosque, the largest mosque in Manchester

Voluntary, Community Faith and Youth

Maulana Mohammad Hussain Sajidul Qadri

Above: Maulana Sajidul Qadri is senior Imam at the purpose built Ghausia Mosque on Able Street, Burnley

Below: Maulana Sajidul Qadri, Imam of the first Muslim Mayor of Burnley in 2000, far left

My name is Mohammad Hussain Sajidul Qadri. I was born in Pakistan in a famous city, Faisalabad. My date of birth is 5th of January 1967. When I left school I was admitted to college and did my BSc in Psychology and then I was admitted to Punjab University, Lahore where I did my Masters' degree in Arabic. My father was an Imam in the village near Faisalabad.

In 1992, I was invited to Britain to become Principal of the Islamic Missionary College in Bradford by Pir Sayyid Mar'uf Hussain Shah who was the organiser of the college, and I worked there for 5 years. Then in 1997 I came here to Burnley. I was invited by Ghausia Mosque and have worked there ever since.

When I left Pakistan, I was educating Ulemas, I was teaching Ulemas in Pakistan because I have several Masters in Islamic sciences. There are about 19 subjects, and Alhamdulillah I've learnt up to Masters level in 19 subjects. When I came here, the circumstances were totally different so I focused on writing. Up until now I have written about one hundred books; eighty-five books have been published and they have been sold all over Europe not just in the UK. In Sunni mosques, the syllabus books are written by me, entitled the 'Teachings of Islam.' At the moment I am working with the young people, so about a hundred people over eighteen years of age are learning from me, Arabic grammar, Qur'an translation, Hadith translation, Islamic law and other various sciences.

Above: Maulana Sajidul Qadri at Ibrahim Mosque meeting with other Imams in response to 7/7 terror attacks in 2005

My interest grew from my family's interest, because we are from the family of Sayyiduna Ali al Murtadha (ra) and my ancestors migrated from Madinah to Baghdad and from Baghdad to Afghanistan and my sixth grandfather, he came to Jhelum. So all of my ancestors were Ulema scholars and they gave great services within Islam. Here in England, I still have the original handwritten manuscripts of a lot of books written by these religious scholars from my family. It meant the environment that I was brought up in was totally about serving Islam and serving people and providing them with the true guidance towards Islam. You could sum up the most important teaching of Islam in just two aspects; the relationship with God and the relationship with fellow beings. Islam is a moderate religion and both aspects go side-by-side, hand-in-hand. There is no negligence to Allah Almighty, nor to his creation, so serving to Allah Almighty in the dimension of worship and serving humanity includes all types of services, particularly in relation to young people as they are the backbone of society, the leaders of the future and in reality young people build and construct society.

In Burnley, the response from the young people has been unbelievable; because a lot of young people go to work at 6 o'clock in the morning and then come here to study rather than going home directly. The people have a very real attraction towards learning Islam and learning all the related humanity, ethics and moralities. Very recently, we started two new classes, on

Sunday and Wednesday. The young people come from sixty to seventy miles away; Rochdale, Manchester, Bolton, and Preston, we start at 8pm in the evening and finish at 10pm. It's often 11:30pm or midnight when they leave for home; the young people have a lot of interest in learning. Really, the inspiration is the faith in Allah Almighty and love for the holy Prophet (peace be upon him), when we speak to them in their language, and they understand, they feel inspired by themselves.

I've seen a big change in Burnley, not just in the young people from the male side, but also in the female side, Alhamdulillah. My daughter is an Alimah (Islamic teacher) as well, and this is the final year of her degree in Psychology; she studies at Burnley College. My wife is also an Alimah, she holds a programme every week and about three to four hundred ladies participate. There's been a big change since I came here to Burnley, just in the mosque there were about 10 to 12 students but they were aged 12 to 15 and now the students I teach are from 14 years of age and they go up to 25. The number 100 is a big number, I think, in this society and we can see that a number of people are in the mosque reading the Qur'an; they are just sitting in the mosque and they have an appropriate attitude and behaviour to other people. That is the main thing, not just that they are learning but they are evolving themselves into the real fold of Islam, which is just kindness and affection to every person because Islam teaches respect and reverence for every single person; and not just for human beings. The Prophet, peace be upon him, says of creation, all creatures are the family of Allah Almighty, and most beloved to Allah Almighty is the person who is most kind to his creation. Alhamdulillah, there is a big change, and I can say a few young people who were not on the right path before – they were drug dealers – but Alhamdulillah, now they're very punctual and regular in offering prayers and coming to mosque and respecting their elders, and stopping other people from going down that path.

Three years ago, I remember, there was a young man and he had no nice record in his past life and we had a congregational seclusion in the mosque in the month of Ramadhan, and there were about 90 to a 100 young people who stayed in the mosque for the full ten days. I worked with them day and night although I had little sleep. But Alhamdulillah, the spiritual work had real impact on the young man. Alhamdulillah, he is married now; he has children, he is living a nice life, he is

100% changed, and he has attracted some other people away from that path, to the mosque.

My theory in this respect is, when we are learning about Islam indirectly, for example if I quote a verse of the Qur'an or a statement of the holy Prophet (peace be upon him), you just have to believe me that it is the true translation, a true interpretation. Also, there is no language to truly translate the Arabic language, it's so sensitive and so broad that you can't translate Qur'an and Hadith because for example, one word has a hundred meanings and the person who is translating does so according to his own capacity and his own ability, not necessarily the true sense of the Qur'an or true sense of Hadith. But when you understand the words of Allah Almighty directly, it has a big and very different effect on the people so my main theme is to teach people the direct words of Allah Almighty and the direct words of the holy Prophet (peace be upon him). When they are reading the Qur'an without any other assistance, by themselves, Allah's words have real effect.

That is the miracle of the Qur'an. That a lot of people, even if they don't understand anything from the Qur'an, as they recite they enjoy the spiritual experience but can you imagine their enjoyment when they also have understanding, as well as the effect on their hearts and souls. And some of my students say when they come to the next lesson, they sit all day and night dreaming about this understanding of Qur'an and Hadith.

In a hundred students you can say that 50 are male and 50 are female, and they, Alhamdulillah range in age from 15 up to their 20s. To me it is more important that the females come because the male is one person, one unit, but the female is a full family. If you teach a woman, really you teach a family, not just the one person, and that is why the Prophet (peace be upon him) did say that paradise lies underneath the feet of the mother because it is the mother with whom everyone has a 100% attachment. If the mother is nice in behaviour and attitude then automatically – even if she is not teaching and she is not training – automatically, her morality, her ethics they will be transferred to the children who are always with her. That's why a very famous poet, Ahmad Shoqi, says "Izaa ta'almtan-nisaa fa adatta madrastan," which translates to 'when you educated a woman, really you constructed a school and university.'

There have been two main barriers. The first

barrier is the barrier of language, so those Ulemas and those scholars who are in my field but are not able to speak English, they find it difficult to attract the students because the students find it hard to understand what they are saying. Secondly, we must have a broad vision, we must not have a narrow vision because Islam is not and never was a narrow religion. For example, some people don't like women coming to mosque... why? Mosques are built for everyone. But we have to come out of that fold that is not the true fold of Islam. Islam is very broad, and Islam is really a natural religion and in nature, the woman and man they both go side by side.

Above: At an inter-faith gathering, Maulana Sajidul Qadri is second from left in the front row

Firstly, you have to present yourself as a model for people to have confidence in you. Show that you are not abusing the people, you are not taking advantage of them, but you are really serving them. People need to believe in you, that you are a true person and truly your mission is to teach and your mission is to train the people and to serve the people. I deliver speeches on Friday so it is a very good opportunity for me to influence the minds of the people, very gradually, indirectly - not directly. For example, when I was to announce the class for women, I delivered some speeches on the main roles of women within the history of Islam, for example, Sayyidah Aisha Siddiqah (may Allah be pleased with her); she was the wife of the holy Prophet (peace be upon him). And the Sahabah (companions) of the Prophet (peace be upon him) used to go to her to learn. She was the teacher of Sahaabah-e-Kiraam and on the Hajj occasions, her tent was in a very prominent place and people from all over the world, they came to Hajj in Makkah-Tul-Mukarramah to learn from her. We learned half of our deen from Aisha Siddiqah (may Allah be pleased with her) and the very first supporter of Islam and the Prophet (peace be upon him) was a lady, Sayyidah Khadijah Tul Kubra (may Allah be pleased with her). So it is said that behind a great man is always a great woman and you can take that example from the Holy Prophet (peace be upon him). When he received the first message from Allah the Almighty, because it was a great message from Allah the Almighty and the Prophet was still a human being, and he was thinking whether he would be able to fulfil his responsibilities or not, then it was Sayyidah Khadijah - a woman – who gave him confidence and said yes, you will do and your Lord will not let you down.

I came here about 14 years ago; at that time Ghausia Mosque was situated in two houses. Now we have the new building for the mosque and we can praise the very generous people of Burnley who donated a lot of money, which allowed us to finish the construction of the new mosque three years ago. The new mosque has capacity for three thousand people, almost all the donations came from Burnley, and we have built a magnificent mosque.

I am proud of it, Alhamdulillah, and everyone is proud of it, that's a sign of the greatness of Burnley really. The mosque has a very, very important role and function from the very first days of Islam. There is still a misconception regarding the mosque as just a place of worship. It is a place of services to community, and not just to the Muslim community, but all human beings. The holy Prophet (peace be upon him) used it for every issue; politics, social affairs - everything can be dealt with and can be served in the mosque. So the mosque has an important role within society; to change the people, to change their behaviour, their attitude, and their ethics.

Ghausia Mosque is open to everyone so delegations from schools, from universities, from colleges, they come to the mosque. They learn from the mosque; we invite them and show them the mosque and, Alhamdulillah, there is a very good response from all the communities here in Burnley. The work that I am most proud of is the congregation of young people around me. I am proud of the young people. That's the main thing to me. I think that there are two main elements; sincerity and ability. If a person is working with sincerity and loyalty, they never feel any hurdle in their way.

We're having an impact in the wider community as all of the students who come to me are really from universities; they are solicitors, doctors, and engineers, so many people are educated in this society, so when they are over 18 they are well educated in different fields. They come because the heart is the same in every person, whether he is an engineer or whether he is a doctor, just sometimes there is a place of love of Dunya, love of some negative things. If you can delete the layers or you can remove them, then the heart is clean; the heart is clean, In sha Allah.

A number of schools have visited the mosque, as well as Burnley College; they have visited two or three times. The police force, judges, nurseries, and the church on Colne Road; they are all working with young people and they have also visited the mosque.

Burnley definitely is home. I am proud of Burnley. When I was leaving Bradford for Burnley, some of my friends said, it's not a wise decision because you are leaving a city and you are going to a village. But Alhamdulillah, I made the right decision because in cities, there is petty politics, but in villages there is sincerity and loyalty, love and real love. The people here showed me a great deal of respect. I did a lot of work here in Burnley, because there was no bickering, there was no hurdle.

Chapter 17 - Third sector

Voluntary, Community, Faith and Youth

Abdul Hamid Qureshi

Above: Abdul Hamid Qureshi is a faith leader who was co-ordinator of Building Bridges Burnley and Chairman of Lancashire Council of Mosques

My name is Abdul Hamid Qureshi. I was born in Pakistan in 1958 in a small village near Jhelum city. When I left school I went to college in Pakistan. I came to the United Kingdom in 1979. My father worked in British companies for 19 years. He spent time there in the oil refineries as a foreman. He came to the UK in 1969 and he used to work at Prestige. I was fond of the army and wanted to join because Jhelum was a city where the army is a strong employment force as well and I really wanted to play a role in it. But my mother opposed that and my father wanted us to join him here in Britain. So I joined them here in 1979. I intended to study, so I joined Burnley College and I started to make my inroads in Burnley.

As I wanted to study, I went on to do engineering and graduated with honours. I've always been someone who loved people and all people. Whilst I was at university, I started to think about how and what challenges we as a society will have in future. At that time, I realised as a general member of society, but particularly as a Muslim, there would be two to three areas that would be very difficult in future. One was the development of young people; how their lives will develop because Islam guides you to live Halal lives, to live lives which contribute to society – how you earn is a very crucial matter, rightful earning is very important. I was very interested because the kind of opportunities that were available for young people here, and the kind of inspiration and kind of engagement that were available to them, was unclear to me. The second point was that I felt that there would be a lot of pressure on our social fabric. It could not sustain itself as it was based on cultural values. I have always believed that we would not be able to sustain cultural values but we could sustain Islamic values and, therefore, how to redefine it and how to reach to that, to cut across cultural barriers and see what the boundaries really are. That's another aspect which I've always argued intellectually and

I've always argued in a sense to try to transform that bit. The third element was engagement as a Muslim, with broader society. So this was three-pronged work which I engaged in. And having that in mind, we established the 'Young Muslims' organisation in 1984 with four objectives. I was the founder member; I love to say that even my non-Muslim friends when they hear about it they say, we can really buy into it. Those objectives were number one, that Islam would provide us guidance in our morality, in our engagement, in our perception, in our behaviour. The second point was that we must excel in education. The third objective was that we should have a concept of organised work. The fourth element was service to humanity. Whenever I look back at the level of work we did at that time, it really was quite forward looking. Many of those people today, whether it's in the arena of politics, education, development of young people and scholarly work, or whether it's professorships in universities, you will find that we made a deep contribution. We managed to cut across sectarian values including our work with both males and females. So I engaged in studying for a Diploma in Management Services, but always spreading the message that it's lifelong learning, it never stops.

Below: Abdul Hamid Qureshi in his office at Ibrahim Mosque

That's where my career developed. I began working with some of the charities within the Lancashire Council of Mosques and that was not a monetary decision. My decision was based on the opportunity to influence the institution where 90 per cent-plus were young people. Therefore, it was important that I saw that we influenced the mosque environments in order to influence the kind of mind set and attitude we would have towards society in future. I was convinced right from the beginning that many of the negativities that we see are culturally based negativities. The recent history was there in the form of colonialism etc which was the baggage carried through into our culture, therefore we needed to think differently. Because now we were in a society which was not lower or higher, which meant all opportunities were in front of us, we were on an equal footing so we should make the difference by actively engaging. That's where my role was; continuously nurturing, continuously forming, hence my work at Lancashire Council of Mosques and Building Bridges, Burnley. It's very important that when you create interfaces, when you create that understanding, when you change perceptions, when you have to have different attitudes, that you come to know that there are small things people do not know so those sensitivities when somebody dies, when somebody's living, when somebody's helping the people how to really engage and connect over that issue are very important. I thank God that I was able to contribute in its development and some of the work that we did was acknowledged nationally and internationally. People were becoming comfortable with one another and they started to get the confidence that it is not all talking about differences; it is that you can live and understand the differences and differences are not always negative. You don't have to be the same, you can be different and yet cohesive. My national role, in a sense, was again about engagement as I worked with the Institution Development in Oldham, which again focused on the creation of future scholars and Imams and community leaders. So I am still in it very actively, that moulding of minds and transforming attitudes and in the coming few years these will contribute a tremendous amount to society.

I have never moved just for a job. I always moved if the work was about cohesion and linked to the concepts I have. I was part of Young Muslims; I love to talk about it because that was one of the best experiences Britain could ever create. I know the American Muslims used to come and learn from us. Then my role with the Lancashire Council of Mosques; I think that I performed quite a sensible role there as well although when I went into the organisation, the organisation was not perceived very well. When I left the organisation, though I am still with it in a different way, everyone - statutory bodies, the voluntary organisations, all felt it was normal to state that we can do business with this organisation. It's because it started to perform the function of engagement; right advice, right attitude, right approaches. Again, I love the fact that the work I managed to do had this impact, I feel very thankful for the work I did with Building Bridges, that opportunity, and what I managed to do in the organisation. With the same

Left: The International Bishops Groups visited Burnley. Bishop John and Rafique Malik sitting and Abdul Hamid Qureshi (fifth in the second row) with Bishops and faith leaders, at a dinner hosted by Burnley Council of Mosques

approach I went into the NHS, and did one and a half years of work engaging the communities and again it was quite a good initiative.

A principle that has always been uplifting for me is that I always clean my heart from the prejudices against humanity. It doesn't matter what kind of person I encounter, negative or hating you. I worked for the 'Interfaith Network UK;' I was their executive member and performed a great role. They were having their 10th anniversary year, organising a big programme, and I was part of the committee. That committee was composed of all kinds of people of different denominations; Muslims, Christians, Jewish people, Hindus, and Sikhs, I managed to work with all of them with a great deal of respect.

Internationally, I am at this moment President of a newly formed organisation which is called the European Muslim Council. It is an initiative which is quite good in interfaith work, based in the UK as society here is more relaxed with one another than many parts of Europe. We have people who may share similar views, with whom we were previously engaging in different parts of Europe. We decided to create an umbrella organisation to engage at a European level, which will slowly develop into political engagements as well as social engagements. Many of the people are immigrant communities for example, they're new to Europe, from Norway to Greece, and a key objective is engaging the young people. Often, people sit and say that somebody's non-Muslim or Muslim and at once other people think that it's a point of distinction, it's a point of discrimination we have created, but when you look really, Islamic values are so beautiful and the narrative creates the mindset that we all are

human beings and God created those human beings. We acknowledge that human beings are the best creation of God, that's what theology tells us. Therefore every human being is worthy of respect. So that's point one. Muslims respect all humanity. The second point is the expression we always use 'back home'. This terminology is not right. A Muslim's home is wherever he lives. A Muslim's contributions and responsibilities shift with the context. My life is in Britain rather than Pakistan. My responsibilities, my role, my contribution belongs to those people among whom I live. Therefore, that means that another principle point is that all the earth, all creation, is created by God. By virtue of that there is nothing which is more pious than the other. This whole earth where we live, the sanctity of it, the defence of it, the good things to generate in it, is again Islamic. The third element was on a sense of choices. Now God created me and God created any other human being. If I have a right of choice for me, that right of choice is also for others -

Below: The Archbishop of Canterbury visits Burnley. Abdul Hamid Qureshi (far left) representing the Muslim community

Above: Cub Scouts from Ribchester visting Ibrahim Mosque. Abdul Hamid Qureshi standing sixth from right

for which we're accountable to God hereafter. Therefore, if anybody transgresses on that choice it is against Islamic values. In terms of choice it is very important. God is going to ask me what have you done for your next door neighbour, for the society you were in, what really have you done for them regardless of their faith and regardless of their orientation to anything? So again, it's my responsibility. Collectively, these few things become a principle for that international organisation and we follow that as a mind-set for the future, which is so beautiful. I think given time, the very point which I was saying (that we will be the great bridge makers) is not something which is just a perception but can, and in some cases, is starting to happen, we are becoming real bridge builders of the future.

Looking back, I remember when the M65 arrests took place – there was a Viva Palestina convoy going to Gaza. That was just after a war in Gaza a few years back. Three vans were going with a few people to be part of that convoy. These vans were taken into custody while they were on the M65, going towards joining the convoy somewhere in another part of Britain. There was a very big hoo-ha stating terrorist arrests had been made and so on and so forth. But at the end, it came to light that that was overhyped activity. There were about six young Imams who were going with the convoy. The way the arrest took place, the way the searches took place, the way the women were treated in the process was very negative. But we got engaged with all groups. Where it was negative we pointed it out, and where they needed support we created that support and a favourable outcome. We also went

into the mosques and explained to them why the incident took place, what happened, what was wrong with it and what was right with it and how we should behave at this particular moment. And therefore, maybe a situation which could have been very volatile instead became very, very amicable in a sense and it has shown the maturity of the Muslim community in relation to the authorities. Lancashire Constabulary is a very good force, they engage very nicely. It showed our relationships over a period of time, it showed that we have resilience; it showed that we can face tough situations and tough questions and yet come out as very good members of society who can work together even if the situations are very difficult. We can make changes, we can improve ourselves, we can engage with societies, and we can contribute in a positive way. So there should be nothing to stop us from engaging with any other human being who lives around us.

Voluntary, Community, Faith and Youth

Anwara Shahid

Above: Anwara Shahid is a committed community leader and popular family worker to Stoneyholme Nursery School

My name is Anwara Shahid. I was born in Bangladesh in 1943. After I left school I did a bit of voluntary work in Bangladesh. My dad had a business, mum was a housewife. I emigrated to England because I married Mr Shahid who was in England in 1965. When I first came to England, I lived in Leeds for 15 years but in 1979 I came to Burnley.

All my children were born in Leeds and I tried to be involved with their school lives. Then my husband and I thought we'd start a business. So we sold our big house and tried to buy a business but we were not business people. My late husband used to sit down at the table and read The Guardian and The Times but he didn't like the business. We didn't want the children to be involved with the business. My husband saw an advertisement for an advisor at Jinnah Development Trust, which Mr Malik advertised. He went for an interview and he got the job. Mr Malik's brother-in-law, Mr Yaqub, was my husband's friend. So I will always say, somehow, Allah sent me to Burnley. In Leeds we used to live in an all white area like a suburb; I never saw Muslim people, just a completely white area, nice and at that time there were no problems. In 1965, my husband enrolled me in a place called Pitman's College in Leeds, to learn typing. I learned English at home as well because my relatives were intellectuals. At that time, English was spoken in my house. Our relatives and adults, when they used to sit down on their own – all lecturers and professors, and they used to sit down and talk in English.

I learned functional English, they used to call it; in the college the teacher used to encourage us to talk as well. I was the kind of person who always grabs something new and enjoys it. Once the language is in your hand then you can communicate. I remember the day after I came, my husband sent me with the wife of one of his friends so that I could learn how to do a bit of shopping and buy something. When we came back, my husband's friend said, "You don't need to send your wife with somebody else, she can shop by herself." So I managed. Not very high class but I managed, with the English I have got.

When my husband got the job here at Jinnah, in the advisory service, we sold the lace business to somebody and came to Burnley. My eldest son was able to get admission into Burnley Grammar School. At that time, only the top one or two students could get in to the school. So Mr Gregson (he's not with us anymore), he was Mr Malik's friend and my husband's and he said it was a good school, so we came and bought a house here in Burnley.

Then when he was in the school, my second son, who is a GP now in Leeds, and then my daughter Ayesha, also got a place there because they were siblings. All of them went to London universities. The day after I came to Burnley, living at 38 Cromwell Street, I went to Stoneyholme School for my son's admission, and at that time Mr Mason was headmaster. Mr Mason asked me, when I was talking to him about my son's admission, he said, "Many people who come here from Pakistan and Bangladesh, especially the children, they can't understand a single word." At that time there was no separate linguist centre. "Please can you help them to understand for one hour, weekly or whenever?" I said, "I'll try." So the next day I went for one hour, and I spent all morning there. The following week, I saw Pakistani and Bengali children - they didn't understand a word in English but the children were intelligent. I volunteered there for ten years and through that I had, you can say, a sort of teacher's training. One day I said to Mr Wills (he became head teacher after Mr Mason), I can see everything but our people, they only need somebody to hold a torch, show them light and I want to try. I want to try to give them light. Apart from Mrs Malik I had nobody, no friends as I didn't know people. I was not used to that environment, the new home or Burnley. Everything was new for me. I said no, once you love the children there is happiness; when you give, then you get. If you give love you always get it back. If you smile, give a smile, just smile.

I realised I could provide community service, I could help people through this volunteering. I wouldn't go to anybody's house but through the school I used to help the community. Parents were not allowed inside at all, no involvement at all. But through my work, the parents were used to my smile, my welcoming them at the school. They used to talk to me and felt that this is not such a scary place. Without parental involvement, you cannot gain anything for their children. Through the volunteering I made all these friends. It doesn't matter where we came from. If you give love, they feel free to talk. I did my bit, but as well as that, a lot of people did well and many children became graduates, lots of professionals. It's my joy in my heart that so many have done well. It doesn't matter whether they were Pakistani or Bengali, they all came to me. Now when I ask a child who his or her parents are, they are often people I used to support when they were children themselves through my volunteering in the school, so I always feel a connection with all of the children. I feel they are mine. They're all my children. When they first had a playgroup at the beginning of '79 or '80, I used to go and work there sometimes. But I kept volunteering in the school. Whenever I went to the school or the class I felt this was my home, they are my children and their welfare is in my hands. Whatever I did for the children it was with love and good intention.

I used to explain to teachers the reason the Asian community could not mix easily in the school was fear of the unknown. They didn't know the language, they were scared. At the beginning they didn't get that love and respect because there was always a kind of misunderstanding. Many that came were rural people; they'd never been to towns because they were needed as a workforce. Somebody came from such and such a village, so highly- educated people didn't come much, in fact, very few. There were very few graduates and still it was difficult even for them to find a good position, they couldn't get a job easily. Mostly, unskilled people were needed; factories were there, and foundries were there. They didn't need any study or anything and with their limited words they managed and they brought their families. Slowly, slowly, we had development. But I'm so glad the people are doing well. I was a bridge, someone had to be a bridge of love, understanding. It was only language that was a barrier.

I remember once, one little boy about four years old, he came to me when his father died. But always, everybody went and consoled his mother at home but nobody talked to the child, comforted him. He used to call me and say, please sit down here outside in the cloakroom. Then he started talking about how his dad went to the tree and got the mango for him, because he wanted to share his feelings and memories of his father with someone. He felt he could trust me and feel safe with me. It was like they were my grandchildren all of them. It was really, really nice, really, really nice.

Now things are changing because now there's parental involvement, lots of language lessons helped new mothers to learn English as a second language, they learn the language and they get more confident. And old fashioned ways are changing; then, mothers would be at home and fathers weren't because they were working. Everyone's learning slowly, slowly. Like forced marriage, they are learning. Nowadays a lot of people are careful, they cannot force anything. Back then there was a lot of pressure on young parents and now it's getting much, much better and girls and boys understand better. Everybody knows their rights. It was hard for elders, generation gaps. There are always going to be gaps with younger people and older people. Also, elders were trying to help family they'd left behind when they came here. And in a way there's something very honourable about helping family. Without money, even in our country when they were in school, pay; medicine, pay; everything you have to pay. In here, we all had no expenses, none of my children were in private school or anything because my husband and I helped them at home.

I could understand both points of view. Well, we all want to be heard, don't we? The whole community, whether it was the English community, the Pakistani, the Bengali, everybody saw me as belonging to all of them. I remember my eldest son used to work in Whitehall, in the Home Office. Then one day on a corridor in Whitehall he passed Shahid Malik who was a

Minister, and Shahid said, "How is aunty?" They were going to an official engagement and the first thing Shahid asks is about me. It's a special bond of love with the Malik family, it's understanding each other because we have the same values; there's a lot of love and affection. My husband used to say my brother Yaqub is there in Burnley. That's true love and understanding each other, it's wonderful, it's very emotional.

Luckily, I come from a background where my mummy and dad always loved and cared for their people when they needed help. Originally, we came from a Sufi family background, so they showed love for God, love for people. A kind of nice thing. You can't choose your parents, you're lucky to be born and learn something from them. Humanity, love each other. There is always give and take, and show respect for each other. Like the Ten Commandments, it's the same teaching for all; I don't find many differences on Eid day. My friends are like sisters, all in retirement now but all from different faiths. It's nice to be loved. Until you love, you don't get it back. Caring. If I go for a few days to Leeds to see my children (and they live in a big detached house, big area, nice), after a while I want to see Burnley's Pendle Hill and children passing by and always, Burnley is like a flower garden to me. It's home, sweet home; it's the love for people, it's very important. It's a very spiritual vision. I was looking at my late husband's desk the other day. He was an

Below: Anwara Shahid retiring as bilingual assistant from Stoneyholme Nursery School in 1999

6 *Burnley Express & News, September 17th, 1999*

Children say farewell to caring nursery nurse Anwara

LANGUAGE differences have never posed barriers for a retiring Stoneyholme nursery nurse.

Caring Mrs Anwara Shahid has left her job as a Bilingual Assistant after around 10 years service at Stoneyholme's nursery and primary schools.

Mrs Shahid's work colleagues and pupils described her as "a little lady with a big heart" and presented her with a bouquet to recognise her dedication.

Although retiring from her fulfiling work, Mrs Shahid will continue to be involved in the life of the school and the community.

Pictured are pupils Tahmina Uddin (three), Minhaj Miah (three), Zainab Mirza (four) and Thanisha Alom (three) presents retiring bilingual assistant Anwara Shahid with cards and flowers with headteacher Mari Nearney and bilingual nursery nurse Shahnaz Begum looking on.
090999/1/1.

economics graduate in 1957, a highly intelligent, religious person, but when I go through his books and see all these big words and the Qur'an that he underlined, now I read. He left 15 months ago, he is in the grave but I find his writing, everywhere, and at a certain age I was busy with the children but now I've got time, I read. His thoughts were highly intelligent, full of goodness, love for people. He also liked helping. Even if he was sick he would send for a student whose dad had died and he would say, this child needs us always. He said family education is the key to success. Mr and Mrs Malik, Mr Yaqub - all showed how to give and these things are taught in the family.

It's the secret for people; we have to give to everybody. Everybody should give, it's who we are. We as Muslims, we love each other. And people should respect and love, not from our outside but our inside. Love is the true colour of Muslims, and we are the messengers of our Allah and this is the way we can share with others.

Voluntary, Community, Faith and Youth

Iris Verity

Above: Iris Verity was a pioneer in Community and Race Relations, both in Burnley and Pendle, daring to carry the flag of intergration at a very critical time in the early '60s

My name is Iris Verity but I'm known as Miss Ford. I was born in Nelson in 1938. My father was a builder, my mother was in business. My parents were native here. I went to a convent school. After leaving school I got a job and went to London where I was a nurse. I did several things actually after leaving school. I also got married. Then when I was about 28 I became involved with the Pakistani community.

The most rewarding part of my work with the Pakistani part of the community was seeing the outcome of it. I enjoyed working with the children; it was very satisfying for me. Mr Bashir, a Pakistani community leader and I started helping the newcomers. We started a school in 1963 in Garfield Street first, and then they bought another property in Netherfield Road and that became the Asian Institute of Learning. The children came and they were taught English customs, well, how to react really to the local community, how to use knives and forks, how to address people. Then they had lessons from the Qur'an there.

At one point I became quite ill and Mr Bashir came to see me in hospital and he said when I was recovered, could I help him form this Pakistani Association? That's how the Welfare Association was started in 1966. I said yes, I would help him. I wrote letters and saw the council and all those things. Then he started with a school in Netherfield Street, but there were very few children; this is over a period of years, obviously. Then the families started to trickle in and we started the school for the children. That was in Netherfield Street in Nelson. There was a committee of men, and of course the English community then started coming to me if they found there was anything they wanted to complain about, they were usually complaining. One of the things that they complained about was

the fact that the property wasn't painted. It was shabby and it wasn't painted. So I went to the committee and told them that we should really paint it, so one of the men went off, bought the paint, and painted the door, it looked beautiful. Unfortunately, I hadn't told him to get gloss; it was emulsion and when it rained it was all down the street. Funny when I look back. So we had more complaints because of this paint. Then they got money together and bought a property in Netherfield Road in Nelson; it was called The Institute of Learning and they knocked the building around and made classrooms. It was quite a nice building. The building in Netherfield Road was quite well known. Then Bashir went back to Pakistan and I thought the whole thing would fold from my point of view, but it didn't.

One of the things I remember specifically is one particular meeting we had at the town hall. One of the things that the English people were against, for want of a better word, was how they saw the treatment of women by the Pakistani men. Wherever I went, I always got this, "Well when they treat their women better," you know, all this business. I remember going to a council meeting at Nelson and they were all men there, and I was representing the Welfare Association at that time. All the same things came up time and time again, "They smell," "Well when they treat their women better", you know, "We will have more time for them," or whatever. And I looked round and I said, "Hmm, yes I can see your point about the women, but I represent a Pakistani Welfare Association, where are your women?" So they couldn't say anything about that, they never brought that up again, because I was a woman representing the Pakistani Welfare Association. It was Enoch Powell's time, and when Enoch Powell was talking about his 'rivers of blood', people were getting really hot under the collar in the community about it. It just brought everything to the surface, and I had my windows broken several times during that period. And, as I said, I had quite a few very nasty letters.

Working with the community was the best time of my life really. I worked for about 20 years with the Association. Of course in the beginning, it was very difficult for me, it was very difficult. I mean my parents didn't agree, my parents were quite against it. As I got better known then it became respectable towards the end. Even my mother saw it as respectable at the end but in the beginning they just didn't; the English people were suspicious of me and the Pakistanis were suspicious of me too! But it was the children that motivated me. When I used to go up to Netherfield Road, there was one particular boy, he had a bicycle and he loved this bicycle. He was a lovely child, and I had a son of my own at that time, my son was three or four and he used to come with me. I used to think, if my son was in another country I'd want someone to treat him properly. That was my motivation. Again, my mother wouldn't babysit for me so I had to take Andrew with me, and then my mother said there was a problem, saying, I was trying to make him Muslim. She was afraid of him becoming Muslim because he was up there (Netherfield Road) and I said, "He's just going with the children."

My son Andrew, he's grown up with the community. He finds no difficulties; he's very at ease with them. He's been to Pakistan, and he's not a Muslim by the way. Now, I'm retired. I'm an old lady. It was difficult at times but, it was enjoyable. As I said, it was the best part of my life really. It still is because I'm still involved, only I don't know anything now, just talk to people! The real significance, as I've found with the community, is the fact that we're all human. There's no difference, and I think that's the impact I made on the family; that, okay I was English and wore a skirt but I was alright!

A big change I've noticed, certainly one of the things, is the ladies. When they came to England; none of them wore the veil. Now the young girls are wearing the veil and I think, from what I can gather, they're trying to persuade their mothers to wear the veil as well. But the veil was never worn. The only time I ever saw a veil was when I went to Pakistan for the first time, and that was a very well-to-do family where the girls were. So that's one big change, in the dress. The other is, I've noticed that because of the halal issue, the community never went into any English cafés. I never saw them, and the reason is because they

didn't know what they were. The other reason was because they didn't know what they were eating and they had these dietary rules. And it's only recently that I've seen Pakistani ladies, or Asian ladies, actually in a café having a drink of tea, or coffee, or whatever. I noticed it the other day in Nelson because we have a very large community. I thought, it won't work in Nelson because there are too many Asian people here, and they certainly won't go into the cafés, but they do. That's a big change that they go, now, and if they're shopping they'll go and have a coffee, which they never used to do before. You never saw any Pakistani ladies, or men for that matter, in cafés. And the thing about halal, I can remember, we had a small number of Christian Pakistanis in Nelson and I'd been asked to go to this house in Poplar Street and when I went in, the lady was at the cooker, and she was cooking sausages and I was horrified. I thought, I wonder whether she knows what they are. I'd never seen any ladies cooking sausages. I thought, should I tell her? She's cooking away, and I said to her, "Oh, I didn't know they made halal sausages." And she looked at me and started to laugh and said, "I'm a Christian, you know?"

I think working with the children meant they changed so they didn't view English women with suspicion. They would say, "Well, we do know someone." They knew someone from the white community, and they'd been to my home and I'd been to theirs. I do feel part of the community. I went to this friend's house yesterday because people have to go and pay their respects when someone has passed away, and I went last night. I rang, and in fact I was quite surprised, they let me know straight away. I had four phone calls to tell me that Bashir had died. He passed away in Pakistan. It's heart-breaking. I mean, we've seen each other grow old. It was difficult, but it was easy, because I knew all the ladies, I knew the family. I know aunts, nephews, nieces, grandchildren; I know the whole family. So I am part of that family. In fact, the man who when I rang yesterday said, which was very sweet, when we were going in, I said to him, "Don't leave me there too long" I explained to him and I said, "I'm not comfortable." I had to go and pay my respects. He sent his daughter in and his daughter said, "When you're ready" you know, "Dad said you can go." When I was coming out, driving back, he said, "Now I have to look after you like Bashir did, it's my responsibility now."

I started writing the history actually, but I've never finished it. There's a photo with me, and I

Left: Iris Verity, aged 10, with her parents, Hartley and Doris Ashworth, at an annual New Years Ball in 1948. These Balls were the highlight of the social calendar from the '40s to the '60s.

think you can see Bashir and I think Mr Malik is on there as well. I think that was the opening of Netherfield Road, the Asian Institute of Learning. And there was a lady here, in Burnley, Mrs Green. She became a magistrate, and she was very active in the Pakistani community in Burnley. We didn't do much work with Burnley because Jinnah Development Trust was formed round about the same time, I think, as Nelson. So as I said, Mr Malik had his brother in law, Mr Yaqub, who was a teacher. You see Mr Yaqub died many years ago but Mr Malik and Mr Yaqub were sort of the Burnley part. They used to come over to meetings and events we held.

We decided to establish Burnley, Colne and Nelson Community Relations Council. In 1967/68 it was later named Burnley and Pendle Racial Equality Council. Once, the townspeople complained to the mayor that the Pakistanis had not cleaned their windows. So we used to arrange for people to go round and meet the Pakistanis. And he was on at me about the windows and I was saying to Bashir, "Just make sure that everybody cleans their windows, for goodness' sake." So we were going around with this party with David Waddington, who was then the Member of Parliament and he came up to meet the family. And everywhere we went, every house we went, the ladies had put a bottle of Windowlene on show! And I was killing myself because I just looked at him and Bashir was trying not to laugh. A bottle of Windowlene in every house down the road.

I was invited to Pakistan, and talking about dress, in the beginning, Bashir never wore national costume, he always wore a suit. Fazal, who was his cousin, he always wore national dress here. When I arrived at the airport in Pakistan it was a big culture shock because Bashir was in national costume with a gun and bandolier round and I thought, my God, what have I come to? Fazal was in a suit with a briefcase! I said, "Why have you got your suit on?" I'd never seen Fazel in a suit, "Why are you wearing a suit?" He said, "It pays to wear a suit here, with a briefcase." I can remember I arrived during Ramadan and I remember breaking the fast in a bicycle shop in Lahore. The fasting wasn't difficult because nobody was eating! I was never expected to do it. They didn't expect me to do it, but I did out of respect. I think Fazal bought me some sugar cane, he said I could have this sugar cane then I went on the bus, and the bus broke down. Then we went to the village by horse and cart, what do they call it – tanga. I enjoyed it, but whilst I was there war broke out and I was the last European person to come out of Pakistan. War broke out when I went which was probably my most memorable experience in Pakistan. It was like a town square, we were in this town square and of course it was Ramadan, and war was declared with India. That was a funny experience as well because we were out on the border, you understand that the border is quite near the village, and they had been told that if the Indians came the women had to go into their fields and hide. I remember there were these tanks, I saw these tanks as I went back and I said, "There are tanks coming up." And I was petrified, actually. Bashir went out, he said, "It's alright, it's ours. They're our tanks." I knew a lot about the political situation because I used to give quite a lot of lectures, and I used to take maps to explain about east and west Pakistan and Afghanistan and all these surrounding areas. So I had a very good knowledge of the country before actually going there. So nothing came as a shock, except war breaking out. I stood there, and it was announced over the tannoy and I said, "What's that?" and Bashir said, "Oh, we're at war." And then there was a big rush to get me back.

Afterwards the Burnley and Pendle Racial Equality Council took responsibility for most of what our Institute of Learning in Nelson and Jinnah Development Trust in Burnley were doing. Mr Malik and Mr Yaqub took a more active part in the Racial Equality Council and I continued working with Pakistani families in Nelson. I am happy that communities understand each other better, far better than they did in the early 1960s.

Chapter 17 - Third sector

Voluntary, Community, Faith and Youth

Mian Abdul Waheed

Above: Mian Abdul Waheed founder Trustee of Abu Bakr Mosque and Ibrahim Mosque, Jinnah Development Trust and a long serving community and faith leader

My name is Mian Abdul Waheed. I was born in the village of Channan in the district of Gujrat, Pakistan, in 1937. I had a very rough time in education because of ups and downs in my life. Sometimes I went to the mosque and sometimes to school. There was only one primary school in our village. My father was a headmaster in the village of Karariwala about a mile and a half away from our village. He began his teaching career there and stayed there until his retirement. When I left the primary school and started high school, one of my cousins called me to his house because he was sent to jail for two years. They were strict Muslims, so no male was allowed to enter the inside area of their house except a family member. Therefore, I missed two years of my education. When he got out of prison, one of my friends, Dr Khan, originally from another small village nearby, moved to our village and he started practising Homeopathy. Because of him, I took an interest in Homeopathy and passed the test. I practised Homeopathy and prescribed medicines from home. I continued my practice for two years before I migrated to the UK as a Homeopathic doctor in 1962.

When I came to the UK, I first went to Nelson because I had a few friends there. I became ill due to the severe cold weather in the UK. For at least two and half months, I had to have bed rest. I met a guy who was employed by British Railways. I also joined British Railways in 1962. I worked in Bury as a deputy collector for five years. In 1967 I drove to Pakistan with some of my close friends. I got free rail tickets for myself and the car, due to my employment with British Rail, from Dover to Calais. We travelled through Belgium, Austria, Yugoslavia, Turkey and Iran and finally reached Pakistan. It took us 21 days to complete the journey. It was extremely dangerous to drive through Pakistan, due to a lack of roads and bridges. I went back again in 1979 by road

and it had significantly improved compared to 1967. In 1967, due to job cuts in British Railways, I was made redundant and came to Burnley. I applied for three jobs at Prestige, Qualitax and Burnley, Colne and Nelson Joint Transport (BCN). Whilst I was sent for a medical fitness test, by Prestige, to a doctor, I also received a job offer letter from BCN. I worked as a conductor and a driver there until 1975. I left the company due to health issues and joined Riverside Knitting Factory in Padiham. I worked there until 1992. I also worked at Jinnah Development Trust for a year.

At Jinnah, my main job was reception work, form-filling and advice work. If someone had an issue with the local council, I used to help the individual, draft a letter to sort out the issue. I was a key member of the group which formed the Pakistan Welfare Association in Burnley. The late Mr Yaqub bought a house on Rectory Road. There were a few differences amongst the community. Mr Malik called a meeting to sort out the dispute. Most people agreed to establish a mosque there, so I donated a large amount in three figures which was quite a lot at that time. We formed a committee. The late Mr Yaqub, Mr Malik, myself, Chowdhary Ghulam Nabi, the late Mr Fida Hussain Bukhari and Mr Afzal Khalid were elected as Trustees of the Mosque in 1968. It was the first mosque in Burnley. It was a corner house and we spent an enormous amount of money to refurbish the building.

We raised funds through collections and donations from the Muslim community. After a while we got the house next door, 1 Holme Road, for about £4, 000 at that time.

The late Mr Yaqub was such a nice and educated person, he used to teach children in the Mosque. Mr Malik was also very social. I must admit that Mr Malik had a very hard life. Sometimes when

Above: Mian Abdul Waheed standing in St Peter's Church before an inter-faith meeting

he was in the toilet, or bathroom, people would ring or knock on his door for different problems. Some had passport issues and some had immigration problems. We supported people without any fee or return. I, the late Mr Yaqub and Mr Malik used to travel to Bradford to collect people's passports free of charge. We did it as our social duty.

There was a flood in Bangladesh in 1967 and Mr Malik organised a fundraising campaign. We collected a huge amount of money. We used to invite the Consul General for Pakistan, Mr Mujahid Hussain from Leeds, who was a really nice gentleman. He used to say, "Tell me the true story and I will issue the passport." Mr Malik, the late Mr Yaqub and I dealt with him and found him an incredibly helpful and genuine person. He was transferred to New York, and we bought him a tea-set with his name engraved on it and presented it to him at a big farewell gathering in the Burnley Lane Baptist Church. My father was a head teacher and I was brought up in a religious environment and the mosque was next door to us in the village. When I was only seven, I began going to the mosque. I arrived in the UK and met the late Mr Yaqub who was also very religious and that is why we decided to build the mosque. I feel proud that I supported Mr Malik and the late Mr Yaqub in this endeavour. Since I joined Mr Malik and the late Mr Yaqub, despite the fact that we had differences on numerous occasions, we never fell out with one another because Mr Malik neither cheated nor mistreated anyone. Mr Malik has got too many good qualities and he is trustworthy. There were many widows in the community and he used to visit them in their own homes and sort out their problems. They found him like their real brother, even better.

He would sort out their pension, immigration, benefits, housing and council tax problems. I used to call him 'Midwife'. This is one of the main reasons why I never left him. Although the late

Mr Yaqub and I were members of the UK Islamic Mission and Mr Malik supported the Pakistan People's Party (PPP), even then we never had any problems. We always treated one another as brothers. Political differences never split us apart.

We always supported each other in social work and community events. If he organised an event and invited PPP leadership, I supported it wholeheartedly and Mr Malik did the vice versa.

The late Mr Yaqub was also an extremely nice person but he had a bit of temper. Mr Malik is a very cool-minded person. Regardless of what people said to Mr Malik, he listened to them humbly but the late Mr Yaqub defended any allegation put against him very strongly.

The late Mr Yaqub was very honest, highly intelligent and humble but an outspoken person. He always tried to help others. He knew his community well and served it well.

The UK Islamic Mission was formed in 1962 in London by some Muslim undergraduates. The organisation spread all over the UK and in 1973/74, we joined them. It was again the late Mr Yaqub who took this initiative along with Mr Qadri, Mr Sattar and the late Mr Roshan Din from Nelson. We set up an Islamic study circle in Nelson at the late Mr Roshan Din's house. We used to study the Qur'an with translation. The late Mr Yaqub invited me to join the circle so I was pleased to be part of the group and we eventually bought a mosque there too.

We felt great. Before, we only used to read Qur'an (Arabic) together and now we had the opportunity to understand its meaning and get the message of God to transform our lives. It allowed us to understand the message better and convey it to others. We began reading the Qur'an translation in Urdu/English and this encouraged us to respect human beings more. I learnt one of the great aspects of Islam. It was, if your neighbour is hungry and you have food you must share it with them or give it to them. If you didn't know about his plight, and he slept hungry, you are not a Muslim.

This is the core lesson I got from the teaching of Islam and the Qur'an that a Muslim's main objective is to serve Humanity in the best possible way. When the late Mr Yaqub returned from Pakistan after his six weeks holiday in 1986, he had a stroke. He was restricted to a wheelchair;

even then he was so brave and courageous that he used to attend all UKIM meetings. I and the late Mr Yaqub also went to Hyde Park to protest against the USSR invasion of Afghanistan in 1979. I used to carry the wheelchair and I pushed it in the park. In 1986, when he was a senior vice-president of Shura and chairman of the education committee, he addressed a Youth Conference in Walsall. After the speech he came and sat with me. When someone raised a question, he tried to get up and answer it. He had another attack then and there and his health deteriorated. One of the doctors examined him and referred him to Birmingham Hospital and eventually he passed away in January 2003. When he passed away, I couldn't bear it. We were so close to each other and I used to share everything with him. He used to listen to me and boost my confidence and morale. There are three key people in my life – the late Mr Yaqub, the late Dr Ghulam Rasul and Mr Malik. I couldn't imagine life without them. We were always honest with each other. Above all, we had similar goals and objectives to serve the local community and humanity in general which kept us together

I am doing a lot of work for the Mission purely to please the Almighty and I don't expect any reward from anyone. I suppose we did the best job for the community. We acquired the building for the first mosque in Burnley. People had differences of opinion and based their mosques on their schools of thought, whereas we opened our doors to everyone in the community. We

had trustees who were of the Shia sect as well as from other sections of the community. We had the late Chaudhry Ahmed Khan, Ghulam Nabi Chowdhary, the late Mr Yaqub and Mr Malik. We all worked together in spite of differences of opinion, and served the community needs.

I am retired now but I used to travel a lot with Mr Malik and the late Mr Yaqub across the country, whether to visit the Home Office, or to attend meetings of the National Federation of Pakistani Association or to attend religious or community events. I was involved in everything that had something to do with the community, at all levels. I was also a governor of Barden Junior School, Barden Infant School and participated in other community work. We were all encouraged by Mr Malik and the late Mr Yaqub to participate and play a fuller role in the community. I was also part of Walshaw Girls High School. The idea was to get involved, get to know people and sort out the issues for the community.

UKIM had a policy to support the political party which served the best interests of the local community. I was in Burnley and the Labour Party was sympathetic to immigrants so we supported Labour throughout our lives. I think it was 1976 when Mr Malik got elected as a Labour councillor. Some people had problems with their tax. Mr Malik requested Labour to announce an Amnesty for those who had given wrong affidavits. It was granted in 1967. Hundreds of people paid the tax arrears they had evaded

Below: National Federation of Pakistani Association (NFPA) at Burnley Lane Baptist Church presenting Mujahid Hussain, Consul General of Pakistan, with a cheque for flood victims in East Pakistan. L-R: Mian Abdul Waheed (behind the Mayoress), the Mayor Alderman Willis, Abdul Mateen, President of NFPA, Consul General, Rafique Malik, Chair of NFPA

and they got their positions regularised. People used to produce fake and forged documents to avoid tax charges and show whether they were single, married, or married with children, to seek exemption from tax. Twice in history, and only by the Labour government, an Amnesty was announced - once for tax evasion in 1967 and then for illegal immigration in 1974. 100s of people had benefitted from them across the country. In April 1974, an amnesty was announced for people who had entered the UK illegally, through whichever means, before 31 December 1972, if they proved that they were here before that. They were granted amnesty and allowed to settle in the UK. It was all down to the leadership of Mr Malik who was a member of the Race Relations Board and understood the system and community issues and was able to present community views across to the top leadership. Since I arrived in the UK, I have observed our community suffer from multiple issues ranging from immigration, tax and health. People came to Mr Malik with particular problems like immigration, bringing their fiancées or wives over to the UK, tax problems and health issues etc. He used to advise me to draft a letter and make enquiries. I always felt great when I saw myself serving the local community. Factory owners used to refuse to provide letters for Asian workers, to support workers' immigration matters despite the fact that they had been working there for 2, 3, 5 or 10 years. One of Mr Malik's friends, the late Mr Mahmood Shah had a problem when he was trying to bring over his family from Pakistan. My own daughter Maryam used to work in Specialist Anodising and her manager refused to supply the required supporting letter. Mr Malik intervened and explained the situation

to the manager and he provided us with the letter. In 1992, I went to Holland, and my daughter Gazala had a problem. The late Mr Yaqub wasn't very happy because she had an appeal at a Manchester tribunal and it was postponed three times. Mr Malik got involved in the case and got her appeal through successfully.

I haven't done anything as an individual; it was our group consisting of Mr Malik, the late Mr Yaqub and myself. When we had a problem, we discussed it together and supported the local community. I strongly believe that unity in the community is the most important aspect of life and I have always professed this strongly. I am nothing without my community and everything is my community. Once there was an election at the Union and I wasn't interested in it at all. But I was encouraged by friends to participate in the election. I discussed the opportunity with Mr Malik and he also encouraged and motivated me to participate in the election. I was told by an indigenous community shop steward who said that it's in the community interest (so his words had profound meaning for me) you were only successful because your community supported you. I have always supported any endeavour. The late Dan Jones, our first MP, then Peter Pike and Kitty Usher, we always supported them because we felt that they were good for the community.

Burnley is my first home and Pakistan is my second home. I have spent nearly five decades in this town since I first arrived in the UK. I have hardly spent more than six months in Pakistan since my arrival in the UK, so absolutely I consider Burnley as my first home.

In Memoriam

Mohammad Yaqub
— 1938-2003 —

- First President of Pakistan Association in Burnley

- First Chairman of the Racial Equality Council in East Lancashire

- Founder Chairman of Abu Bakr Mosque

- First Pakistani heritage school teacher in Burnley

- First Pakistani heritage Deputy head teacher at Brunlea Special School

- First Pakistani Justice of the Peace in Burnley

- Senior Vice President UK Islamic Mission

- Community activist

Dan Jones
—— 1908-1985 ——

- Former MP for Burnley (1959-1983)

- Champion of Family-Reunions for minority ethnic workers

- Proposer of Mohammad Rafique Malik as first Pakistani heritage councillor for Burnley

Raza Shah
1939-2007

- Graduate of Punjab University

- Founder member of Jinnah Advisory Service

- Voluntary co-ordinator of Family Bereavement Support Service at Jinnah

- "Exceptional orator of Alama Iqbal poetry" by Mohammad Rafique Malik

- Community activist

Florence Green
——— 1927-2003 ———

- Former Liberal Party member

- Local postmistress

- Secretary of the Racial Equality Council in East Lancashire

- Justice of the Peace in Burnley

- Community activist

Ahmed Khan
1934-1994

- Shia Founder member of Abu Bakr Mosque

- Community activist

- Founder chair of Burnley Bereavement Support Service 1981-94

- "Tower of strength for all local community groups" by Mohammad Rafique Malik

Ken McGeorge
———— 1929-2007 ————

- Former Mayor of Burnley

- Leader of Burnley Borough Council

- Burnley Councillor

- Labour Party Member

- Champion of equality and diversity

- Coummunity activist

Mohammad Yousuf Moghul
——— 1939-1987 ———

- Community activist

- Secretary of the Burnley's Urdu Literary Society

- Volunteer at Jinnah Advisory Service

- Secretary of Burnley Bereavement Support Service

- Secretary of Burnley Islamic Trust

Afterword

As the Mayor of Burnley during the year that this book was published, I was pleased to see these important stories collected together.

The accounts of the pioneer immigrants to Burnley from Pakistan are fascinating, and they will be of interest to anyone who wants to understand the history of our borough.

I am struck by the variety and diversity of the stories here. Contributors to this volume have made their mark in business, health, public service, politics, sport, voluntary work, the law and in many other fields.

People talk about their family lives, their friendships, and the way their hopes and ambitions have played out through education, work, and community life.

It is noticeable that many of the people writing here have been inspired by their faith to seek integration in the town and promote building bridges.

Most of all, I am struck by the positive commitment to Burnley and the future of the borough that runs through all of these pages. Some people tell their stories of being born in Pakistan and moving here. Others are born and bred in the borough. All have made a big contribution through their work – paid and voluntary – to the quality of life we all enjoy in our town.

Important social history – and a great read! My congratulations to the Jinnah organisation and to all who were involved in creating this book.

Councillor Frank Cant
His Worshipful the Mayor of Burnley
August 2013

Appendix

Contributors

- Sobia Malik
- Safdar Baig Mirza
- Mohammad Rafique Malik
- Mohammad Najib
- Shahid Malik
- Sajda Majeed
- Shufkat Razaq
- Fara Sharif
- Khalida Sharif
- Wajid Khan
- Safdar Baig Mirza
- Dr Ahsanul Haq
- Dr Misfar Hassan
- Susan Hughes
- Abid Sharif
- Hafiz Riaz Khan
- Muzzamal Hussain Ahmed
- Abdul Aziz Chaudhry
- Munsifdar Mirza
- Afrasiab Anwar
- Ghulam Nabi Chowdhary
- Abdul Majeed
- Waseem Chowdhary
- Riaz Ahmed
- Basri Chowdhary
- Iftekhar Chowdhary
- Adnan Ahmed
- Nazia Khan
- Mohammad Younas
- Maulana Abuzar Afzal
- Alamzeb Khan
- Nasreen Malik
- Maulana Mohammad Iqbal
- Abdul Haq Mian
- Father James Petty
- Shahzad Ahmed Qadri
- Maulana Mohammad Hussain Sajidul Qadri
- Abdul Hamid Qureshi
- Anwara Shahid
- Iris Verity
- Mian Abdul Waheed
- His Worshipful the Mayor of Burnley, Councillor Frank Cant